SMITHSONIAN SERIES IN ETHNOGRAPHIC INQUIRY

William L. Merrill and Ivan Karp, series editors

Ethnography as fieldwork, analysis, and literary form is the distinguishing feature of modern anthropology. Guided by the assumption that anthropological theory and ethnography are inextricably linked, this series is devoted to exploring the ethnographic enterprise.

Los Pastores

History
and
Performance
in the
Mexican Shepherd's
Play of
South Texas

Richard R. Flores

SMITHSONIAN INSTITUTION PRESS
Washington and London

Copy Editor: Vicky Macintyre
Production Editor: Jack Kirshbaum
Designer: Janice Wheeler

Library of Congress Cataloging-in-Publication Data

Flores, Richard R.
 Los pastores : history and performance in the Mexican shepherd's
play of South Texas / Richard R. Flores.
  p. cm.
 Includes bibliographical references (p.   ) an index.
 ISBN 1-56098-518-6 (alk. paper)
  1. Pageants—Texas—San Antonio. 2. Pastores (Play : Granado-
Tranchese version) 3. Mexican Americans—Texas—San Antonio—
Social life and customs. 4. Christmas plays, Mexican—History and
criticism. I. Title.
PN3211.S27F66 1995
394'.2'66309764351—dc20   95-16781

British Library Cataloguing-in-Publication Data is available

Manufactured in the United States of America
02 01 00 99 98 97 96 95 5 4 3 2 1

⊗ The paper used in this publication meets the minimum requirements of the American National Standard for Permanence of Paper for Printed Library Materials Z39.48-1984.

Jacket illustrations: Photographs by Richard Flores of *Los Pastores* in performance.

To the memory of my grandparents,
        whose perseverance infuses still;

For my mother and father,
        whose supportive proddings never cease;

For Christine,
        whose heartfelt song as yet resounds;

For Katherine, Rebecca, and Rachel,
        this is your *herencia*.

Contents

Preface

"All mysteries which mislead theory into mysticism," Marx writes in the eighth thesis on Feuerbach, "find their rational solution in human practice and in the comprehension of this practice." But can the same unriddling be found in performance and its comprehension? What is the rational solution made explicit in this form of cultural practice? If performance offers a means of comprehension, what is the "said," "expressed," or "solved" that beckons comprehension? And does a maxim such as Marx's apply to a performance of the mystery of the Christian nativity? Furthermore, how are we to understand the continued enactment of a centuries-old genre of folk-religious practice without ourselves falling intellectual victims to mysticism. Or, just as critical, how are we to make sense of Mexican-American social actors "acting" the parts of medieval shepherds and devils without further mystifying their performance as an exotic anomaly in the secularized modern world? These are some of the questions that, after my initial investigation, induced me to explore more fully the present-day performances of *Los Pastores* in South Texas. And even as this book provides a synthesis of my thinking, the issues raised and topics discussed remain subject to further readings and discussion—performative expressions always are.

In some ways, the mystery of cultural performance is no mystery at all—it is a social phenomenon that speaks to the deepest reserves of human activity by condensing, into various generic representations, the conundrums of the social world. And although such a position suffices for some of the queries listed above, it fails to answer why one group of Mexican Americans dramatically express their experience in this manner. Even though such questions are complex, the response given by the performers to them are not. They perform, they tell me, "para el Niño Dios" (for the Christ Child). But how are we to comprehend, in practical terms, this reply in a way that is consonant with their intention without ourselves falling victim to the mystification of intellectualism. Performing "para el Niño Dios" cries for comprehension, not because it renders the world simpler (it does not), but because it articulates social and numinous desires that yield for its performance community a perspective of their own social world.

There is much to explore here, and by way of introduction, let me comment on one aspect of this exploration: the social dynamic of gift-giving. Chapter 7 demonstrates that gift-giving is an important feature of performing Los Pastores—a variety of oblations are offered and reciprocated at different moments in this event—and it is one that merits special recognition because generosity is implied in such a process. Here I am referring to the generosity of all the performers of *Los Pastores* who accepted my presence and intrusion into their dramatic world. They not only allowed me to question the rationale for their performative endeavors but they cloaked me with the role of a shepherd, teaching me about Los Pastores from the performer's point of view. This book could not have been accomplished without the support, approval, and immense generosity of all the troupe members. *¡Gracias pastoralistas!*

My interest in the study of Texas-Mexican folklore and cultural performances stems from an influence that cannot be underestimated—that of my parents, Richard and Elizabeth Flores. Because they were raised, at various stages of their lives, in the neighborhood where *Los Pastores* is performed in San Antonio, this study is in many ways about a world they inhabit and that continues to inform their way of life. This book, then, is actually about getting to know them; it is about recouping a collective cultural memory—in place of bringing memory to silence—and allowing that memory to speak in a voice that melds with my own. My parents—by their life, love, and labor—provided me with an opportunity to discover part of them in me. This, I suggest, is what a dialectical hunger of memory could be.

Over the years, a number of teachers, friends, and colleagues have been instrumental in shaping my own social biography. Two high school teachers merit special recognition, Mike Canfield and the late Phil Osborne—the first for teaching me about a world inscribed in books, the second for making me write. Upon the encouragement of another teacher, Jim Barlow, I found myself enrolled at the University of Notre Dame, no thanks to my high school principal, who informed the Notre Dame recruiter that no one from my class would ever make it there. Three of us did. I found Notre Dame to be a place of warmth and challenge, even in my first blizzard. During those years I read Augustine, Aristotle, Nietzsche, Marx, and Jung and slept through Thomistic philosophy. They planted in me a seed of the scholar's moral weight and social responsibility. And when Professors Bill Storey and Don McNeill suggested that I consider returning to Texas and contribute something to my community, the seed germinated into social action.

It was at this time that I met Christine Mecchella, now my wife. Her capacity for solicitude and insight have guided me throughout this work, as she has been equally committed to its completion. With our daughters, Katherine, Rebecca, and Rachel, she has been a supportive companion and gentle reminder of a compassionate life bearing witness to the surrounding world. Her encouragement through the hours spent writing it made this book possible. My brothers, sister, their families, and other family members in Texas and New York, especially Robert and Grace Mecchella, never failed to spur me on and were all sources of support at different stages of this project.

While working at the Mexican American Cultural Center in San Antonio, Texas, I discovered how anthropology, as a mode of intellectual inquiry, emerged from critical scholarship forged to the lives and practices of real people. Several friends and mentors at this stage of my career bear mentioning: Roberto Piña, Leonard Anguiano, Yolanda Tarango, Rosa Maria Icazas, Virgil Elizondo, Joe Forman, Tom Basile, George Pyle, and Jorge Cuellar.

My intuition about anthropology was confirmed when I encountered works of Professors Américo Paredes and José Limón. In their writings I found impeccable scholarship wedded to the lives of people I knew and experienced. As teachers, they were incisive, demanding, yet understanding; as mentors they have been supportive, generous, and still incisive. Their example of critical scholarship coupled with a deep humanism has provided me with a model of academic life. Others at the University of Texas, some no longer there, merit special recognition for their guidance and continued friendship: Richard Bauman, Beverly Stoeltje, Joel Sherzer, Steve Feld, Ramón Saldívar, Greg Urban, Amy Burce, and Frances Terry, who led me through the maze of academic bureaucracy with her good humor and institutional adeptness.

A Danforth-Compton fellowship, administered by Sarita Brown, and a graduate assistantship at the Center for Mexican American Studies at the University of Texas made graduate work possible. Subsequent research support from the Graduate School of the University of Wisconsin—Madison and the Institute for Race and Ethnicity, University of Wisconsin System, allowed me to revisit and rework the material of this book.

A number of colleagues provided critical comments, probing questions, and useful advice at various stages of this project. Among them are Frank Salomon, Emiko Ohnuki-Tierney, Neil Whitehead, Kirin Narayan, Anatoly

Khazanov, Jack Kugelmass, Francisco Scarano, Jim Escalante (who helped with the graphics), Nayith Pedroza-Garbisch, Ben Márquez, Ruben Medina, Steve Lee, Olga Nájera-Ramírez, Myrna Castrejón, Jonathan Stephens, Laura Duggan, and Harry West. Peter Nabokov merits special recognition, not only for reading the entire manuscript but also for his special sense of friendship; and again, José Limón, whose judgment and critical insights have made this project all the better.

A special word of appreciation to Daniel Goodwin, Jack Kirshbaum, Vicky Macintyre, and other staff members of the Smithsonian Institution Press. Collectively, you have made this book a reality; individually, you have been supportive, critical, and professional at just the right moments.

This book is a testament to the dedication, commitment, and social desires of the performers of *Los Pastores*. I hope, with a certain degree of accuracy, it articulates and makes comprehensible the vitality and experience of this mystery play from the Old World to those who read it. Its failures and omissions, however, are my own.

A version of chapter 5 appeared in the *Journal of Historical Sociology;* and portions of chapters 6 and 7 appeared in *American Ethnologist.*

Introduction

Before every enactment, in a voice made strong from nearly fifty years of performing, the director of *Los Pastores* declares: "La gente ya no viene por devoción sino por diversión" (the people no longer come for devotion but for diversion). Initially, the significance of these words did not register, but after hearing this exhortation repeated at every performance and on every recording I made, their meaning began to emerge. In ways I have come to appreciate and interpret, the polysemous tension between devotion and diversion forms the crucible in which this analysis of *Los Pastores* is forged. As this book demonstrates, devotion and diversion are not merely rhetorical stances that inform one's posture toward *Los Pastores* but are themselves metonyms for the historical trajectory, symbolic logic, and cultural scheme that informs the making of this event.

This book explores the ritual practice and cultural performance of *Los Pastores* among South Texas *mexicanos*. *Los Pastores* is a nativity play, performed entirely in Spanish, that descends from medieval Spain. Its generic names are *pastorelas, coloquios,* or *autos sacramentales*. The Spanish missionaries brought this dramatic form to the New World, including the southwestern United States, where it has flourished for over a century.

Most versions of *Los Pastores* have a cast of characters that includes shepherds, angels, devils, Mary and Joseph, a hermit, a statue of el Niño Dios (the Christ Child), and others. The narrative begins with the shepherds in the hills watching their sheep when the Archangel Michael appears to them, announcing the birth of the Messiah. Upon deciding to journey to Bethlehem, bearing gifts for el Niño Dios, the shepherds encounter Luzbel (Lucifer) and his legion of devils, who attempt to thwart their efforts in a series of comedic routines. In the end, the Archangel Michael defeats Luzbel, banishing him to the dungeons of hell, and the shepherds arrive in Bethlehem offering their humble gifts to el Niño Dios.

My general thesis is that this event, and the poetics from which it is artisti-
cally rendered and historically derived, is a collective representation that
"speaks," like other forms of symbolic alignment, to the social desires, sacred
longings, and personal motivations of its performance community. As both
ritual practice and cultural performance, the enactment of *Los Pastores* in
South Texas has undergone numerous transformations, diffused in multiple
variations, and has meant any number of things to those who have witnessed,
participated in, or sponsored it. Like other forms of ritual spectacle and festi-
val, *Los Pastores* is a multivocal, polysemic, and multifunctional event. In my
view, this cultural performance is inseparable from the economic, geographic,
and social location of its performance community—South Texas *mexicanos*.
Furthermore, cultural performances in general, and *Los Pastores* in particular,
are not mirrors of the real but events constructed from the same historical
and social processes of the everyday, aesthetically reconfiguring the world of
those who produce them.

In 1913 Don Leandro Granado began organizing performances of *Los Pastores* in San Antonio, Texas. Like most Mexicans who came to Texas at that
time, Don Leandro arrived with few economic resources, and he made his
living selling *raspas* (snow cones) and *melcocha* (taffy) from a wagon he carted
through the streets of San Antonio's West Side *barrio* (neighborhood). Before
leaving his home in Irapuato, México, Don Leandro had committed to memory the text of a shepherd's play, and, upon his arrival in San Antonio, inscribed his memorized text in an old ledger, in the care of the current director.
When performed in its entirety, Don Leandro's pastorela lasted up to eight
hours. In 1949, the Reverend Carmelo Tranchese, S.J., of Our Lady of Guadalupe Church, edited, translated, and published Don Leandro's pastorela, entitled *Los Pastores*.[1] Today, the performers at Our Lady of Guadalupe Church
in San Antonio, the heirs of Don Leandro Granado, perform *Los Pastores* using
Tranchese's published text as their guide.

Historically, this drama is connected not only with religious devotion, but
with the festive and popular humor of the Middle Ages.[2] However, the social
critique found in the popular traditions of the Middle Ages, a critique rooted
in parody and satire, has been displaced: urbanization, bureaucratization, ra-
tionalization, and other manifestations of the modern world have led to a
decline in public cultural performances like the one considered here (see Sennett 1974). How, then, are we to make sense of *Los Pastores*? Is it merely a
remnant, a cultural survival, of the past? Has its meaning been reinscribed
by a modern desire for "authentic" representations and experiences of the
premodern "real"? Have the popular critique and humor of its medieval pro-

genitor been lost, the social play eroded by the logic of a different social, political, and economic order? My response to these questions is found in the various analytical and interpretive arguments that inform my exegesis of the symbiotic tension expressed by the director as that between devotion and diversion.

PERFORMANCE AND ETHNOGRAPHY

In the fall of 1987, after having spent two weeks observing rehearsals, asking questions of the performers, and consuming more than a few beers with the men, I was asked to join the troupe of *Los Pastores* as a performer. Several new people who were to join it never did, leaving several roles vacant. Before rehearsal one Sunday afternoon, the assistant director turned to me and said: "If you really want to know what the pastorela is all about, then you need to perform in it." Agreeing, I was given the *papel,* the role of one of the minor shepherds. From that moment on, members of the troupe took me into their care, instructing me in the rudiments of costuming, staging, and relating stories of past events.

When I became a performer, my ethnographic role took on dimensions that I had not expected. But this had its advantages. It legitimated my presence and gave me the status of an insider at the different locations in which "we" performed. Furthermore, it allowed me to be present at all the rehearsals, discussions, bus rides, and performances and to study *Los Pastores* through the event itself.

My new-found role was also limiting, however, for I was less free to interview audience members. Instead of mingling throughout the performance, being more attentive to the audience and to their reaction and participation in the drama, I had to observe such matters from the "stage." I was free, however, to talk with audience members before and after the performance and during one of the scenes in which the shepherds were not performing.

Another important element marked my presence in the field: my ethnicity. While the troupe knew quite well that I was not from the *barrio,* my Spanish surname and dark complexion provided them with points of reference they recognized—I did not appear, at least upon visual scrutiny, to be an outsider. The fact that I knew, however slightly, several members of the troupe from the time I had lived and worked in the area a few years earlier also facilitated my initiation into the troupe.

On several occasions, a former "Anglo" (the one and only) performer visited our rehearsals or performances. He had acted with the troupe in the late 1970s and early 1980s, during which time he produced an educational film on *Los Pastores.* His visits always stirred up a sense of excitement and enthusiasm, his participation being remembered with fondness and warmth. But his presence also juxtaposed the two of us in an interesting way. On every occasion of his visit, members of the troupe walked over to me and whispered that they had taught him the rudiments of performance, as well as Spanish. These actions cast him as the outsider to my insider position.

At the same time, I was not one of them. As an ethnographer from the university I did not share their social location, a difference that manifested itself in a certain attitude I sensed among the leaders. On several occasions they inquired about my commitment to the performance (would I really last the entire performance season?), and questioned if I really believed, in a religious sense, in el Niño Dios. In a way that is quite legitimate, they wanted to know what I thought about their own cultural practice by questioning mine. Addressing this first concern, I told them that I would indeed stay for the entire year, and possibly the next. It was not, however, until late in the season, having been through several performances in 30-degree weather (the most challenging of all circumstances!), that members of the troupe became convinced that I was serious about remaining for the entire performance season. After this point, no one directly questioned my commitment to participate in *Los Pastores,* and I never felt isolated or excluded from the joking and drinking sessions conducted by the men before and after rehearsals and performances. In my second year with the troupe, all traces of this sentiment disappeared.

The ambivalence regarding where I stood on the issue of "religion"—that is, if I believed in el Niño Dios—was more lingering. This tension surfaced primarily in talk of the "miracles" that el Niño Dios had performed, especially those experienced by the director. According to him, as well as other members of the troupe, the director's presence in this event after a second stroke was the result of a "miracle." While I listened to such stories quite intently, it was inferred on several occasions that my status as a university researcher prohibited me from believing in miracles. This ambivalence stemmed, I know, from my own anxiety about participating in a ritual activity whose religious sentiments I did not fully share. My response, calmly stated, was straight from every ethnographic field guide I had ever read: "I was not there to judge whether their beliefs were appropriate or not, and I took their religious sentiments as valid, honest, and truthful evaluations of their own experience." While my personal beliefs never became an issue of dissent, I could read the skepticism in their eyes, especially after my overrational and objective response. I am sure that if my Anglo counterpart had been present, members of the troupe would have been whispering in his ear about my intellectualizing of their deepest experiences. Such are the conundrums of a positioned ethnographer.

I suggest that ethnographers not only build on discursive traditions and historical contact from both an insider and outsider position (Pratt 1986), but that we also situate ourselves in the field so that certain elements of our subjectivities (like ethnicity and religious belief) align us with our informants, while other aspects produce incongruent relationships. In essence, ethnicity, and other elements of our social selves, combine to form our particular "web of significance" and, eventually, our own aspect of signification. The issue is not whether one's social position offers a clearer, therefore less opaque, understanding of social life, but whether it facilitates or hinders our communication with others—our particular prejudices and assumptions, forged from personal encounters and ideological assumptions, are never quite buried. The old anthropological adage that one is too close to study one's own culture is, I believe, more ideologically motivated than theoretically proven: all of us have prejudices we need to encounter and qualify. The issue is not the identity of one's position, but ability to communicate, in dialogical fashion, with our ethnographic interlocutors. Any tools we bring to such a dialogue, whether they be those of language, personal history, or a commonly perceived social self, are merely resources that must be put to the ultimate task of communication. Only naive ethnographers, not native ones, think otherwise.

In my initial stage of fieldwork, a sense of shared identity allowed me to enter the field more easily. But it was not until I had proven myself—through cold, wintry-night performances, returning for a second performance season, and during that time, creating a network of social relationships—that I began to know my way through the field.

STRUCTURAL ORGANIZATION

Los Pastores, as a folk drama of considerable length, historical longevity, and aesthetic complexity, consists of multiple levels of textual and performative elements. Such genres offer particular problems of focus: Does one analyze the text, the literary tradition, or the enactment? How about the multiple relationships within the genre: there is poetry, song, music, dance, and movement, overlapping at times or standing alone. What about the distinction between ritual, drama, and cultural performance: Which of these best articulates the dynamics of the event and its understanding by those who perform and attend it? These issues do not offer simple solutions, and in dealing with them I have melded my ideas to the event itself, drawing from multiple approaches to the study of art, its production, and its place in social life. This relationship, especially as expressed through ritual, drama, and other forms of cultural performance, is the source of much debate (Bauman 1986b; Bruner 1986; Kapferer 1986; Turner 1974, 1986). My view is that through art, social life is reflected upon and rendered poetic; the everyday is the place where experience occurs, historically, cognitively, and symbolically aligned into creative expressions of culture.

In order to fully explore and articulate the interrelationship between the various levels of text and performance of *Los Pastores*, I have divided this discussion into two related parts: the dramatized event and the dramatic event. My use of these categories is not meant to imply a strict separation between them; on the contrary, by building on the same processual cognate, "drama," I intend to emphasize the irreducibility of the dramatized to the dramatic, and vice versa.[3] Performance, as the culmination of the dramatized and dramatic, is realized in the dialectically emergent frame: one event, two lenses.

The Dramatized Event

Los Pastores is both narrated story and enacted drama, exhibiting various literary devices and dramatic structures (see figure 1). By focusing on *Los Pastores* as a dramatized event, I attempt to capture several of its critical aspects. The first is its textual tradition. *Los Pastores* evolved from liturgical religious drama, of the golden age of Spanish literature, and the indigenous traditions of México. As such, it has undergone various textual and literary changes and developments, providing this event with its particular literary characteristics (see chapter 2).

A second aspect of *Los Pastores*, one that is more central to its dramatized qualities, is its embodiment of story and structure (see chapter 3). As story, *Los Pastores* contains a narrative line that unfolds in the linear performance of the event; as structure, it releases dramatic tension by juxtaposing characters from different symbolic domains. Together, story and structure form the narrative and dramatic elements of *Los Pastores*, or the linear and paradigmatic combinations that produce its dramatized form. Several properties that do not categorically fall under the rubric of story or structure but that are indispensable to each are costumes, staging, and characterization. These are also discussed under the heading of the dramatized event.

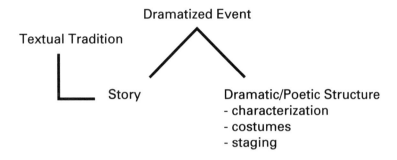

1. The dramatized event.

As a dramatized event, *Los Pastores* also exhibits various aesthetic qualities that are critical to its dramatized production. The poetics of performance (chapter 4) explores the aesthetic features of the dramatized event, delineating the multiple dimensions of artistic elements that are part of its performance.

The Dramatic Event

Besides the various textual and performative features that are part of this drama, the enactment of *Los Pastores* constitutes an event in itself (see figure 2). Through this rubric I explore the relationship between *Los Pastores* as a dramatized event and its historical and contemporary enactment. Furthermore, by looking at how *Los Pastores* and its performers have been inscribed by the dominant discourse, I hope to place this event within the broader discursive struggle of South Texas cultural politics and social identity (see chapter 5). *Mexicanos* were not always a subaltern class in Texas—they were once landowners under the banners of Spain and México. Their demise, necessitated by a changing economic order, was carried out through murderous violence, treacherous deceit, and American political self-interest. *Mexicanos* responded in ways that included armed resistance, civil disobedience, acquiescence, and forced assimilation.

If it is true that cultural performances are cut from the same social cloth of everyday practice, then in theory, one should be able to "locate" the dialectical interplay between the performance of *Los Pastores* and those practices grounded in political and social life. By focusing my historical narrative on the way *Los Pastores* has been fashioned by the cultural poetics of the dominant, I intend to demonstrate how cultural form and dominant political practice co-

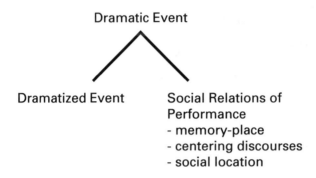

Dramatic Event

Dramatized Event   Social Relations of
                        Performance
                        - memory-place
                        - centering discourses
                        - social location

2. The dramatic event.

incide in one social frame. This leads not only to an understanding of the demarcation of particular cultural practices as "other" and "traditional" but to the sociological process of "othering" and "traditionalizing." This dichotomy heuristically attempts to capture the active process of "folklorization" instead of accepting such practices as historically given. My intent is to "to discover where folklore study and social action come together, . . . [and] how traditions reveal the points of tension within and between groups and the inequities that arise in any stratified society" (Bauman and Abrahams 1981:4). The fact that *Los Pastores* has been performed in South Texas by Mexicans who have been relegated to a marginal role by the social powers that be is critical to an understanding of its historical and contemporary significance.

In chapters 6 and 7 I look at this event and its present performance in three different domains or locations: the *barrio*, local churches, and a tourist event at one of the historic missions located in San Antonio. As a dramatic event, *Los Pastores* is related to the production of memory, the politics of "gifting," and performance for tourism. Let me briefly state that my interpretation of *Los Pastores* cannot be separated from either its historical significance or religious intent. That is to say, the present meaning of *Los Pastores* emerges from the conjuncture of the narrative and dramatic form of the text and the numinous desires and sociological place of its performance community. I argue that the significance of this event is found in the way it negotiates, on multiple planes, the historically particular forms of social domination experienced by its performance community.

In the conclusion, I provide an interpretive essay that situates the meaning of *Los Pastores* within the context of the modern world. This line of inquiry considers the relationship between the narrative and dramatic structure and its relationship to *Los Pastores* as a work of culture. The structural underpinning of *Los Pastores's* narrative and the sociological experience of its performers cannot be separated, if one takes seriously Fredric Jameson's (1971:329) Marxian understanding of form as the "working out of content in the realm of the superstructure."[4] Following this line of inquiry, I show how an interpretation of *Los Pastores,* as a dramatic narrative form, must be grounded in the social and historical conditions of modernity. As such, the specific case of *Los Pastores* and its place in the repertoire of *mexicano* cultural practice provide a discriminating lens through which the social and cultural processes of modernity can be viewed. The relentless persistence of *Los Pastores* derives from the way narrative and dramatic form converge with the social and historical experience of its performers and audience, demonstrating how the "dialectical forces (historical, social, and cultural) in the content of the lore" (Bauman and Abrahams 1981:6) form an experiential totality that is the locus of the critical meaning of *Los Pastores.*

TEXTUALITY AND PERFORMANCE

I ground this study in the historical and ethnographic experience of *Los Pastores* as a cultural event, incorporating a wide range of historical and sociopolitical factors that aim to integrate elements of history and social process. The performative meaning of *Los Pastores* depends as much on the social and political conditions of performance as on the artistic competence and religious beliefs of its actors. My intent is to show how historical conditions and the processes that structure social life in this community are negotiated through performance. *Los Pastores,* as a cultural text that has been and often continues to be performed in a social climate that is indifferent, if not antagonistic, to its cultural makeup, is an effort by its performers to negotiate that same environment.

Overall, my approach to Mexican-American folklore, one that I view as both resistant to the dominant social pressures as well as constructed in relation to them, is influenced by the work of Américo Paredes, specifically by his book *With His Pistol in His Hand: A Border Ballad and Its Hero* (Paredes 1958a). Both in its social and critical approach to folklore, as well as its influence as a cultural text during and after the Chicano movement, this work has affected my own personal, cultural, and intellectual thinking. In its own distinct way, this study is an attempt to continue an intellectual tradition initiated by Paredes and continued by Limón (1992), Saldívar (1990), Peña (1985), and others who understand Mexican-American folklore in Texas, like the border *corrido*, as "embedded in a history of social conflict, and therefore, as a text [that] continually signifies and refers to the confrontation of larger social forces defined by ethnicity and class" (Limón 1986:12–13). Through song, dance, jokes, and legends, the folklore of *mexicanos* in South Texas has been constructed over and against the forces of class and ethnic alienation.

There are multiple levels of texts in this study. First, a number are written texts. One is the original text that Don Leandro wrote in an old ledger back in the early 1920s (not to mention the written or oral text from which he himself learned and which is inaccessible to us). The current director maintains the original, although several copies have been made. One that I had the opportunity to analyze is held in the archives of the folklore library at the University of Texas at Austin. Another is the published text of Don Leandro's ledger that was edited and translated by Tranchese and printed in 1949; this was eventually republished with musical notation in 1976 and is now the text from which all contemporary members of the troupe learn their parts.

Second, there are the performed texts of *Los Pastores*. Here, I draw on Paul Ricoeur's (1979) "The Model of the Text" as the theoretical basis that allows me to "read" performances of *Los Pastores*. But even here, each enactment, formed by elements of improvisation and changing social contexts, creates a distinct performative text.

I deal with this situation in two ways. First, I follow the precedent set by Ward Keeler (1987) and restrict my analysis to those events that take place in the frame of performance. In this way, the common thread of all performances is taken to be the performance itself, creating a sense of equivalency among them. Second, and more important, this common thread that unites these events becomes, for my purpose, a composite text that is the focus of my analysis. In this endeavor, I follow Américo Paredes (1958a) who, in analyzing the ballad of Gregorio Cortez, reconstructs his own composite text from the many variants he collected. Whereas his reconstruction is based on collected variants, my reconstruction is based on the variations created by each performance. Therefore, I focus my analysis on the "text" created by the cultural enactment of *Los Pastores*, an enactment constituted by the convergence of written texts and impromptu speech, performed in different social settings. And although at different points in this study I analyze specific elements of speech, these may or may not be replicated in every act of performance but have been reconstructed from those I recorded.

PART I

Tradition, Story, and the Making of *Los Pastores*

Jilguero, how sweet you sing,
With your sweet clarion voice.
Go, wake up the souls,
It is not time to sleep.
　　　　　—TEBANO, *LOS PASTORES*

One thing only we pursued all our lives: a harsh, carnivorous, indestructible vision—the essence. For its sake what venom we were given to drink by both gods and men, what tears we shed, what blood, how much sweat! Our whole lives, a devil (devil? or angel?) refused to leave us in peace. . . . this essence went by many names; it kept changing masks all the while we pursued it. Sometimes we called it supreme hope, sometimes supreme despair, sometimes summit of man's soul, sometimes desert mirage. . . . And sometimes, finally, it seemed to us like an integral circle with the human heart as center and immortality as circumference.
　　　　　—NIKOS KAZANTZAKIS, *REPORT TO GRECO*

Two Errors: 1. to take everything literally, 2. to take everything spiritually.
　　　　　—PASCAL, *PENSÉES*

1

The Social and Dramatic Stage

Los Pastores is both ritual and drama, which is to say it is one aspect of the reflexive, coded, and symbolic means of human communication. As the Durkheimian tradition posits, the ritual aspects of *Los Pastores* are part of the "profoundly social" through which people experience themselves, their history, and their place in the social order (Durkheim [1915] 1965). And yet, as a cultural performance, the sociability, ludic behavior, drinking, eating, and general festive atmosphere that emerge in each enactment are equally as important as the devotional and ritual aspects of this event.

As a folk production, *Los Pastores* is not, by any measure, a professional event but one enacted by neighborhood people who have no technical or formal training in theater or music. Members of the troupe are not paid for their effort, nor are performances undertaken for a wage; monetary profit or gain is not even a consideration, since there is none to be had. An offering of dollar bills is sometimes given to performers during an intermission, but this is rendered as part of a ritual offering and does not constitute a wage. There is also a money offering at the end of the event, given by audience members as a donation, but the amount collected is minimal and given to Guadalupe Church as a donation by the troupe. The one place money is negotiated is at a performance sponsored by the San Antonio Conservation Society at San José Mission. The Conservation Society pays $150 for the event, a performance that creates its own kind of tensions and conflicts, which I explain in later chapters, along with the ritual of presenting money.

SAN ANTONIO'S MEXICAN-AMERICAN COMMUNITY

In 1718 the Franciscan Friars founded their first mission along the banks of the San Antonio River for the native inhabitants of Texas. Soon afterward, a military presidio was established as an outpost of the Spanish military, and in 1731 fifty-five Spanish colonists from the Canary Islands settled across the river from the mission and presidio, establishing the town of San Fernando de Béxar. By the 1820s, these three communities formed what was to become the city of San Antonio.[1] The early inhabitants of San Antonio consisted of elite Spanish and Mexican families, poorer Mexicans, mostly mestizos (known as *mexicanos* or *tejanos*), and Texas Indians.

These settlers were key players in the early history of Texas, shaping the Spanish and Mexican colonial frontier. By the 1830s, however, Anglo-American families in this Mexican territory outnumbered the Mexican citizenry. Although Mexican officials were wary of the growing Anglo-American presence, life on the frontier required mutual respect and a certain degree of cooperation. In Béxar, a "consonance of Tejano concerns with those of the Anglos" helped build an early cooperative spirit (de la Teja and Wheat 1991:23). In 1834, however, Santa Anna annulled the Mexican Constitution of 1824, seizing central power for himself, and men like Lorenzo de Zavala, Juan Seguin, and José Antonio Navarro played critical roles in forging an Anglo-Mexican alliance that favored Texas independence. But soon after the founding of the Republic of Texas in 1836, Mexicans—including Seguin who served as a captain in the Texan forces and as mayor of San Antonio from 1840 to 1842—suffered a vengeful backlash from the Anglo-Texans. The social place of Mexicans was further eroded after México lost the war with the United States and saw Texas and much of the Southwest incorporated into the United States, under the Treaty of Guadalupe-Hidalgo of 1848. The ensuing years brought various forms of ethnic conflict and discrimination. Beginning in the late 1850s, San Antonio's Mexicans were increasingly segregated from the growing Anglo-American population, and by 1883 the West Side was already recognized as the Mexican side of town (De León 1982:32).

Between 1880 and 1920, South Texas underwent a radical shift in economic organization that displaced many traditional Mexican families from their ranch and cattle homesteads to the agricultural fields where they found employment as wage labor farm workers.[2] The result of this shift, David Montejano (1987:114) writes, was that "Texas Mexican people had generally been reduced . . . to the status of landless and dependent wage laborers." Various expressive cultural forms, including *Los Pastores*, mediated the economic deterioration and growing tension between the Anglos and Mexicans (see chapter 5). Prominent among these forms is the Texas-Mexican *corrido*, or folk ballad, a genre whose influence extends to contemporary Chicano and Chicana literature (Flores 1992; Limón 1992; Paredes 1958a; Saldívar 1990).

San Antonio's *mexicano* and *tejano* population reacted to their social and economic dislocation in various ways. For example, Mexican lawyers, doctors, and business leaders resisted the social encroachments of the Anglo power structure through political maneuvers and open discontent; their political standing and financial independence allowed them to engage in politics and to organize against the changing social climate. Most *mexicanos* did not have the same opportunity and put most of their effort into attending to their families' financial needs. By 1900, however, not even wealthy *mexicanos* could stop the growing isolation and marginal status of their economically less secure compatriots. In spite of their dwindling economic base, *mexicanos* continued to resist the erasure of their constitutional rights, lack of educational opportunities, and poor living conditions by participating in and organizing labor strikes and early civil rights complaints (De León 1982; García 1991; Limón 1974; Montejano 1987; Nelson-Cisneros 1975, 1978).

When Don Leandro Granado arrived in San Antonio in the early 1900s, he was one of thousands of Mexican immigrants to settle on the West Side. This well-established Mexican *barrio* offered a network of business opportunities, familiar social networks, and a predominant Spanish-speaking environment. With the emergence of this Mexican enclave and the need for unskilled, cheap labor to sustain San Antonio's growing industrial sector, the Mexican segment of the town's population increased from 25.7 percent in 1900 to 46.3 percent in 1940 (García 1991). Although a number of wealthy Mexicans fleeing the political turmoil of the Mexican revolution between 1910 and 1921 adopted San Antonio as their home, most new immigrants were not from the elite classes. Contributing to the arrival of México's lower classes was an open immigration policy to the south. That is, the literacy test required of all European immigrants under the Immigration Act of 1917 was waived for Mexican immigrants as a result of pressure from commercial agricultural interests. The arrival of lower-class Mexican immigrants, coupled with the depression-era movement of Mexican agricultural workers from rural areas to urban centers like San Antonio, increased the size and density of the West Side. This Mexican *barrio* had long been inhabited by both poor and middle-class *mexicanos,* whose economic and social conditions only grew worse in the 1930s.

Today, San Antonio is the third largest city in Texas, with a population of over one million. People of Mexican origin constitute 54 percent of the population and 70 percent of those living in poverty. Of the many reasons why poverty has continued to plague the Mexican-American population of San Antonio, the two leading ones are the lack of education and unemployment. In 1980, only 50 percent of Mexican-American males in San Antonio received a high school diploma, compared with 80 percent of their Anglo counterparts (Cardenas, Chapa, and Burek 1993). This difference in high school completion rates is due in part to the fact that for years Mexican Americans in Texas have been isolated in poor school districts with low budgets and few resources (San Miguel 1987). Not only has this resulted in an inferior educational environment, but its effects on the economic stability and employment of Mexican Americans have been quite disturbing. In 1988 the ratio of Anglo to Mexican employment in San Antonio was 4:1 in managerial and professional jobs, 6:1 in technical occupations, and 2:5 for unskilled labor (Cardenas et al. 1993). Low educational attainment has transferred into low-skilled jobs. Mexican Americans know how to achieve economic stability and success; what has been denied them in many cases is equal opportunity to enter the educational and business institutions that provide it.

Mexican Americans can be found in every part of San Antonio and in every social and economic class, but it is the West Side that has maintained its identity as an economically poor *barrio mexicano*. It contains a mixture of public housing, low-wage industry, single- and multiple-family homes, and urban renewal programs. Violence, both domestic and drug-related, is high in the area, as is unemployment. In the past twenty years, city and community leaders have targeted this area for public money to fight the ills of urban poverty. But, like many of the inner cities throughout the country, it has experienced an increase in poverty and a decrease in economic resources over the past decade.

One of the many prominent institutions in Mexican-American social life is the Catholic Church. It is not surprising that when Don Leandro arrived in San Antonio and began organizing performances on the West Side, he affiliated his drama with Our Lady of Guadalupe Church. The parish had gained a reputation as the "Mexican church," especially under the tutelage of Father Carmelo Tranchese, who was influential in a number of community projects, including the establishment of federally subsidized public housing. Tranchese's relationship with Don Leandro, discussed in chapter 5, is an important aspect of this analysis—one that is related to the contemporary meaning of *Los Pastores* as both devotion and diversion—especially in his role as editor, translator, and publisher of Don Leandro's text.

Tranchese's early social and political efforts have been reinvented in the past twenty years through the presence of Communities Organized for Public Service (COPS), a neighborhood-based political organization modeled on the political work of Saul Alinsky and the Industrial Area Foundation he started. COPS has worked diligently and unceasingly at changing the social, political, and economic face of the West Side, and with a measure of success. Many

West Side churches, both Catholic and Protestant, have supported COPS's work from its inception. Our Lady of Guadalupe Church, staffed by politically minded Jesuits, has been an important stronghold of COPS, and its staff have been key players in this organization. My own experience with COPS goes back nearly twenty years to the time I was a college volunteer and drove a parish bus providing transportation to elderly women and men, depositing them at city council meetings, where, in voices filled with emotion and frustration, they expressed their deep desire for social change.

It is not surprising that church leaders, following the efforts initiated by Tranchese and continued by his contemporary successors, like the Reverend Edmundo Rodriquez, S.J., see *Los Pastores* as a critical element of Mexican-American social life. These efforts are not limited to the Jesuits at Guadalupe Church but include the Reverend Balty Janacek whose parish assignment, Christ the King—another landmark of the West Side—has sponsored performances of *Los Pastores* for at least fifteen years. Although I am critical of church-sponsored performances of *Los Pastores* in terms of the cultural production of meaning they enact, for the most part these churches have been a beacon of light supporting political and economic change on the West Side for decades. Even as this neighborhood continues to be marred by poverty, crime, and other urban ills, the positive influence of *barrio* institutions like the church cannot be dismissed.

The relationship between *Los Pastores* and the cadre of citizens who are dedicated to the social improvement of the West Side has another interesting component. At the time of my involvement with the troupe, it was common to see neighborhood leaders at church performances. One of the benefits of *Los Pastores,* I suggest, is the long-term presence of a cultural event that functions as a public reminder of the history and culture of Mexican Americans. As one young woman reminded me, "We need our traditions to be noticed in America." (I discuss this aspect of the relationship in part two.)

Guadalupe Church has continued to support *Los Pastores* by furnishing a vehicle for transporting members to performances, as well as providing them with a place to rehearse. Some performers maintain close ties to the church and are involved in a number of its activities, such as the choir and men's club, but church affiliation is not a prerequisite for joining the troupe.

THE SOCIAL ACTORS: GENERATIONAL PROFILES

The two seasons I spent performing afforded me an opportunity to interact with and interview the more than twenty members of the troupe. Performers encompassed three generations: elders, middle-age adults, and adolescents (in 1993, one of the young women had her four-year-old daughter performing, adding a fourth generational presence). A number of characteristics are consonant throughout the troupe, despite the wide span in members' ages. The most evident is their shared commitment to *Los Pastores:* members spend hours on weekends rehearsing, not to mention memorizing lines and decorating costumes. Performers also come from the same socioeconomic class—all of them were employed or had been employed in low-skilled or semiskilled jobs—and some participate in various government assistance programs. Whereas a few of the performers have relocated to other predominantly Mexican-American neighborhoods, most troupe members live well within the boundaries of the West Side. In addition, all the performers are of Mexican origin. Even if they construct their subjective identities differently—indexed by various self-referents like *mexicano*, Mexican-American, or Hispanic—it is an identity keyed to their Mexican ancestry. And, except for one young man who spent only several months with us, all the performers are U.S. citizens.

In the past, *Los Pastores* was an all-male event.[3] Over the past twenty years, however, women have become central to its continuation, and during my tenure with the troupe, almost all the shepherds were women. Today, only the devils maintain their male identity, refusing to allow women into their numbers, although the young women have been needling the director for a chance to perform these roles, but with little success.

Despite the similarities among the performers, a number of differences in values and social identity persist. Not surprisingly, most of the variance is a function of age and gender. In order to portray both the similarity and variance of the performers, a composite—based on generational and gender grouping—is proffered, highlighting the social characteristics of the troupe. These generational profiles are constructed as I knew the people concerned in 1987–89 and 1993.

The Elders

Among the elders were six or seven male performers who, because of their age or years performing with the troupe, were treated with respect and endearment. Three of the men had been performing for nearly thirty years and the director for close to fifty years. Only one elder was still employed. Some had retired with a pension, whereas others were living only on their social security benefits. The one elder who was still working had to quit at the end of my first season because he could no longer fulfill the tasks of lifting and hauling heavy objects required in his job. These men ranged in age from fifty-eight to seventy.

Vicente Manuel is the current director, and if his health permits, he would like to perform through the 1995–96 season, which will mark his fiftieth anniversary with the troupe. He has played numerous roles during his tenure as a performer, but it is his current role of Luzbel that brings him recognition. He is often featured on local television programs or in newspaper accounts, and he uses these opportunities to publicize *Los Pastores*.

He recollects knowing Don Leandro, but it is Chencho, who directed *Los Pastores* until the late 1970s, whom Vicente Manuel recognizes as his mentor. Chencho was a strict, brusque, disciplined, but respected leader who directed *Los Pastores* for many years. Vicente Manuel is Chencho's heir and has molded his own leadership style after his predecessor, although he is more relaxed in temperament and the way he directs the troupe. *"La gente* don't stay," he claims, "if you are too strict." Vicente Manuel is quite knowledgeable about *Los Pastores* and remembers the various earlier troupes that used to perform in the city but have not survived to the present. None, he claims, were as "authentic" as this troupe.

Guillermo, the lead shepherd, had recently retired as a school maintenance worker and, in spite of coronary bypass surgery several years before, was one of the more active members. A performer with the troupe for over twenty-five years, he knew almost all the *papeles,* or roles, and often assisted newer members with their lines. In 1990, Guillermo underwent heart surgery for the second time, and on my return visit in 1993 I found him performing once again, this time as the hermit. He never failed to explain various aspects of the performance to me, whether it had to do with costuming, speechplay, or the general rules of comportment for the performers. Like Vicente Manuel, he had a vast knowledge of *Los Pastores* and often discussed related performance forms like *coloquios* and how they differed from the *pastorela*. Guillermo was also a religious person and would not miss an opportunity to tell me of his devotion to el Niño Dios. Over the years his granddaughters have also performed, something his own daughter never did because, "in those days, *hubo muchos viejos*" (there were too many old men). Although his wife is not a performer, she was present at most performances, talking and helping the hosts in various tasks, or sitting with other women or family members in the audience. Not having gone far in school, Guillermo placed great emphasis on education and was quite excited to see members of his family take their education seriously.

Mr. Solis was no longer a regular performer. His family did not allow him to participate because they feared he would fall and break a bone on his frail frame. But on several occasions, after his family tired of his insistence, they entrusted Guillermo with his care and allowed him to play the hermit, a role he had perfected over many years. Mr. Solis could not hear well, and his eyesight was also failing, but Guillermo would cue him his lines, whereupon he would respond with the words he had memorized some thirty years earlier.

Juan, in his mid-sixties, could not read or write, yet over the years he had performed a number of roles, all of them shepherds. He never forgot a part once he knew it, and he took great care in instructing younger members. He also had a wonderfully clear baritone voice, singing harmony to Guillermo's lead melody. He had lost one leg from diabetes, and his eyesight was also poor, but he was always present.

These men have been the core of *Los Pastores* for many years, spending weekends from September to February for the past twenty to fifty years rehearsing or performing. But during my last visit in 1993, only two of them were performing regularly: Vicente Manuel and Guillermo. There was another elder male present, but he was a recent arrival and had not been with the troupe long. Vicente Manuel often bemoaned the fact that it was difficult to get men to participate: "too much television and *bailes* [dances]," he said. Men just did not want to participate any more; they were more interested in Sunday afternoon football than in donning masks or crooks and singing the praises of el Niño Dios.

Women were absent from the group of elders for two reasons. To begin with, none had been performing as long as these men, since they had only been admitted into *Los Pastores* in the past twenty years. More important, even if they had participated as long as the men, the male-centeredness of this genre would have prevented the male elders from recognizing the leadership of these women.

Middle-Age Adults

Most of the women who did participate in *Los Pastores* were middle-age adults, in their mid-forties to late fifties. Confined to the roles of shepherds, these women had taken roles left vacant by the male performers. Carmelina had been performing the longest, joining in the mid-1970s, outlasting several of her daughters who had also been troupe members. She was known for her strong voice, and on occasions when Juan or Guillermo were absent she would sing the lead role. More vocal than the other women, she was very proud of her participation in *Los Pastores* and often spoke excitedly of her

daughter's ability to capture an audience's attention when she was still performing the role of Gila. Carmelina was also deeply devoted to el Niño Dios
and often mentioned that she had survived every difficult situation in her life
because of her deep faith in him.

Like the men, the women lived on fixed incomes, either from their own
wages, their husband's, or various forms of government assistance. Some, like
Carmelina, continued to work, supporting their families, and at times, extended families. Like most of their male co-performers, they held low-paying
jobs with few benefits, some working several jobs to provide the basic needs
for their families.

If it had not been for the two men who performed as devils—one the son
of an elder—men of this generation would have been absent altogether.
These men were younger than their female generational cohorts and, being
employed in industrial jobs, were financially more stable than the elders. One
characteristic they shared with their male elders was the propensity for *chingaderas,* or verbal "screwing around," which José Limón (1989) has identified
with lower-class, male, speechplay. It was quite common for both elder and
middle-generation men to occupy a portion of rehearsal time with their latest
jokes they had learned. It certainly made for an entertaining field experience.

Ricardo was employed in an industrial job that gave him a decent wage to
support himself and his family. His dedication to *Los Pastores* was unquestion-
able, but he was less verbal about his devotion to el Niño Dios. It was not that
he lacked such devotion, only that he was not outspoken about it. Ricardo
had been performing for nearly twenty-five years and on several occasions
hinted that he would not be returning the next performance season. He was
of the *baile* generation that the director often referred to—younger and more
influenced by the modern world—an age group with little involvement in
religious and cultural affairs.

Men and women of this generation seldom interacted, more out of prescribed gender roles and lack of shared interests than any notion of dislike.
During breaks from rehearsals or performances, the men kept to themselves,
as did the women—at least those in this age group—while the younger generation interacted out of a different set of norms.

The marginal income of elders and middle-age adults was further threat-
ened by health problems. When medical care was required, both men and
women attended community clinics, or veterans' or county hospitals, since
few of them had private insurance. One of the male performers even delayed
surgery to repair a hernia for more than a year, which forced him to quit the
troupe because he could no longer stand or walk for long periods of time.

The Adolescent Generation

The adolescent group was made up of both males and females. Most of the males performed as devils—except for one young man who acted the part of Joseph—while the women acted as shepherds or the angel. The young performers had no problem interacting with each other. They often discussed school activities and events, and they enjoyed each other's attention. This group was quite energetic and looked ahead to high school, going to college, and finding secure employment. Some spoke of joining the military—a way out of the *barrio*—or becoming police officers, teachers, or just "getting a job." During my 1993 visit, I found one person enrolled full-time in college and planning to graduate the next semester; another had just been discharged from the marines and was hoping to transfer his military-learned skills into a well-paying job, while others, after taking some college credits, were employed full-time, supporting their parents or their own families. Most had taken jobs in light industrial plants around town and found themselves "caught" in jobs they were not particularly excited about.

Marisol had performed with the troupe for eight years, all of them as a shepherd. When I first met her, she was taking classes at a junior college, studying to become a pharmacy technician. Four years later, she informed me that she was working in a factory for one of the corporations that had a twin plant across the border in the maquila industry. She was the oldest in her family, and when her mother became ill she was forced to work full-time. While her father was still employed, the family required more than one income to meet their basic financial needs and growing medical costs.

Sonia, another shepherd, was quite active in her high school and had participated in several organizational clubs. In 1993 she was in her last year of college and considering a teaching career. Few in her family had completed college, and her ability to continue school and succeed made them very proud of her. Sonia was quite articulate about her goals, as well as her impetus for performing. Although no less a devotional affair for her, *Los Pastores* was central to her identity as a young Mexican-American woman, she told me. Like so many of her generation, she did not grow up speaking Spanish; her participation and commitment to performing was a matter of recovering and learning about her culture. She spoke out about the plight of Mexican Americans in San Antonio and criticized what she considered racism against herself and other Mexican Americans.

The elders expected much from this generation; their presence meant that *Los Pastores* would continue in the future. The young adults met this expecta-

One of the younger members of the troupe. Notice the decorative pictures, trinkets, and ribbons on the cloaks and staffs of the shepherds.

tion with enthusiasm, especially the young women, often speaking of the need to continue this centuries-old performance. As we drove back to the church in the bus after a particularly lively performance, it was not uncommon for the young women to begin reciting the text in its entirety. They were inspired, they said, by men like Vicente Manuel and Guillermo, and for those who knew him, Chencho. *Los Pastores,* they claimed, was part of their history, cultural identity, and tradition; their task was to ensure that it continued in the years to come.

REHEARSAL AND PREPARATION

Despite their years of experience, members of the troupe begin rehearsing in late September under the old covered sidewalk adjoining the school of Our Lady of Guadalupe Church. They meet every Sunday afternoon, regardless of the weather, and keep doing so until mid-December, when the first official performance is given. Rehearsals vary in length but generally last three to four hours, even if the amount of time actually spent rehearsing is less. Admittedly, between jokes, stories, and a few beers, a good part of Sunday afternoon is spent talking instead of rehearsing. But this interaction is important and no less significant than the performances themselves.

During rehearsals, participants tell stories about past events, their travels, and cold evenings warmed by more than a few drinks. These stories range from personal narratives about first performances to other memorable events experienced by an individual or the group. They are informal events marked by joviality, sociability, and entertainment and function not only as preparation but as initiation. Although they are still a serious endeavor, today the atmosphere is much lighter, I am told, than ten or fifteen years ago. In general, rehearsals are a congenial and social event during which the time spent practicing is rounded out with men drinking and women gathering in conversation. It is not uncommon for some narratives to reflect a sense of nostalgia and loss while others are told as the inevitable ways of the present. This is especially true when talk focuses on the way rehearsals were conducted under Chencho's supervision; in those days there was little talking or joking, and performers were expected to memorize all their lines before the first performance of the year.

When rehearsing does begin, the shepherds gather at one corner of the sidewalk while the devils gather at the opposite end. The groups rehearse apart from each other, coming together at least once in an afternoon to work together. Members of the troupe already have their *papeles* or roles, which are decided upon at the last meeting of the previous year. If a particular role has not been filled, members are asked to recruit potential candidates who they believe would make good performers.

It has not always been necessary to recruit performers. According to one member of the troupe, twenty-five years ago there were more than enough people, primarily men, who wanted to perform. But "now, with television and all the modern stuff, people don't have time for this anymore."

As the month of December approaches, more time is spent discussing the coming performances. The director relays information regarding the time and place of engagements and transportation, since many of the members do not drive or own cars. Guadalupe Church allows the troupe access to its bus, when the vehicle is functioning properly: Guillermo makes his round through the neighborhood providing transportation to and from performances.

Since the same costumes are used from one year to the next, there is little discussion about them. The cape is the most elaborate of the costumes, and newcomers are usually loaned one from previous years. The *ganchos,* or staffs, are not difficult to make but they are also passed on to new members. The shepherds are asked to buy their own hat, if they do not own one, and decorate it in the manner of the others. In general, information about costumes is transmitted informally from veteran members of the group to neophytes.

In addition to being urged to learn their lines, performers are told that being a member of *Los Pastores* carries a certain "responsibility" and requires proper comportment. As the director emphasized a few weeks before our first performance, *diciplina* (discipline) is all-important:

> Los pastores no deben tocar los diablos. Son invisibles a todos, sino el Ermitaño y el ángel. Recuerden, que los pastores son humildes y respetuosos. Si juegan durante la pastorela la gente sabe que no están haciendo una obra seria. Hay que tener diciplina.
>
> (The shepherds should not touch the devils. They are invisible to all of you except the hermit and the angel. Remember that the shepherds are humble and respectful people. If you fool around during the performance, the people will know you are not being serious with this work. You need to be disciplined.)

Skill and competence, while stressed at different times during rehearsals, are not the primary factors in the selection of personnel. The reason, in part, is that there is some ambivalence and tension about whether *Los Pastores* is a ritual act or a performed drama. As drama, competence in performance would surely be emphasized; however, as ritual and devotion, the personal disposition of the performers in relation to the ritual act is more critical. Competency in verbal art is deemphasized in two ways: first, little effort is put into training performers—especially those who speak through a mask—to project their voices. The devils, because of the difficulty of projecting through their masks, are not always heard. Although some project better than others, on the whole their voices are difficult to hear. Some of the shepherds, although not hindered by masks, sing or speak softly or quickly, or both, and their lines are often just as difficult to understand as those of the devils. The audience adds to the problem because it is often noisy.

Second, there is little, if any, effort put into musical training or improvement. Luzbel and the lead shepherds, Parrado and Tebano, have excellent singing voices as far as range, pitch, and projection are concerned, but other members, including myself, do not. As a result, the musical quality of the performers is quite uneven. Because of the emphasis on ritual, at least on this point of production, artistic competency is not a primary concern. As explained in chapter 4, other factors point to a more performative understanding of this event.

Two devils dancing as they prepare to approach the shepherds.

In both rehearsal and performance little effort is made to develop a dramatic presence over and above the recitation of lines. There is help for those who are unable to remember their lines. Guillermo, reading from a copy of the text, often cues performers, providing them with the first few words of their lines when the need arises. At times, however, verbal competency is stressed, especially if a large audience is present. Then performers are told to project loud and clear so that they can be heard above the background noise.

As a display of communicative competence, *Los Pastores* is uneven and varies from performer to performer, and at times, from one enactment to another. In a recent description of performance, Richard Bauman (1986a:3) states, "Performance thus calls forth special attention to and heightened awareness of both the act of expression and the performer." Although this is true for certain aspects of the drama (the attention given to the hermit for his performance skills), this notion of performance does not hold true for *Los Pastores* as a whole. In this case, the performative aesthetic is more collective—it is the performance of *Los Pastores* as "an event" that warrants attention and by which competence is judged. It is not the display of individual competence that is important, but the endeavors of a collectivity that display their performative skill as a group that mark this event. An example of this occurred one evening when, in the midst of a performance, Roberto, a shepherd, grew ill and could not walk to the *nacimiento* (the manger) to adore *el Niño Dios*. While members of the group and audience helped him to a nearby chair, another shepherd quickly walked to the *nacimiento,* bowed his head, and recited his lines. At this moment, bringing the act to completion and keeping the text intact were more important than performing it correctly.

The official beginning of the performance season varies. I was told that the first performance is hosted by Our Lady of Guadalupe Church on December 24, but earlier performances are also scheduled. Most of these performances occur in surrounding communities outside the city and are considered "dress rehearsals" for the Christmas Eve event. After Christmas, performances continue until the *candelaria,* the feast of the blessing of the candles, on February 2. Traditionally, this day is celebrated as the *levantado del niño,* or the sitting up of the child, in Mexican folk religious practice. On a few rare occasions, a performance may be scheduled after this date. Between Christmas and early February, performances are scheduled every Saturday and Sunday, and now and then there are three in one weekend. Performances are arranged by invitation, with some local churches and communities having hosted this event for fifteen years or longer. *Los Pastores* is performed in three different venues: the backyards of *barrio* homes; churches; and Mission San José, one of the historic missions located in the city, where the performance is sponsored by the San Antonio Conservation Society.

CHRISTMAS EVE: *LAS POSADAS* AND THE *MISA DE GALLO*

Christmas Eve at Guadalupe Church is a combination of folk tradition and Catholic liturgical practice. Before the *misa de gallo* (midnight mass, or, literally, the cockcrow mass), church personnel organize *las posadas,* a reenactment of the story of Mary and Joseph looking for lodging in Bethlehem. This practice varies from one community to another, but in general it features a couple dressed as Mary and Joseph, if statues are not used, going from house to house seeking a place to stay for the night. At the last house, they are given hospice and a *fiesta* (party) ensues with native Mexican festive dishes like *tamales* and *buñuelos* (cornmeal dough rolled and stuffed with meat and a thin wafer of fried and sugared dough). Children are entertained with the breaking of a *piñata,* a papier-mâché globe formed in the shape of an animal or cartoon character and filled with candy. Once those participating in the posadas have returned to the church, the Christmas Eve performance of *Los Pastores* begins. This is the only performance that is preceded by *las posadas.*

The Christmas Eve performance is held in the old church, which has been converted into a meeting hall and senior citizens' meals center. The atmosphere is calm and casual, although a few of the audience members arrive dressed in clothes indicative of the holiday season. Depending on the weather, there can be thirty to sixty people gathered for this annual event. Many members of the audience are from the local community and have participated in this particular performance for years; others are newcomers to *Los Pastores*, wanting to experience this event for themselves and their children.[4]

People are still entering and taking their seats even after the performance begins. Opposite the performers sit some of the wives of the shepherds and devils, talking, knitting, making coffee, and warming tamales for those who have gathered. When the performance begins, these women continue with their conversation, catching up on news and events that have passed since they last saw one another. Meanwhile, the children in the audience can be found speaking to parents and friends, running in and out of the hall, or laughing at the sight of the devils giving chase to the hermit. The hall is filled with noises ranging from the shepherds' and devils' voices to the chatter of friends, children running to and fro, and the sounds of cooking utensils clanging the insides of pots and pans. Those who expect a solemn and quiet scene of religious devotion will be disappointed. Between the performers who speak in soft voices and the surrounding noise, hearing the drama can be quite difficult.

Right after the performance, people are invited to attend the *misa de gallo*. While audience members meander toward the church, the performers gather to discuss the next performance, getting directions and exchanging stories about the first performance of the year.

The shepherds, because of their role in *Los Pastores*, have a special part in the *misa de gallo* that follows. They are invited to sit in the first few pews of the church and lead the congregation in a special hymn during the liturgical service. Although almost all of the shepherds attend and participate in this service, none of the devils are to be found. Instead, they stay to dismantle the *infierno* (the hellmouth where the devils congregate when not performing), drink a few more beers, and leave. It seems their dramatic roles influence their participation in the *misa de gallo*. The shepherds, those who journey to see el Niño Dios, participate in the official religious service of the evening; the devils, those who attempt to thwart the shepherds, do not attend and have no special part in the official liturgical event of the evening. Even though the Christmas Eve celebration is, in a sense, the high point of the year for the performers, it is just the beginning of the performance season, which will last for the next month and a half.

DOMAINS OF PERFORMANCE

As already mentioned, *Los Pastores* is performed in three domains, or venues: neighborhood homes in the *barrios* of San Antonio's West Side, local churches, and San José Mission. In distinguishing between these three domains, I demonstrate that each domain is a frame, or setting, that demarcates a place for the differential construction of social relations and the concomitant meaning of *Los Pastores*.

The *Barrio*-Home Performance

Little additional work needs to be done in preparing for a *barrio* performance of *Los Pastores*.[5] Costumes and characters have long been chosen, and if someone is absent, that person's role is dropped or taken up by another performer, who will work both parts. Most planning and effort goes into transporting the *infierno* to the site of the performance, and although this is not a difficult task, it takes several people because of its cumbersome size. If the family or hosting group has not constructed an *altarcito* (home altar) and *nacimiento* (manger) for el Niño Dios, the players set up their own small manger.

Performers usually arrive between thirty to forty-five minutes before the scheduled beginning of an event. But schedules, especially for performances in a home, are quite flexible. It is not unusual to begin an hour after the stated time while waiting for food to cook and for neighbors or family members to arrive.

During this time, social interaction divides along gender lines. Male members of the troupe usually stand outdoors, talking, telling jokes, drinking beer or whiskey, and socializing among themselves and with the male members of the hosting family. It is not unusual to find the men outdoors, huddled around a makeshift bonfire, deep in conversation. Female members of the troupe, if not outdoors socializing with the other women, are indoors talking with members of the hosting family or helping out in the kitchen as they prepare food for the festivities. The mothers and wives of the performers are almost always present, and have been associated with the performance as long as their husbands, children, or grandchildren. Many of them help indoors with the cooking and serving while others spend time in conversation catching up on news. Although not performing themselves, spouses are just as dedicated as their acting family members, having been part of this event for many years.

The usual place of the performance in a *barrio* setting is the driveway or backyard. Often, combination driveway and carport provides an elongated, rectangular area in which to perform, as well as shelter from wind or rain. Little consideration is given to any formal stage setting or the decor, although in some cases families string Christmas lights and candles around the area. None of this is necessary, and the decision to do it is left to the discretion of the hosting family.

Before the performance begins, the host, usually the woman of the family, introduces and thanks the performers for coming. In the majority of events in which I participated, the performance was arranged as part of a *manda,* or dyadic vow, fulfilling a *promesa* (promise) made to a saint or the Virgin. In these cases, women of the family made specific reference to their *promesas,* citing their spiritual request, and thanking el Niño Dios or La Virgen for having answered their religious supplication. This is a critical factor in home performances, as discussed in chapter 6.

As in the Christmas Eve performance, the home is marked by an informal character. Members of the audience sit close, bundled in blankets, sipping hot cocoa or coffee, watching and talking among themselves. Children may be still for a while, but they end up wandering around, playing, and enjoying themselves. When the devils appear, the children usually come back for a closer look, as they are impressed and awed by the masks and costumes. The men usually become absorbed in the performance, although it is not uncommon to find them off to one side drinking and conversing. For the most part, the women of the family are inside ensuring that the preparations for the meal are progressing. Elderly members of the family usually stay inside and help cook, especially in colder weather.

The home location is one of interest, partial participation, conversation, movement from indoors to outdoors and back, neighbors wandering over from down the street, and shepherds marching, singing, while Luzbel rants and fights with the angel. In all, this scene is marked by the familiar—the troupe members interact with the audience more loosely and readily, gathering in conversation, helping with the preparation, and engaging in joking before and after the performance. During the performance, shepherds are more flexible, laughing at comical scenes, occasionally talking among themselves about events unrelated to *Los Pastores.* In this domain, it is more common to shorten a performance if the weather is extremely cold or wet, so as to allow people to leave early or move indoors. When not performing, the shepherds and devils are likely to be found inside keeping warm or gathered around a bonfire.

After the performance, food is served by the women of the hosting family, with the spouses of the performers helping, at least marginally, by directing traffic indoors and arranging chairs. When all is done the performers move slowly back to the bus or cars, sitting and waiting for the trip back to the church; the devils begin to dismantle the *infierno,* loading it in the truck, so it will be ready to be taken to the next performance.

The Church

Although the number and places of performances vary from year to year, several churches have sponsored *Los Pastores* for a number of years. Christ the King Church, for example, has sponsored a performance for the past fifteen years. Because of early announcements and excellent weather, the performance in January 1988 saw approximately three hundred people in attendance. Several other churches, both local and in the outer areas of the city, also sponsored performances.

The most striking difference between the home and church domain has to do with sociability. Although there is still a sense of familiarity in the church domain, and enthusiastic communal and communicative relations between performers and audience, there is less social interaction at the church than at the home. Before a performance starts, the members of the troupe are less likely to interact with members of the church audience; and, audience members, having the church as a geographical and social focal point, tend to interact among themselves more than with the performers. Being a less familial location for both performers and audience members, this domain is marked by a distance not found in the home environment. Even family members of the performers are less likely to associate with the audience in the hosting institution, before, during, and after the performance.

Everyone's behavior is affected by the physical site itself. The religious context of this domain enhances the ritual dimensions of *Los Pastores.* The smell of candles, the incense, and religious iconography all help to produce a different sentiment from what is experienced in the *barrio*-home, an issue I discuss as memory-place in chapter 6. Performances usually take place in church halls, which tend to have a large open space that creates a less familial and more distant atmosphere. There is little to suggest it is particular to the community, although posters and artwork mark its religious character. Furthermore, per-

Luzbel and the other devils heading to the dungeons of the Earth after their defeat.

formances inside a church are usually less flexible than those in the *barrio:* aisleways and fixed benches restrict the use of space and movement. One advantage of these indoor performances, however, is the acoustics, which in church buildings are usually good and allow voices to carry quite a distance. Performances outdoors, on church grounds, usually have ample space but less sound control. Open spaces give people more room to walk about and thus create a sense of constant motion and disengagement from the performance.

Another important feature of the church domain is the number of people who can watch the event. I noted earlier that Christ the King Church had about three hundred people at a performance it sponsored. This size of audience also affects the way the performance is experienced. First, in the physical arrangement of space, performers are situated so that they speak to one another and not out toward the audience. Since they do not use any amplification, this makes it difficult for people in the audience to hear over the noise of the crowd.[6] A second factor is the crowd itself: the sheer number of people creates a more festival-like atmosphere. In spite of physical limitations and distractions, the church venue maintains the potential for large group responses to the drama. At Christ the King Church, the crowd roared, clapped, and shouted *gritos* (shouts of approval) in response to the hermit's interaction with the devils. And when Michael the Archangel defeated Luzbel, the atmosphere was filled with jocularity and dramatic tension, and the group response was unlike that found in the home.

For the performers, this domain constitutes a more dramatic frame in which some members of the troupe enhance their performance. In general, however, the performative practice of most members—that is, the way in which they recite their lines, move, and sing—remains the same, although the atmosphere is certainly less relaxed in this location. In the home, the shepherds are more at ease and jovial and talk from time to time in the midst of the performance. In the church, performers are more serious and less likely to talk with one another, and more prone to feel they are on display. When one of the women shepherds was asked to take over the lead and sing for the ailing Parrado at a church performance, she grew nervous and tense and remained that way throughout the entire event. Even though she had performed in *Los Pastores* for more than twenty years, this new role in front of a church audience was enough to change her entire demeanor. Later, she admitted to me that if it had been a smaller audience and a home setting, she would have had no problems taking over the lead role.

Another distinction between the home and the church domain is related to the festivities after the performance. Food, except that served to the performers, has to be bought. In place of a home setting where food is a gift of the hosting family, in the church domain food is served cafeteria-style, with set portions and commercial food products, and audience members are charged for refreshments during the performance and afterward. The intimacy of the home table, the social nature of family cooking, and the relations that are constitutive of this process are lacking in the church venue.

Interaction after the performance is also less intimate. Instead of socializing with members of the hosting family, the performers often sit together as a group and do not interact with the audience members. On several occasions, some of the performers who had finished eating went off and sat in the bus, waiting to depart. Similarly, audience members are more likely to interact only with themselves, and few stay for any of the postperformance activities.

Mission San José

Since the mid-1940s the San Antonio Conservation Society has sponsored a performance of *Los Pastores* at San José Mission. San José is one of five Spanish missions from the colonial period and is now under the joint control of the Catholic Church and the National Park Service. The San Antonio Conservation Society sponsors at least one performance a year in this historic setting. This domain differs rather sharply from that of the church and home in that the event is attended by tourists and others.

One of the distinctive features of mission performances is the use of a translator, an idea initiated by the Conservation Society. Translation into English is provided by a well-known local radio announcer who, for many years, has been associated with the San Antonio Missions, hosting brief historical documentaries produced for radio broadcast. He acts as a master of ceremonies, providing a brief synopsis or translation of the dialogue while the actors are performing in Spanish. The result of such an arrangement is one of narrative distance and disjuncture, since the translation is not verbatim and is done for the large tourist and non-Spanish-speaking audience. As a result, people are only partly engaged in the performance and rely on the emcee for their specific knowledge of the narrative. The quality of the performance is also affected since the master of ceremonies speaks over a microphone whereas the performers do not use any amplification. As a result, the voice of the announcer sometimes drowns out the voices of the performers or takes attention away from them.

The large number of tourists in the audience also affects the event. There were about 150 people at the performance in 1988, about 400 in 1989, most of whom were tourists and non-Spanish speakers. As a result, they depended on the emcee's summaries of the narrative and jocular asides, and although they may have known the plot of the drama (those aspects related to the traditional discourse on Christmas), the verbal artistry and cultural-specific codes went unnoticed by this group. This led audience members to wander away from the action, talk more loudly among themselves, and become disengaged from the performance.

The physical arrangement of the mission also affects the performance. *Los Pastores* is performed in a large open space in the mission enclosure. The rectangular staging area found in the other domains is replicated here, although much longer, with audience members sitting around the entire rectangle. The temperature in 1988 was 26 degrees Farenheit, with the result that people tended to move to the periphery, where barrels filled with burning wood helped keep them warm. Many people, especially those unfamiliar with the Spanish language, stayed around the barrels, coming in only for an occasional view.

Because of these distinct features, performers treat the mission more formally than the other two venues, and thus there is little interaction among the actors outside of their prescribed roles. It is rare to find performers and audience members interacting, except for the occasional request for a photograph. Even members of the San Antonio Conservation Society keep to themselves, only engaging audience members and performers to encourage them to purchase food from the booths strewn throughout the area. This lack of interaction, I suggest, is due to the fact that there is no social context for interaction, except for this event. As demonstrated in chapter 6, audience members, performers, and members of the conservation society inhabit distinct social locations that offer little or no areas of social convergence. Therefore, once the performance is over, people leave having experienced little interaction since audience members and performers have no other social, political, or religious arenas in which they directly interact.

Relations between the Conservation Society and the performers, especially the director, have become strained recently because of the fee the society pays the troupe, an amount that, like all other donations, goes to the church and not to the performers. In the past several years the performers have been asked to produce two performances without an increase in the fee, but the director has refused. This is the only group for whom he has refused a performance because of the amount of money involved.

Another controversial issue that has not yet been made public concerns the use of Spanish in the performances. The master of ceremonies, having participated in this event for a number of years, has on several occasions urged the director to switch to English. This, he says, will appeal to a wider audience and make the drama more accessible to the non-Spanish-speaking audience and hence more marketable as a tourist event. The director has refused to even consider this possibility.

Before I explore the more intricate aspects of *Los Pastores* as the enactment of particular narrative, poetic, and structural devices—which constitute its dramatized structure—it is important to trace its generic tradition, which goes back to medieval liturgical ritual and popular cultural practices that made their way into New Spain soon after the conquest of Mexico. This is the subject of chapter 2.

2

From Spain to South Texas: Tracing a Text

The text of *Los Pastores* brought to San Antonio in 1913 by Leandro Granado from Irapuato, México, while unique in its textual variations, cultural enactment, and the meaning it renders for this particular performance community, shares a broader literary tradition with its generic progenitors. This textual history—an eight-hundred-year span that begins in medieval Spain, moves to the New World at the time of the conquest, then north to the southwestern United States as this terrain is explored and settled—reveals a complex assemblage of texts that coalesce at different historical moments into various guises or genres known more commonly as *pastorelas*. At each historical juncture, the local cultural practices and social ambiance of its performers influenced, and at times altered, the narrative forms and symbolic resources of this event. Still, these texts, like the one that is the subject of this study, have maintained many of their distinctive traits throughout this long and tenuous history, notably, their poetic form, stock characters, and ludic components.

THE ORIGINS OF THE *PASTORELA*

Religious drama has long been a part of European custom, especially in Spain, where it has flourished since the Middle Ages. Some scholars believe these performances originated in Italy and from there moved to Spain as early as the eleventh century. Richard Donovan (1985:8), in his revisionist study of Spanish liturgical drama, claims that these events began in Byzantium in the tenth century as part of the Easter liturgical cycle known as the *Quem quaeritis*, an Introit of the Easter mass in the Roman Catholic Church. Unfortunately, this evidence does not come from the East, but from the West, in the text of *Regularis Concordia* found in England. By the year 1000, this Easter play was already being performed in France, as well as Germany (Donovan 1985:12).

Christmas liturgical dramas follow the Easter tradition and were likely modeled after the *Quem quaeritis*. Few dramatic presentations seem to have developed from the Introits of the Christmas liturgy. Donovan states that "the dramatic element for Christmas was often supplied at Laudes rather than at Matins. As such, it was not the *Quem quaeritis* trope that formed the core of the play, but the antiphon *Quem vidistis, pastores, dicite,* or another similar to it, *Pastores, dicite, quidnam vidistis* (Donovan 1985:15). In his seminal work, *The Drama of the Medieval Church,* Karl Young (1933:II) refers to these antiphons as the *Officium Pastorum,* or Office of the Shepherds. These are the same antiphons that Stanley Robe (1954) later attributes to the earliest forms of liturgical shepherds' plays. Donovan dates this Christmas play, and its Epiphany counterpart, to the eleventh century.

Three versions of the *Officium Pastorum* emerged between the tenth and thirteenth century. The first is from the cathedral at Padua, Italy, and is found in an *ordo,* or ritual book, of the thirteenth century. The second is from the cathedral of Clermont-Ferrand in France, and the third and most elaborate of the three is found in the liturgical traditions of Rouen, France, dating from the thirteenth and fourteenth centuries (Young 1933:II). Common to all these texts is a manger prepared at the side of the altar with the images of Mary and Jesus placed next to it. An angel, usually a young boy, narrates the Annunciation from the Bible; during this narration, the shepherds enter the church. The chorus joins in the singing of the Annunciation, which is followed by the Gloria. The shepherds are greeted by several midwives; then a curtain is pulled revealing the images of Mary and Jesus. The midwives recite a passage from the prophet Isaiah, and the shepherds sing the Alleluia (Pearce 1956:79). These texts were performed inside the church and staged in front of the altar or, at times, just below the choir. Once they became more elaborate and required more space, they were staged in the atrium of the church. When they shifted to the vernacular and were popularized, they were moved outside the church altogether and eventually to the town square (Ravicz 1970:27).

The *auto sacramental* and the *coloquio* are two forms of religious drama developed in Spain and are precursors to the tradition of the *pastorela*. The *auto sacramental* began in the fourteenth century with the merging of allegorical elements of the morality play and historical and dogmatic elements of the mystery play. This merging created a new theological dramatic form that incorporated material from both the Old and New Testaments of the Bible. *Loas,* or introductory material that is salutational, along with special endings of *villancicos,* or carols (Ravicz 1970:29), were also features of this new form. The *auto* was originally performed during the feast of Corpus Christi, but it became so popular that its form was reproduced for most of the major Christian feasts, including Easter, Epiphany, and the Saints' Days.[1]

The *coloquio* is a simpler dramatic form written in dialogue, prose, or verse form, with little plot. In Spain, it was usually performed in processions, preceded by the recitation of prayers or *loas*. Often its dramatic parts were broken up by musical interludes, with the whole *coloquio* terminating in a verbal summary of the entire program. These *autos* and *coloquios* were the generic forms of the early shepherds' plays in Spain, and many of the *pastorelas* in México and the southwestern United States maintain these generic names (Campa 1934a, 1934b; Robe 1954, 1957).

The *Auto* (or *Misterio*) *de los Reyes Magos* is the oldest preserved example of a shepherds' play produced for use outside the church liturgy that uses vernacular elements. It dates from the early to middle part of the twelfth century (Crawford 1911; Ravicz 1970; Robe 1954). Unfortunately, only 147 lines of this play are preserved, and there are no other similar dramas from this period.

The *Siete Partidas*, the code of Castillian law introduced by Alfonso X in the middle of the thirteenth century, substantiates the existence of Spanish liturgical dramas at this time. It encourages clergy to develop and produce religious dramas, especially those "dealing with such subjects as the birth of Jesus, the Annunciation of the angel to the shepherds, the Adoration of the Magi, and the Resurrection" (Robe 1954:4). At the same time, the clergy were prohibited from producing "juegos de escarnio, porque los vengan á ver gentes" (contemptuous or mocking plays, because they are seen by the people) (Crawford 1911:378). In spite of the concern over the ludic components of this young dramatic tradition, one of the defining characteristics of the *pastorela* was its popular humor, as is also the case today.

By the latter part of the fifteenth century, several other texts had emerged, and with them, characteristics common to contemporary *pastorelas*.[2] In 1480 Gómez Manrique composed *La representación del nacimiento de Nuestro Señor*. This play, written for the nuns at the convent at Calabazanos, is the earliest preserved vernacular descendant of the *Officium Pastorum* (Crawford 1911:377). It was no longer performed in the Catholic liturgy in the church, but in the convent, an entirely different domain. And the text's last song, *Canción para callar al niño* (a song to quiet the child or lullaby) is similar to songs found in almost all shepherds' plays that appear at a later date (Crawford 1911:377).

Another text, the *Vita Christi* written by Father Iñigo de Mendoza, dates from the same year. In this play, the shepherds speak their own vernacular and incorporate elements of play, terror, and gluttony, all of which overshadow the nativity itself (Crawford 1911:380).

The next major development is found in the work of Juan del Encina, who wrote, among other texts, the *Egloga de las grandes lluvias* in 1498. With his work, the shepherds take on their own distinct, festive, and comic characteristics, acting like rural pastoral folk and speaking a coarse Spanish from the region of Salamanca. Encina's literary technique is notable because it encompasses another significant literary tradition: the pastoral. This classic literary form is recognized by its contrast of the idyllic and mythic past with the more urbane and complex present. In Encina, the shepherds of Virgil's eclogues fuse with those of the nativity to produce an authentically Spanish, and religiously utopian, genre: the *pastorela* (Estrada 1974). After Encina, the presence of poor, naive, gregarious shepherds in a romantic comedy that idealizes the simple life of the country can only be interpreted as part of the classic pastoral tradition.

Another of Encina's conventions was his introduction of the presentation of gifts to the Christ child by the shepherds, an element borrowed from the story of the Wise Men (Robe 1954:5). Encina is an important figure in the historical development of the *pastorela* and of religious drama as a whole because he "revivified the liturgical drama by the introduction of these realistic elements. It is not surprising that his influence spread even to America, since his religious and pastoral dramas were models for other authors for more than half a century" (Marie 1948:41).

The next literary figure to contribute to this genre is Lucas Fernández. No date has been found for his drama, *Auto á farsa del nacimiento,* but it appears to have come from this same period. His work is quite similar to that of Encina, except for two new features. First, he uses this genre to convey religious doctrine, and as a result, it displays a strong clerical style (Crawford 1911:285). Second, he introduces the character Pascual, an early prototype of the gluttonous shepherd found in future texts.

In 1503 Gil Vicente wrote the *Auto dos Reis Magos,* a drama that offers a satirical picture of the friars, and *Auto da Mofina Mendes* (in Portuguese), which features the character of Barba Triste, the prototype of the lazy shepherd, Bartolo, who appears in many of the Mexican *pastorelas* (Rael 1965:17).[3]

It is during this period that the Devil and Vice appear as comic figures, frequently associated with Bobo, another stock character of the *pastorela* (Crawford 1911:397). The introduction of the devil is significant since Luzbel, or Lucifer, soon becomes a primary figure of the genre. With the writings of Lope de Rueda in the sixteenth century, *Bato* and *Gila* become standard characters of the *pastorela* and are present in the version of *Los Pastores* featured in this study.

A striking characteristic of the Spanish religious dramas that appeared at the end of the fifteenth century was their use of popular and festive humor. Although they originated as Christmas plays, these *autos* and *coloquios* now focused on the activities and pranks of the shepherds, and if religious elements were maintained, they were overshadowed by the ludic antics of these characters.

It is clear from the writings of Bakhtin (1984), who in fact speaks of this genre and its development in Lope de Vega, and from others, that such carnivalesque representations functioned as a means of oppositional culture in the Middle Ages.[4] Although many spectacles and public cultural events have been drawn into the mainstream of postindustrial society and thereby have lost much of their public commentary (Sennett 1974), the *pastorela's* long tradition of social humor continues to be a significant feature of the genre.

THE *PASTORELA* IN MÉXICO

Drama was an important part of life for the indigenous cultures of México. Aztec society, which was dominant in México at the time of the Spanish conquest, was highly ritualized and aesthetically sophisticated: its dramas and other literary expressions included comic and farcical elements. Troubadours called *tlaquetzqui* traveled from village to village singing myths and reciting traditional oral histories and religious stories. They were well versed in theatrical and dramatic techniques and thus were known as *boca florida*, or flowery or poetic mouth. Some in this group specialized in obscene and farcical poetry depicting humorous interludes between clowns, prostitutes, and other comic characters (Ravicz 1970:17). The *Codex Ramirez* has the following account:

> After having eaten, all the people gathered there and the actors [*representantes*] came out and performed farces. They pretended to be deaf, seized with colds, limping, blind, and maimed, all coming to ask health of the idol. The deaf were acting ridiculously, those with colds [were] coughing and wheezing, and the lame were limping and listing their many miseries and complaints. All this made the people laugh greatly. (Ravicz 1970:21)

The importance of the arts in Aztec culture is also confirmed by the presence of schools—run by indigenous priests in their capacity as educators, known as *cuicacalli*—that specialized in the training of musicians, singers, composers, and dancers (Ravicz 1970:20).

Following Spain's conquest of the Aztecs and other indigenous groups of México in 1521, the social and religious worlds of these native populations disintegrated. Through war, forced labor, and disease, the Spanish were responsible for the annihilation of many of these groups, as well as the destruction of indigenous life, as it was known.

Hernán Cortés, in his effort to Christianize the natives, called upon Pope Leo X for missionary support. A papal bull issued on April 5, 1521, granted his request, and within two years the first twelve Franciscan missionaries arrived, soon followed by Dominicans, Jesuits, Augustinians, and Carmelites.[5] These men hoped to build a new Christendom, the "Iglesia Indiana," motivated by the hope of a new millennium, issuing in the "third stage" of Christianity spoken about by Joachim of Floris (Lafaye 1976:31). As Christian educators, the missionaries often used the traditions of the indigenous cultures, specifically their epic forms, as a framework for Christian stories, catechisms, or histories of the Catholic Church (Ravicz 1970). The missionaries also authored literary and dramatic plays, produced and performed for indigenous audiences. In 1530, for example, the *auto, Conversión de San Pablo,* was performed in México City, at San José de los Naturales, in Náhuatl; it featured indigenous actors.

Other early dramatic works include *El Juicio Final,* written by F. Andrés de Olmos, one of the first twelve missionaries to come to México and well known for his linguistic abilities. The exact year of the performance is still unknown, but Joaquín G. Icazbalceta, the Mexican historian, linguist, and folklorist, speculates that it occurred between 1535 and 1548. José Rojas Garcidueñas (1939:xii) claims that the first drama produced in the New World was the *Representación del fin del mundo,* performed in Tlatelolco in 1533. Although some sources disagree with this date, it is safe to say that it was one of the earliest performances of religious drama in México.

F. Bernadino Sahagún, the early Spanish historian, missionary, and ethnographer, wrote 365 short plays—which contain lively dialogue, song, and gesture—one for each day of the year. The date of Sahagún's writings is uncertain, but it would have to have been after 1529, the year he arrived in New Spain (Marie 1948:49). Perhaps the most well known of these early dramatists was a secular priest, Fernando Gonzalez Esclava, who wrote *Coloquios Espirituales y sacramentales y poesias sagradas,* which were published in 1610 and which Icazbalceta considers the finest work of the entire period (Marie 1948:51). In *Historia de los Indios de Nueva España,* F. Toribio Motolinía says he saw nine different plays in Tlaxcala in 1538. These were performed on the occasion of the major feast days, including the nativity. Icazbalceta suggests that Motolinía wrote these plays himself (Marie 1948:35).

Another of the early missionaries to participate in this endeavor was F. Pedro de Gante, who founded the Colegio de San Francisco in México City as a place for teaching arts, crafts, and special trades. He even built a special church with an enlarged atrium for the purpose of staging his performances. Among his many religious productions were a number of *autos sacramentales* written in the sixteenth century (Garcidueñas 1939; Marie 1948).[6]

Other sources mention shepherds' plays from this same historical period. In his *Historia Ecclesiástica Indiana*, F. Gerónimo de Mendieta wrote about the Christmas and Epiphany *coloquios* he saw performed in México around or after 1554 (Marie 1948:36). In 1587, F. Alonce Ponce, the commissary of the Franciscan missions in New Spain, saw *Los Pastores* and the *Adoración de los Reyes* in Tlaxamulco and when he inquired about these performances was told they had been going on for at least thirty years (Marie 1948:37). In 1596 in Sinaloa, *mitotes*, or ritual dances, with *coloquios* and *villancicos* were performed in the indigenous languages and were most likely written by the Jesuits who worked in the area (Garcidueñas 1939:xiv).

The popular humor that was characteristic of the Spanish texts was also present in the shepherds' plays of New Spain. Moreover, it was also used by these early writers. In fact, the plays connected with the feast of Corpus Christi, the most important of the genre, were not allowed to be performed in 1544 or 1545 because Bishop Zumárraga objected to their farcical elements (Marie 1948:53). "A thing lacking in reverence and most shameful to see," declared the incensed bishop, "is the procession of men in masks and grotesque costumes representing women that precede the consecrated Host, as they move along, jumping and dancing with dishonest and suggestive gestures, preventing, with their noise, the songs of the Church from being heard" (Castañeda 1932:431).

Zumárraga's edict failed to prevent the expression of popular humor, however, as noted by the *Documentos inéditos muy raros para la historia de México*, edited by Genaro García. García states that the Third Church Council of 1585 prohibited presentations in churches "of dances, ballets, representations, and profane songs, either on the day of the birth of Our Lord, or on the fiesta of Corpus Christi, or on other similar occasions" (Ravicz 1970:77).

It is not surprising that the shepherds' plays were among the most popular dramas performed at the time. Having begun as a didactic device by the early missionaries, these plays diffused into the folk theater repertoire of mestizo communities, adding to the secular humor of other *comedias*. The format of the *auto* and *coloquio* allowed a variety of themes and styles to be incorporated into the text, which explains in part their popularity. In addition, their music and narrative structure were highly adaptable to a number of circumstances and open to individual and indigenous changes and contributions (Robe 1957:2).

Juan Rael's (1965) historic-geographic study of the *pastorela* concludes that all of the texts found in México and the southwestern United States, but one, were of Mexican origin. The exception appears to have been written in California, and only three of the texts he examined had fragments from earlier Spanish texts (Rael 1965:315).

In most respects, the authors of these Mexican texts continued the Spanish *pastorela* tradition of imitating the comic and festive style, the poetic form, and the performance occasions. Even the names of characters in the Spanish texts were kept in their Mexican counterparts (Robe 1954:7).

LOS PASTORES IN THE SOUTHWEST

The performance of the *pastorela* in the Southwest coincides with the earliest Franciscan presence in what is now New Mexico, which arrived with the expedition of Juan de Oñate in 1598. The colony de Oñate established in New Mexico lasted until 1690, at which time an Indian revolt forced the inhabitants to move to an area north of what is now El Paso, Texas. Several works written during this period bring to light some important details about these performances. First are the historical records of Father Esteven de Perea, who was custodian of the Franciscan province in New Mexico. In his *Relación*, a report on the mission written about 1629, he makes reference to a talented Franciscan, Roque de Figueredo, who taught ecclesiastical chant at the missions in Zuñi or Hawikuh. In addition, the *Memorial of Fray Alonso de Benavides*, which is a report presented to the commissary general of the Indies on the missions in New Mexico (with a presumed date of 1630), mentions the teaching of organ chant along the Rio Grande. These two chants, organ and ecclesiastical, are "recognizable in the chant which survives today in the *letras* in the extant *pastorelas* and other religious plays" (Marie 1948:65).

Second, a catalogue of books recorded by F. Francisco Atanasio Domínguez of the Custody of New Mexico lists *Ortus Pastores* under number 35. Since the word *ortus* does not exist in the Spanish lexicon, several scholars have concluded that this was an error and most likely should have read *Autos Pastores*

(Marie 1948:74). If correct, this would verify the presence of the *pastorela* in New Mexico in 1776.

During the Enlightenment, México passed a series of secularization laws forcing the Franciscans out of their established missions and replacing them with secular or diocesan priests (Diekemper 1985:47). These laws were extended to New Mexico in 1787 and Texas in 1794. Few secular priests answered this call, however, so that following the retirement and death of the priests already on the frontier, their numbers declined greatly. By 1828 only six Franciscan friars were left in the New Mexico area, and the situation in Texas was much the same. Although historical records offer only sketchy evidence on the religious practices of this time, they do suggest that folk religious practices became the foundation for spiritual experience. Early settlers in this region were left to fend for themselves in matters of religion, organizing worship services and festive celebrations for Good Friday, Corpus Christi, and other feasts (Diekemper 1985:48). Carlos Castañeda, in his work on the history of the Catholic Church in Texas, states: "By the time the Secular Interlude occurred, this sponsorship of simple devotions of the people, during the absence of the priests at one or another of their numerous posts, became widespread" (quoted in Leyva 1951:60).

The Franciscan presence, although insecure, still had an impact on the diffusion of the *pastorela* in the Southwest. Rael (1965:51–54) has traced three lines of distribution from México to the United States. The first point of diffusion begins in Zacatecas and runs north to southern Colorado, with versions of the same text in Fresnillo, Durango, Las Cruces, San Rafael, Albuquerque, Galisteo, Las Vegas, and Colorado. Rael's second line of distribution, not as direct as the first, finds versions of the same text in California and at the Colegio de San Fernando in México City, Colegio de la Santa Cruz in Querétaro, and the Colegio de Zapopán in Guadalajara. And his third major line of distribution is from Zacatecas to San Antonio, Texas, with versions found in Saltillo, Monterrey, Brownsville, and Rio Grande City, Texas. Zacatecas's influence is due to the presence of a major Franciscan seminary, the Colegio de Nuestra Señora de Guadalupe, housed in that city.[7]

Rael identifies three central texts of U.S. origin: those from Rio Grande City, Texas, studied by Bourke (1893) and Cole (1907); San Rafael, New Mexico, studied by Cole (1907) and Campa (1934a; 1934b); and another version in southern Colorado, which is unpublished. Several scholars have disagreed with Rael, among them Pearce (1956), who identifies two other important New Mexican texts. In his list, Pearce includes a *pastorela* from Agua Fría–Las Palomas and a second entitled *El Día de la Nueva Aurora*. Despite the historical evidence that Rael's work brings to the scholarship on the *pastorela,* his results remain inconclusive. The number of texts he has identified greatly misrepresents the diffusion of this dramatic form. John Igo (1985:136), in his work in the *pastorela* in San Antonio, has collected or heard of at least fifteen manuscripts in the Texas area; and the Heinrich Collection at Our Lady of the Lake University Library in San Antonio, Texas, contains twenty manuscripts.[8]

During the Mexican colonial period the *pastorela* went through several important changes. Originally intended as a didactic device for the indigenous populations, the *pastorela* was adopted by the growing mestizo communities. Once incorporated, instead of serving as a pedagogical tool of the Spanish missionaries, the *pastorela* became an instrument of religious maintenance and cultural identity. This change in the performance community distinguishes those plays produced by the missionaries in México from their Spanish antecedents. The *pastorela* had run a course from medieval liturgical drama in Spain to missionary production in México to folk practice in México and the southwestern United States.

LOS PASTORES IN TEXAS

The most well-known published account of *Los Pastores* in Texas is by John G. Bourke in the *Journal of American Folklore* in 1893 concerning the Rio Grande City version he saw performed in 1891. This version was later translated by M. R. Cole (1907) in one of the early studies of the *pastorela*. Américo Paredes has published excerpts of another manuscript, belonging to Juan Manuel Perez of Brownsville, Texas, dated October 14, 1891. As Paredes (1964:466–67) states: "It would be strange indeed if Juan Manuel Perez and his group had not presented this particular variant of the *'pastorela'* in Brownsville during Christmas of 1891, at the same time Captain John G. Bourke was witnessing another." In 1899 Father Pierre Fourier Parisot of San Antonio included in his memoirs an account of a *pastorela* he saw in México. Instead of describing the Mexican *pastorela,* however, he discusses a San Antonio performance that Cordelia Brodbent told him about (Igo 1985:133). This may well be the performance at the cathedral reported by the *San Antonio Express* in 1888 (Everett 1975:39).[9] In 1908 Sarah S. King wrote a small book, *Los Pastores: An Interpretation,* and in 1913 she staged a version in San Antonio that was a "collation of the British *Second Shepherd's Play, Los Pastores, Las Posadas,* and elements from Spanish dramatists, probably Lope de Vega" (Igo 1985:131).[10]

The present study concentrates on the text that Leandro Granado began

The cast of *Los Pastores,* ca. 1955. (Courtesy, the Institute of Texan Cultures, San Antonio, Texas)

performing in 1913 in the *barrios* of San Antonio. He learned the text in México, and once here, inscribed it in an old ledger. This *cuaderno* was edited and translated by Father Carmelo Tranchese, S. J., of Our Lady of Guadalupe Church, and published in 1949 by Treviño Brothers Printing and Lithograph. In 1978 a second edition was published with musical notation added by Sister Carmela Montalvo, O.S.B.

The *pastorela* in San Antonio has worked its way into local popular literature. In 1938 Janette Sebring Lowery published *Annunciata and the Shepherds,* which tells the story of *Los Pastores.* Its main character is Mr. Pomegranate. Although it would seem that she based her story on Don Leandro Granado's troupe, since "pomegranate" is the English translation of *granados,* her foreword suggests that she was writing about the Gertrudis Alonzo troupe, which is now defunct but was performing at the time. In 1940 Lillie May Hagner included a section on *Los Pastores* in her artistic representation of San Antonio, and in 1955 Julia Nott Waugh gave an account of *Los Pastores* in her book, *The Silver Cradle,* about the Gertrudis Alonzo production. Most recently, Mary

Ann Smothers Bruni (1985) has written a fictionalized story around the performers in the Granado version of *Los Pastores*. This book, *Rosita's Christmas Wish*, is well illustrated and depicts the performance with a sensitive eye.

Some of the popular literature on the *pastorela*, like much of the early scholarship, sees *Los Pastores* as a quaint and romantic endeavor of poor, uneducated Mexicans. Parisot (1899:165) has even gone so far as to depict Mexican performers as "unscrupulous and ignorant men," while the comments of Bourke (1893), one of *Los Pastores*'s first chroniclers in Texas, offer a similar sentiment. The attitude of these writers is a clear indication of the social place "assigned" to the performers of *Los Pastores,* which is used to justify their economic and social displacement in South Texas. This is a critical issue, as chapter 5 demonstrates, since the contemporary social critique embedded in *Los Pastores* concerns its ability to mediate such a discourse.

This textual survey is intended to provide a basis for further exploration into the significance and meaning of this cultural event. Meaning is not found in tradition alone, however, but is related to the way literary discourse becomes inscribed in the multiple layers of performative texts and contexts. These concepts are taken up at various points in the remainder of this study.

3

Story and Structure: The Dramatized Event

Los Pastores is composed of a variety of texts, both narrated and performed. These include the script of the drama published by Tranchese, the improvisational texts that are added during particular performances, textual material that is routinely performed but not part of the script, and elements of audience interaction and dramatic tension. In other words, Los Pastores is the product of two interrelated and variously enacted events: the "dramatized" and the "dramatic." The dramatized event is the performed narrative, including the plot, structural patterns, and poetics; the dramatic event is the product of the performed narrative as it emerges in different places, replete with changing social functions and contexts.

As a dramatized event, Los Pastores is the conjuncture of "story" and "structure": story and structure form two dynamically related processes of signification that constitute, in a single, interrelated frame, the performance of Los Pastores as a dramatized event. By "story" I mean the narrative scheme that emerges in its performance. This scheme is composed of six movements and unfolds in linear fashion, as depicted in figure 3.1. The unfolding or linear narrative is always performative; that is, it is not merely the script that I am exploring, but the narrative as performed. This mode of analysis is concerned with the story beyond the scripted text and takes into account improvisation and audience interaction. Several prefixtures to the event—those of costumes, staging, and characterization—are also elements of the dramatized event.

The narrative scheme is augmented by dramatic and narrative tension arising from the interaction of three structural domains: the cosmological, the liminal, and the referential. These domains are inhabited by three categories of agents: Luzbel, his cohort of devils, and Michael the Archangel; the hermit; the shepherds; and Mary and Joseph. These characters inhabit separate domains, and it is the interaction of both the characters and their domains that gives rise to dramatic tension in Los Pastores, as described below. A separate

48

I.	II.	III.	IV.	V.	VI.	VII.	VIII.
Introduction	1st Encounter	Break	Infernal Council	2nd Encounter	Climax	Adoration-Shepherds	Adoration-Audience

3.1. The structure of *Los Pastores* as story.

domain of interaction, one that incorporates the audience, exists as an un-marked entity. As such, the event is the unmarked space that envelops all three structural domains and its situated performance before an audience (see figure 3.2).

PREFIXTURES TO STORY

The story dramatized by *Los Pastores* is a familiar one: a group of shepherds is visited by the Archangel Michael and told of the birth of the Messiah. The shepherds, upon hearing this news, decide to embark on a journey to Bethle-hem to visit the new king. On their way, they meet a hermit, who, after hear-ing about their journey, decides to accompany them. Luzbel and his legion of devils, after also hearing of the news, attempt to thwart the journey of the shepherds and the hermit. However, the archangel, after a series of confronta-tions, defeats Luzbel, thereby allowing the shepherds to complete their jour-ney with no further interruptions.

Several features of this event make it more comprehensible and cohesive: the characters, costumes, and stage.

Characters

Los Pastores dramatizes the exploits of the shepherds and the Ermitaño (her-mit) as they are tempted and taunted by Luzbel (Lucifer) and the other devils on their journey to see el Niño Dios (the Christ Child). María and José (Mary and Joseph) play no significant role in the drama and have only small parts in the introduction and conclusion. The original Granado text and Tranchese's edited version do not even include the characters of Mary and Joseph, which were added by later performers to create a sense of biblical realism. El Niño Dios is represented by a statue of an infant.

As mentioned above, the characters in *Los Pastores* fall into three groups:

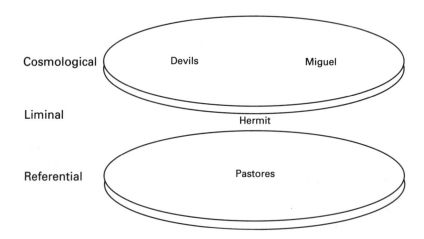

3.2. The structural domains of *Los Pastores*.

the shepherds with Mary and Joseph; Luzbel, his devils, and Michael the Archangel; and the hermit.

The shepherds are led by Tebano and Parrado, whose position is indicated by the number of lines they speak, as well as their role as song leaders. The names of the other shepherds are Melicio, Toringo, Gerardo, Bato, Bartolo the lazy shepherd, Nabal, Mengo, Tulio, Lisardo, Gila (a shepherdess), and Cucharón. As a group, the shepherds also act as a chorus at different moments in the performance.

Of the devils, Luzbel is the main figure. From the number of lines he speaks and the time he spends on stage it is clear that Luzbel has the largest role of the entire cast. This is not unique to the Granado version, as the role of Luzbel was the most coveted of all in the *pastorelas* Marie (1948) was familiar with in New Mexico. The other devils are Satanás, Esturiel, Belzebub, Astucia, Asmodeo, Pecado, and Astarot. Except for Satanás, the other devils appear primarily during the *concilio infernal* (infernal council), although they can often be found chasing and causing trouble for the hermit.

The hermit is a liminal character in this performance, marked by his license to see and interact with the devils, his age, and his religious vow. Two other characters listed in the written text are Doristo and Indio but they no longer appear in the performance.

It is important to note that the shepherds cannot see the devils, except for those times when Luzbel or Satanás are in disguise. They are only visible to the hermit and the Archangel Michael. This blindness creates some humorous interludes between the devils and the hermit, as they taunt and chase each other around the stage, unbeknownst to the shepherds.

Costumes

The costumes of the players are the most elaborate part of the performance. Mary wears a long white dress with a blue shawl draped over her shoulders and head, reaching to the ground. Joseph is clad in a long brown cloak, usually an old monk's habit. Michael wears a short, white, dresslike outfit with detachable wings, white stockings with white shoes or sneakers, and a white crown with a cross extending from the top. He also brandishes a sword. It so happens that Michael is played by a young woman, but from accounts of previous years, this same dresslike garment was used even when Michael was played by a young boy.

Gila, the only shepherd whose character is cast as a woman, is attired in a long white dress. In previous years she wore ballet slippers laced up the calf but now dons any type of shoe, usually white sneakers. The other shepherds, the majority of whom are played by women, are male characters with male names. They all wear brightly colored capes made of satin with their individual names written in glitter along the back. A few of the shepherds who have been part of the cast for years wear satin pullover pants and shirts to match their capes. They also wear a hat, usually made of straw and often covered with the same satin material as the cape, with a flower sewn to the left side. Each shepherd carries a *gancho* (a shepherd's crook or staff), which is decorated with tinsel, ribbon, streamers, bells, religious banners, and other assortments. Besides having a semiotic function, the *gancho*s are used to tap out the various rhythms of the performers' songs.

The hermit wears a rough brown fabric, most likely chosen for its indexical relationship to medieval hair shirts. Around his neck hangs a large rosary with an extra large cross with which he gives chase to the devils, who, in Dracula-like fashion, turn their faces at its sight. The hermit also dons a mask depicting an old man, which adds a white beard and wrinkles to his already frail frame. The mask reflects the hermit's role as the elder of the group, and during the *adoracion,* or adoration, he is referred to as *tatarabuelo,* or great-great-grandfather. Instead of using a *gancho,* as the shepherds do, he has a cane to help him walk and dance, which he wields in lively fashion against the devils.

The devils' costumes are the most elaborate of the cast. They are clothed in black pants and shoes with a red or black satin shirt and black capes with multicolored names glittering across the back. Each of them carries a sword.

Luzbel and his cohort of devils conferring at the beginning of the Infernal Council.

Except for Luzbel, each devil dons an elaborate mask made of papier-mâché or wood. Some years back, masks were made of tin and crafted by a former director who played Luzbel. The masks are painted red and black, with horns protruding from the tops and sides. Several of the masks are made of fabric and resemble giant bear heads with horns extending from the top. One of the devils changes masks during the performance, switching from a traditional one mentioned above, to a plastic face-mask of a skull. In place of a mask, Luzbel wears an elegant black headpiece. It is similar in style to that worn by Michael, except that it is black and in place of a cross has a fluff of black feathers extending from the top with a black veil falling over his face. Beneath the top piece is a wig of long brown hair that drapes over Luzbel's shoulders. He wears black pants with sequins down the sides; his cape is longer and more elaborate than the capes worn by the other devils: it has a red lining and the outside features a skull outlined in glitter and sequins. When in disguise, Luzbel folds the cape over and pins it back to hide the image of the skull and his name written on the back.

The Stage

The staging varies with each performance, depending on where *Los Pastores* is performed: a private home, with the driveway or patio functioning as a

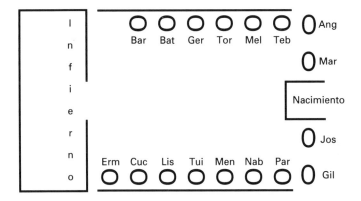

3.3. The stage and position of the actors.

stage; at local churches; or at San José Mission. Each of these venues usually has a narrow rectangular space that can be used as a stage; the space ranges from 30 to 50 feet long and 10 to 20 feet wide (see figure 3.3). On one end sits *el infierno* (hellmouth), a four-walled enclosure with a curtained doorway. The devils congregate in this enclosure when not performing, and Luzbel enters and retreats through the opening.[1] The infierno also serves as a dressing room and a place to gather before and during the performance. It is not uncommon for the devils and other male members of the cast to gather inside the infierno (before, during, and after a performance) for a few *tragitos* (shots of whiskey), especially in cold weather. A small bucket, kept in one corner, is used as a urinal. It is available to all the male members of the troupe, but the devils, who have more access to it, use it the most.

Opposite the *infierno*, enclosing the other end of the rectangle, are four chairs where Michael, Mary, Joseph, and Gila sit during most of the performance. Between the chairs of Mary and Joseph is a *nacimiento*, or manger, where the statue of el Niño Dios is kept.

The size of the entire staging area depends on the performance location. In the driveways of private homes, the area is much narrower than it is in the courtyard of a church. This does not affect the staging, as long as there is enough room for the *infierno*, since it takes up an area of about 7 by 10 square feet. Members of the audience sit around the rectangle, usually along the length of its sides, depending on the available space.

The shepherds are aligned on the stage in rather simple fashion. They stand near the end of the stage where the *nacimiento* is kept, in two rows along the edge of its length, facing in toward one another. They maintain this position throughout the performance, except when they march back and forth along the sides of this area, or when they leave during the infernal council. Although the number of shepherds may vary with each performance, their alignment remains the same. On the left side, facing the *nacimiento,* stand Tebano, Melicio, Toringo, Gerardo, Bato, and Bartolo, and on the right side stand Parrado, Nabal, Mengo, Tulio, Lisardo, and Cucharón.

The hermit, freer in his movements than the shepherds, stands at the rear of the line, usually on the right side. He dances back and forth in this area or chases the devils around the stage. There are no stage props other than the infierno, the chairs for Michael, Mary, Joseph, Gila, and Parrado (the health of the actor makes standing for the entire performance quite difficult), and the *nacimiento.*

STRUCTURAL DOMAINS

The structural poetics of *Los Pastores*'s dramatic and narrative form gives rise to tension, ambiguity, and meaning. What interests me here is the way the structural poetics of *Los Pastores* is related to larger critical issues such as the patterning of performance in folklore theory (Bauman 1977), the structure of ritual and dramatic processes in comparative symbology (V. Turner 1974, 1982), and the poetics of symbolic and literary forms influenced by structuralism, linguistics, and semiotics (Barthes 1972; Culler 1975; Jakobson 1960; Lévi-Strauss 1963). All these perspectives are united in their effort to explicate an implicit logic of symbolic and linguistic forms.

As pointed out earlier, the narrative of *Los Pastores* is formed by the association, intersection, and interaction of the three distinct domains inhabited by the three sets of characters: (1) the referential, or day-to-day domain inhabited by the shepherds; (2) the cosmological domain inhabited by the devils and Michael the Archangel; and (3) the liminal domain inhabited by the hermit (see figure 3.4).

The Referential Domain

The interaction in the referential domain involves the shepherds, alone or with the hermit and the devils. This domain is that of the concrete and the real. Although this is an analytical distinction, it is based on the comments of

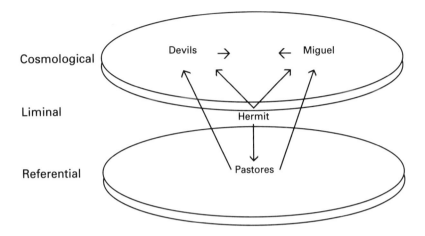

3.4. The intersection of the structural domains.

the performers, who state that the shepherds cannot touch the devils since they are invisible to them, and that only the hermit can see them.

In the referential domain, the shepherds revel in their earthly realism. Primarily through the character of Bartolo, but not necessarily him alone, the shepherds take delight in eating, joking, singing, laughing, and enjoying the festive world they create. That world is not without contradiction, however. Bartolo is often reprimanded for his crude ways and sleepy habits; Gila, the shepherdess, is busy cooking and complaining about her work; and as a whole, the group is ambivalent about fighting off the temptations of evil.

The referential domain, then, is that of the denotative: it is the allegorical "real" of the story. Although the shepherds are concerned with finding the Messiah, they are mainly preoccupied with their need to sleep, stay warm, and satisfy their hunger. Their presence is marked by continuous contradiction: on the one hand, they desire to pay homage to the Messiah and take him offerings of linen, cheese, and oxen; on the other hand, they are hungry, sleepy, busy tending their flock, and concerned with matters of pastoral life.

Contradiction, however, is not exclusive to the shepherds. In the opening dramatic sequence, Mary and Joseph are searching for shelter on the night that she is to give birth. Although this action is eclipsed by other elements of the drama, its occurrence at the beginning of the performance captures the dramatic (and theological) tension that follows: the Messiah, the Son of God, is born to human parents in a stable filled with animals; shepherds—hungry, tired, and coarsely mannered—are the first to hear the news of the new-born king.

The Cosmological Domain

The cosmological domain consists of interaction between the devils and Michael the angel, and among the devils themselves. This domain, like the referential one, emerges through the perceptions of the performers, who stress the invisibility of the devils to the shepherds and the recognition of the angel as a celestial character. In other words, the domain inhabited by the devils and Michael is beyond the referential domain of the shepherds but philosophically supports their spiritual journey. It is a place Luzbel and his legions vie with Michael the Archangel over the meaning of human nature. In his opening soliloquy, Luzbel boasts about his temptation of Adam and Eve and their resulting fall from grace in the Garden of Eden. Accordingly, his role is to make sure that sin continues in the world. When Luzbel meets with the infernal council, the seven sins form the substance of their discussion and narratives. In essence, Luzbel and his fellow devils represent evil and sin. But all is not well with Luzbel and his cohorts: they fear that the birth of the Messiah, foretold by the prophets and made known by the angel Michael, will cause all their work to be lost.

The representation of Luzbel in *Los Pastores* is similar to that found in popular medieval literature, which depicted the cosmos as "a battleground between the forces of good and evil" (Russell 1984:87). Indeed, many of the devils' characteristics, both aesthetic and dramatic, stem from the popular beliefs and literature of this period. The tradition of showing Luzbel with a holy book when he first meets the hermit, for example, dates back to earlier times, as do the hosts of devils and their names, and the color schemes used in their costumes (Russell 1984).

Michael the Archangel is represented as the opposite of the devils. He defends the righteous and spreads the message of goodness, announces to the shepherds that the Messiah is born, and defeats Luzbel in battle. Like that of Luzbel, the character of Michael follows many of the patterns found in medieval popular forms: he initially banishes Luzbel from heaven, announces the birth of the Messiah, and fights off the continued encroachments of Luzbel on the world of the shepherds (Russell 1984).

The actions of the devils have a direct impact on the referential domain of the shepherds, as when Luzbel tempts the shepherds and Michael helps them fend off their tempters. This, however, is only part of the role Luzbel and

Michael play. Dramatically, they personify good and evil: when Bartolo refuses to pay homage to el Niño Dios and instead goes to sleep, it is the devil
who literally holds him down. When the hermit is tempted to lose his virginity, it is the devil, in disguise, who urges him on. As Bakhtin (1981:150) notes,
this domain is the personification of the metaphysical world that functions as
the site where thoughts and instincts, represented by Luzbel and Michael, are
acted upon in the referential domain.[2]

Contradictions can also be found among the devils. Satanás cannot believe
that a child, a man, and a woman can cause Luzbel so much concern. In his
disbelief, he approaches the shepherds himself to see what has made Luzbel
so distraught. It is only then, after his own confrontation with the shepherds,
that his strength wavers and he admits that Luzbel's concern about the birth
of the Messiah is legitimate.

The Liminal Domain

Liminal refers to a structural place that is situated outside the realm of everyday social interaction, and in some cases, between two distinct structural
planes (Van Gennep 1960). Furthermore, special license is accorded the members who occupy this space. Such license is connected to behavior that, under
ordinary circumstances, would be unacceptable in the public domain and that
in some cases is the inversion of everyday practice (Babcock 1978; Turner
1969). The hermit fits both of these qualifications: he interacts in both the
referential and cosmological worlds yet is not restricted to either, and he has
special license to display the ludic behavior typical of this genre.

By virtue of his age and religious vow, the hermit negotiates the tension
between the referential and cosmological domains. This is a privileged role
since he is the only human character to interact with or see the devils; and it
provides him with a license for ludic behavior. This aspect of the hermit's
character is recognized by the performers, who claim: "Ya es señor grande
que ya se perdió la vergüenza" (He is an old man who has lost all shame),
thereby granting him the freedom to act in otherwise unacceptable ways. It
should be noted that tension and crisis also exist within each domain and not
just across them, for example, between shepherd and shepherd, and between
devil and devil.[3]

As is characteristic of the privileges found among liminal figures, the hermit is the only human to see the devils and interact with them. Although it is
true that on several occasions Luzbel appears to the shepherds, he does so in
disguise, unbeknownst to them. It is the hermit alone who recognizes the

The hermit, true to his ludic role, entertains members of the audience.

devils, chasing them off with his oversized rosary.[4] In this betwixt-and-between role, the hermit associates with the shepherds but, having lived a religious vow of poverty and chastity, is not one of them. In fact, the text contradicts itself since at the beginning the hermit first interacts with the shepherds as if he is part of the group but a few scenes later arrives, having emerged from his cave, as if meeting them for the first time. So although the hermit is human, he is not one of the shepherds, who are the main occupants of the referential domain.

It is usually in his role of fending off the devils that the hermit displays his ludic behavior. He will mock the devils, teasing them with his religious ornamentation, and take humorous jabs at them, using his skill as a verbal artist to invert their words in humorous fashion. By and large, much of the festive character of *Los Pastores* depends on the hermit's ability to spontaneously interact with the devils and the shepherds.

THE CONJUNCTURE OF STORY AND STRUCTURE

To reiterate, the dramatized story of *Los Pastores* is the conjuncture of a narrative scheme with three overlapping structural domains. The resulting dramatic form is composed of multiple levels of signifying plot and drama.

Introduction: "Bienvenidos Damas y Caballeros"

The performance begins with the director of *Los Pastores* offering a brief introductory statement. If the audience is fortunate and no more than a few drinks have already been consumed, his comments are brief. Whether short or extended, the message is the same: *Los Pastores* is performed because "la gente no sabe el verdadero significado de Navidad, especialmente, los niños. Hay que mantener y hacer vivas nuestras tradiciones, para educar nuestros hijos en nuestras tradiciones" (people do not know the real meaning of Christmas, especially the children. We need to keep our traditions alive, to educate our children in these traditions). People no longer come to see *Los Pastores* as they did in the past, he states, stressing that "la gente ya no viene por devoción, sino por diversión" (the people no longer come for devotion, but for diversion). Another task of the introduction is to inform the audience of the ground rules, to ask parents to keep their children out of the staged area, for example, because the devils carry swords "con filo y punta" (with an edge and a point). The director also describes the activity of the performers as *"trabajando,"* or working, a critical insight into how the performers interpret their own aesthetic practice.

Once the introduction is finished, the shepherds march toward the *nacimiento* singing,

PASTORES:

Saludemos al pueblo querido,	We greet the beloved community,
y rendidos estaremos ofrecemos,	and we submissively offer to serve,
a servir aunque no merecemos,	although unworthy,
ocupando lugar como aquí,	occupying a place like this,
ocupando lugar como aquí.	occupying a place like this.

Upon finishing, Mary and Joseph walk from the *infierno* to the *nacimiento,* discussing the birth that is imminent. Once there, Mary and Joseph stand while the shepherds bow their heads and kneel, shaking their *ganchos,* capturing the audience's attention. At this time, the director enacts one of the more visibly religious, and culturally coded, acts of religious devotion in the performance. Beginning at the *infierno,* he crawls on his knees, with the statue of el Niño Dios in his outstretched arms, to Mary standing by the *nacimiento.* This scene brings a hush to the audience. The friction over whether *Los Pastores* is drama or ritual is momentarily displaced, since the director's actions clearly mark this as a ritual event.

Once he reaches Mary and Joseph he presents el Niño Dios to them, and they lay him in the manger. This scene was added to the Granado text by the director as a response to the miracles el Niño Dios has performed for him. Now in his late sixties, he has had two strokes, the first at a young age, which left him partly paralyzed. After much prayer, he recovered fully from his paralysis. He now makes this offering at the beginning of each event as a way of fulfilling his ritual vow of thanksgiving. The director owns the statue, having purchased it in México. It is made of ceramic materials, and he takes it to every performance in a special carrying case with a hard shell. This scene, like others, is formed through the juxtaposition of the cosmological and the referential domains, represented by the birth of el Niño Dios into the world of human agency.

The juxtaposition of time, one that will continue in the scenes that follow, is also important. Once the director finishes his introduction to the audience, the performance moves from the present to dramatic time, signaled by the entrance of Mary and Joseph; then it returns to the present with the director's ritual act. Instead of watching a dramatic presentation framed in the semihistorical past, the audience on this and other occasions engages the performance from various representations of time, creating another form of dramatic tension.

The First Encounter: "Ay Qué Linda es la Noche"

Once the director's introduction and ritual act are completed, the shepherds begin with the main part of the drama. "¡Qué hermosa noche! Todo es calma y tranquilidad" (What a beautiful evening. Everything is calm and tranquil), begins Tebano, as the shepherds keep watch in the fields. Then, without warning, the Archangel Michael appears to them, announcing the birth of the Messiah. Upon hearing this news, the shepherds depart for Bethlehem, taking whatever simple possessions they have to present as gifts to the new-born Messiah. On the way, they sing and march, exalted with expectation, stopping only to camp for the evening. Once they are settled, Gila prepares dinner while the hermit searches for a cave in which to pray.

Then, in a loud, howling voice, from deep within the *infierno*, one hears the voice of Luzbel: "Por aquel monte silvestre veo venir pastores . . . Luzbel soy. Luz hay en mí, luz en mi nombre se ve" (On that wooded mountain I see shepherds coming. . . . I am Lucifer. There is light [*luz*] within me; light is seen in my name). Luzbel dashes from the *infierno* and begins a long eloquent monologue on the majesty of God, the wonders of creation, and his own fall from Grace. From the mouth of Luzbel spews a lofty narration on the miracles and mysteries of the world. Soon, Luzbel is joined by Satanás and the other devils, if only briefly, as they raucously lament the rumor of the birth of the Messiah.

In the next dramatic sequence, the devils have returned to the *infierno*, and Luzbel, now disguised as a man bearing a Holy Book, appears to the hermit. With flare and vigor, Luzbel teases and tempts the hermit to leave his life of prayer and chastity and take Gila as a wife.

LUZBEL:
Anda y haz lo que te digo,
y no me pongas réplicas.

Go and do what I say
and do not object.

ERMITAÑO:
¿Pero si yo he conservado
voto de virginidad,
que ¿no será más pecado
quebrantar la santidad?

But, if I have preserved
a vow of virginity,
wouldn't it be more sinful
to break this sanctity?

LUZBEL:
Más pecas con despreciar,
el más eminente fruto,
pues ponte a considerar,
que el demonio es muy astuto,
y aunque te quieras guardar,
puede ser que en un minuto
te engañe y te haga pecar.

You sin more by rejecting
the most lofty fruit.
Go and consider
that the devil is very astute,
and although you want to be careful,
he could deceive you in a minute
and force you to sin.

ERMITAÑO:
¿Pero cómo me prevengo
con disposiciones tan extrañas,
sabiendo que me mantengo
con hierbas de estas montañas?

But how will I defend myself
with such strange arrangements,
knowing that I maintain myself
with herbs from these mountains?

LUZBEL:
No me tengas que porfiar
ya veo que tú eres solo,
pero tú puedes casar
con una hija de Bartolo
que yo te sabré ayudar.
Porque mira,
todos esos ganados son míos,
me los hurtaron los pastores.
Ya que ellos los han logrado

Do not argue with me.
I see that you are single,
but you can marry
a daughter of Bartolo.
I will help you.
Because, look,
all those flocks are mine;
the shepherds stole them from me.
Now that they have benefited from

es mejor que tú los logres,	them, it is your turn to do so.
te los daré para el dote.	I will give them to you for the dowry.
También te puedo casar,	I can also marry you.
yo también soy sacerdote	I am also a priest,
y nadie me ha de estorbar.	and no one will hinder me.
Mira, ¿quieres que te enseñe	Look, do you want me to show you
la novia?	the bride?

When Luzbel finally departs, the hermit rejoins the shepherds, who offer him something to eat. This scene reveals one of the many contradictions of the text: the hermit who had previously been with the shepherds now encounters them as if for the first time.

The popular humor of this genre, though slightly tempered, is evident in this scene with Bartolo, who wants nothing else but to sleep and eat, and Gerardo who wishes his daughter married, freeing him from all of life's responsibilities.

LISARDO:

Yo les daré una noticia.	I will give you some news
Que supe ayer en el poblado:	that I learned yesterday in town.
Me dijeron se casaba	They told me the daughter
la muchacha de Gerardo.	of Gerardo was to be married.

GERARDO:

A mí no me la han pedido.	They have not asked me for her.
Pueden haberlo pensado.	They may have thought about it.
Vale que si se casara,	I wish she would get married
se me quitaría el cuidado.	so I would not have to worry.

BATO:

No quiera Dios que suceda	May God not allow
lo que yo tengo pensado.	what I am thinking.
Porque viniendo el avío	Because, when the bonus comes,
con Gila he de ser casado.	I will marry Gila.

BARTOLO:

Gila, hija, el sueño me vence.	Gila, my child, sleep overpowers
Ya sabes que yo padezco	me. You know that I suffer
de estas flojeras inmensas.	from this immense laziness.
Mientras yo duermo, tú velas.	While I sleep, you keep watch.

GILA:

Buena está la tragedia.	What a disaster has
Buena a mí me ha sucedido.	befallen me. I did not
Que para eso no me casé,	marry for this, to keep
para cuidar las ovejas.	watch over the sheep.

BARTOLO:

Yo no entiendo aquí de quejas.	I'm not interested in your complaining.
¿Hay algo que merendar?	Is there something to snack on?
Y si no dame aquí ese bule	And if not, pass me that jug
que ahora me he de emborrachar.	for now I will get drunk.

The scene ends with the shepherds singing and dancing.

Next, Luzbel has his first encounter with the Archangel Michael, who reproaches him for his pride and lack of fear of God. Luzbel does not recognize Michael as his celestial adversary, however, and is surprised that this brave shepherd recognizes him for who he is.

ANGEL:

Bárbaro, ¿quién como Dios?	Barbarian! Who are you to behave like God!

LUZBEL:

Dime quién eres	Tell me who you are and stop,
y acaba que me acobarda tu voz.	for your voice intimidates me.

ANGEL:

Soy un rayo fulminante	I am a thunderbolt
para altivos y engañosos,	for the proud and deceptive,
siendo de los envidiosos	for the envious,
un cuchillo penetrante.	a penetrating knife.
Soy aquel que tú no entiendes	I am he whom you do not understand
a pesar de tus rigores,	in spite of your power,
defensor de estos pastores.	defender of these shepherds,
A quien engañar pretendes,	whom you want to deceive.
y ya verás finalmente	And you will finally see,
aunque me ves pequeñuelo,	although you think I am so small,
te he de rendir por el suelo,	I will squash you beneath my feet,
a tí y al que se presente.	or anyone else who may appear.

LUZBEL:

Pues bien, Mancebo imprudente,	Very well, imprudent young boy,
bien se conoce que ignoras.	it is clear that you are unaware
Lo valiente de mi pecho altivo.	of my great pride.
¡Agradéceme que vayas vivo!	Thank me that you leave alive!
Que si no fuera cobardía,	If it were not cowardly on my part,
valor en darte muerte por tu	I would kill you because
villana valentía.	of your rustic boasts.
Mira, vete, vete ya de mis ojos	Now get out of my sight, and
y no me causes más enojos.	do not cause me any more anger.

ANGEL:

¡Si tu traición piensas que la	You think that I ignore your
ignoro!	treason! That God that created you!
¡Ese Dios que te crió!	is the Lord I worship,
es el Señor que yo adoro,	and even though you once were
y aunque tan alto y elevado fuiste.	very mighty and high, for
Por tu soberbia todo lo perdiste.	your pride, you lost it all.

LUZBEL:

¡Bien informado estás	You are well aware of
de quién yo soy!	who I am!

They banter back and forth, exchanging hits with their swords, until the Archangel Michael leaves in disgust over Luzbel's unrepenting pride and sin.

These scenes, like those before it, are formed by the intrusion of and interaction among the inhabitants of the three structural domains. Second, they are marked by the lack of sequential or linear time. The sequence opens with the shepherds singing about the beautiful night on which the Messiah is born: "Ay qué linda es la noche cuando Jesús nació" (Oh, how beautiful is the night when Jesus was born). As of that moment, however, Michael has yet to appear to them announcing the birth of the Messiah.

Here, all three worlds are present as in figure 3.4. First, there is the encounter between the liminal and the cosmological worlds represented by Luzbel and the hermit. And second, Luzbel tempts the hermit with elements from the referential domain represented by Gila.

In this encounter, the hermit exhibits another contradiction involving time when he states: "El verdadero Jesús me libre de todo mal, pues digo por la señal de la Santa Cruz" (May the true Jesus deliver me of all evil, I say this through the sign of the Holy Cross). Here, the hermit is invoking the name

Michael the Archangel pulling the enchained Luzbel after their battle.

of Jesus and the cross on which he died at the very moment that his birth is being announced.

Then Michael arrives to fend off Luzbel. Although Luzbel does not yet recognize him as the angel who banished him from heaven, he does recognize him as a powerful and brave person. This is the first scene between these two characters who will compete for dominance of the cosmological domain. It ends with Michael leaving Luzbel in a state of frustration, sensing that his evil reign is about to end, all because of the events that have taken place among "un pastor, un hombre y una mujer" (a shepherd, a man, and a woman).

Intermission and the Gifts of the *Madrinas*

At this point there is a break in the action for the presentation of symbolic gifts by the *madrinas* (female ritual sponsors). Although this is not the practice at every performance, it is customary for women from the audience or family hosting the performance to pin small gifts on the cloaks of the shepherds and devils. The gifts vary from pins—like those bearing a picture of Pope John Paul II that were issued to commemorate his visit to San Antonio in September 1987 or those of Our Lady of Guadalupe—to ribbons with the name of the sponsoring church written in glittering letters. Another common gift is a dollar bill, which is pinned either by itself or in combination with other ribbons. In most cases, the money is given in recognition of a good performance. The hermit almost always receives the most recognition, because of his comic improvisations and his taunting of Luzbel and the other devils. After the *madrinas* have presented their gifts, all but the devils leave the staging area.

This is the second time that dramatic time is interrupted by the present. This action, then, serves not only as a break in dramatic time but as a commentary on the ability of the actors. Structurally, this device pulls the audience back to the present, and unlike the ritual actions of the director in the beginning, reinforces the dramatic and performative aspects of this event over its ritualistic ones.

Infernal Council: "Ay Satanás, un pastor, un hombre, y una mujer"

Immediately after the break for the *madrinas*, the infernal council begins with Luzbel, disgusted and dismayed by his fear that the Messiah has arrived, summoning Satanás and the other devils.

SATANÁS:
Qué es esto, príncipe augusto,
qué es esto, monarca altivo.
¿Qué ocasión o qué motivo
te causa tanto disgusto?

What is this, august prince?
What is this, proud monarch?
What occasion or what motive
has caused you so much disgust?

LUZBEL:
Ay, Satanás,
un pastor, un hombre, y una mujer,
hoy me han venido a poner asombro,
miedo y pavor.

Oh, Satan, a shepherd, a
man, and a woman, today
have come to bring me
dread, fear, and terror.

SATANÁS:
¿Es posible, gran señor.
De cuyo poder adverso, ha temblado
el universo con las criaturas
que abarca?
Dame licencia y verás
que mi orgullo es sin segundo.

Is it possible, great Lord,
whose adverse power has shaken
the universe with all the
creatures in it?
Give me license and you will see
that my pride is without second.

| Pondré a tus plantas | I will put at your feet |
| el mundo y ese monarca rapaz. | the world and that boy king. |

In their attempts to devise a strategy to rid the Earth of "una mujer, a un infante, a un vil rapaz, y a un hombre" (a woman, an infant, a despicable young boy, and a man), the devils call forth the seven sins of hell. They praise the works of evil and scoff at the name of God as they comfort Luzbel in his dread. Then Pecado reads the list of the seven sins from a special book.

PECADO:

Manda el príncipe Luzbel,	Prince Lucifer has ordered
que por vengar su afrenta,	that his insult be avenged,
invente el Averno cruel,	that the cruel Avernus
una campaña sangrienta	contrive a bloody campaign
contra el pueblo de Israel.	against the people of Israel.
Y para tal intención,	And for those reasons,
los que su caverna encierra,	those enclosed in hell
han sido de su opinión	are of the opinion
que cubran toda la tierra	that the whole earth will be
de luto y maldición.	covered with sorrow and evil.
De vicios llénase el mundo,	Fill the earth with vices,
de rencores y lamentos,	with rancor and lament,
que hasta el sabio más profundo	that even the most wise will
experimente mil tormentos.	suffer a thousand torments.
Que no haiga choza,	Let there be no cottage or
ni aldea que maldecida no sea,	village that is not cursed,
que haiga terrible rencor	let there be terrible rancor
en toda la gente Hebrea.	among all the Hebrew people.

ASMODEO:

Yo pondré todo mi esfuerzo,	I will do everything to make sure
en dar a esos un mal almuerzo.	they have a terrible breakfast.
	(Laughter by the devils.)

PECADO:

Siete vicios principales	Seven principal sins
son los que tengo dispuestos,	are at my disposal,
para hacer a los mortales	to cause the mortals to
caer en gravísimos males.	fall into very grave woes.
El primero es la soberbia.	The first is pride.

Upon hearing the names of the seven sins, the devils laugh, mock, and gloat at the mention of each one: *soberbia* (pride), *avaricia* (greed), *lujuria* (lust), *ira* (anger), *gula* (gluttony), *envidia* (envy), and *pereza* (sloth).

The infernal council ends with the devils marching, brandishing their swords, and singing their praise and support of Luzbel.

ALL THE DEVILS:

A la lid vamos todos,	To the battle let us go,
a la lid sin temblar.	to the battle without fear.
Que hoy, debemos perder	For today, either we lose
nuestro reino, o guardar.	our kingdom, or preserve it.
A la lid vamos todos,	To the battle let us go,
a la lid sin temblar.	to the battle without fear.
Que hoy, de Luzbel el trono	Today, we must save
debemos conservar,	Lucifer's throne.
debemos conservar.	We must save it.

LUZBEL AND SATANÁS:

Guerra, guerra terrible y eterna,	War, terrible and eternal war,
muera todo lo que es celestial,	let everything celestial die,
queda solo Luzbel en su trono,	leaving only Lucifer on his throne,
como el dueño de la humanidad.	as the master of humanity.

Structurally quite different from the other parts, the infernal council begins with the shepherds, angel, hermit, as well as Mary and Joseph, leaving the stage. With these characters absent, this part of the drama is less dynamic, performatively and structurally, as indicated by the increased level of noise and interaction in the audience. It is not unusual to find the audience leaving their places to get something to eat and drink at this point. Analytically, this is quite predictable. If, as stated earlier, the dynamics of the performance are constituted by the dramatic tension created by the intersection of different structural domains, it seems reasonable this part, totally contained within the domain of the infierno (cosmological), would lack a certain amount of drama. This lack of tension is also evident in the staging area. Normally the area is overrun with devils, shepherds, the angel, and Gila. In this scene, however, the devils are the only ones present, and thus the tension is lowered.

The infernal council, constructed primarily from dialogue between Luzbel and the devils, has little dramatic action, and the narrative consists of doctrinal and philosophical discourse on the nature of sin. Throughout the entire discourse, the shepherds say little, if anything, of philosophical or theological substance—it is the devils, and primarily Luzbel, that comment on the ontological nature of their world. As is characteristic of medieval morality plays, the doctrinal voice of the church now issues from the mouths of Luzbel and his legion of devils.

The Second Encounter: "No es Mesías ese que han visto"

At this point in the performance, the devil Satanás, seeking the source of Luzbel's torment, visits the shepherds. He pleads with them to forget their journey to Bethlehem: "Déjense de ir a Belén; ¡Que es camino muy riesgoso! Hay frío, hay nieve, hay hielo horroroso, hay feroces animales" (Stop your journey to Bethlehem. It is a very dangerous road. It is cold and snowing, the ice is dreadful, there are fierce animals). His petitions end in failure, and he despairs, as did his leader, "¡Ay! Lucifer, Lucifer . . . reniego de ser quien soy, reniego de mi poder, que un pequeñuelo Pastor, un hombre y una mujer hoy me han venido a poner asombro, miedo y pavor" (Ah! Lucifer, Lucifer . . . I curse who I am, I curse my power, that a very small shepherd, a man and a woman, today have caused me dread, fear, and terror).

Folding over the writing on his cape to reveal only the red underside, Luzbel once again decides to visit the shepherds. Cucharón, sent to keep watch over the sheep, encounters Luzbel. A play on words, based on the similarity between *mesías* (Messiah) and *Matías* (Matthias), takes place.

LUZBEL:

Dime, pastor,	Tell me, shepherd, if you
si has oído decir en tu pueblo,	have heard talk in your town,
habrá nacido el mesías,	about the birth of the messiah,
o que dicen, vendrá presto.	or if they say he is to come soon.

CUCHARÓN:

Un primo tengo, Matías,	I have a cousin, Matthias,
que hace dos años enteros,	it has been two whole years,
que por una muerte que hizo	since he was exiled
lo echaron a un destierro.	for a murder he committed.
La parte le han perdonado	The other side has forgiven him,
aunque vendrá como un trueno	although he will come like thunder,
que si acaso no ha llegado	if he hasn't already;
pienso no vendrá lejos.	I believe he cannot not be far.

LUZBEL:

No te pregunto por Matías,
lo que digo es, buen vaciero,
si sabes si habrá nacido
ese mesías de los profetas.

I do not ask about Matthias;
what I say, good shepherd,
is if you know if the messiah
of the prophets has been born.

CUCHARÓN:

¡No hay tal, Señor!
por más señas que me acuerdo,
que le ví circuncidar,
y estuve allá en su petena,
y le pusieron Matías,
por ser hijo de Mateo,
primo carnal de mi padre,
pariente, de Malavelo,
que casó con prima hermana.

There is no such thing, sir,
for many signs I remember,
I saw him circumcised,
and I was there on his feast
and they named him Matthias
for being the son of Matthew
first cousin of my father
related to Malavelo,
who married my cousin.

Concerned that Cucharón has been absent far too long, the hermit wanders off in search of him. Walking in the direction of the *infierno* and calling Cucharón's name aloud, the devils taunt the hermit, one by one, pretending to be Cucharón. The hermit, nearly blind from age, is fooled every time until at last Cucharón returns and, reunited with the shepherds, they begin to sing once more. The archangel again appears to Luzbel, demanding that he leave the shepherds alone, and again they battle with swords. Then upon Michael's cajoling, Luzbel takes a good look at his opponent and recognizes, with astonishment, that Michael is the angel who banished him from heaven.

This second encounter is critical, as it leads to the climax of the performance. Here Satanás and Luzbel, both in disguise, attempt to get information about the birth of the Messiah, continuing the intersection of structural domains found in earlier parts. When Cucharón takes off to watch the sheep, however, he encounters Luzbel and is taken into the *infierno*. With Cucharón's entrance into the *infierno*, the cosmological domain of the devils and the referential domain of the shepherds come into direct conflict. It is the hermit who mediates this conflict, by searching for and finding Cucharón. During his search, the hermit calls out the name of Cucharón as the devils exit from the *infierno* one by one, taking their turn taunting and teasing him. Finally, led by the hermit's cries, Cucharón finds his way out of the cosmological domain of the *infierno* and moves into the referential domain of the shepherds.[5] If the symbolics of this action go unheeded, the proclamation of Nabal, which directly follows Cucharón's return, highlights this event as *un anuncio milagroso* (a miraculous announcement). While Nabal's announcement is about *nuevas del cielo* (news from heaven), its placement immediately after Cucharón exits the *infierno* and returns to where the shepherds are gathered suggests that the *anuncio milagroso* is about the importance of maintaining the structural worlds in their proper order.

The Dramatic Climax: "¡Yo rendirme!"

Upon Luzbel's recognition of Michael, the two begin to battle and Luzbel is humiliated and defeated once again. Michael enchains him and leads him to a place in front of the *nacimiento,* where he tramples him beneath his feet. Defeated, disgusted, and shamed, Luzbel cries out:

Aprended, flores, de mí.	Learn, flowers, from me.
Ya llegó la redención	Redemption has arrived
y yo quedo avergonzado,	and I have been humiliated,
si soy padre del pecado.	for I am the father of sin.
Miren si tengo razón,	See if I am not right,
Adán metí en confusión,	I led Adam into doubt,
de la malicia en que estoy,	from the malice in which I live.
si fuí, si he sido, si soy,	I was, I have been, I am.
suéltame Miguel valiente,	Free me valiant Michael,
que veo el mundo diferente.	for I see the world differently.

The devils, forming a chain of clasped hands, attempt to free their leader from Michael's hold. But their efforts are thwarted by the hermit, who chases after them, brandishing his crucifix as a weapon. Finally, Michael banishes the defeated and fearful Luzbel into the dungeons of hell for all eternity.

ANGEL:

Levántate, fiera horrorosa,	Arise, horrid beast, and
y sepúltate en el abismo	bury yourself in the abyss
donde castiga Dios mismo	where God himself punishes
tu malicia perniciosa.	your pernicious malice.
Crújete cruel, venenosa serpiente,	Cringe, cruel and poisonous serpent,
que de la tierra al abismo,	from the earth to the abyss,
Dios te destierra y con amor	God exiles you, and with supreme love,
soberano le deje al linaje	leaves to the human race
humano armas para darte guerra.	arms to wage war on you.

With this, the devils, led by Luzbel and Satanás, sing and march back into the *infierno*. While the hermit mediates the clash between the cosmological and referential worlds, it is Michael who finally decides the outcome of the cosmological domain.

The defeat of Luzbel and his return to hell forms the dramatic climax of the performance. With the boundaries between the cosmological and referential domain restored and the devils safely contained in the *infierno*, the shepherds can now continue their journey to pay homage to the Messiah.

The Adoration: "Lléguese a adorar a ese tierno Niño que está en el portal"

The shepherds complete their journey to Bethlehem, where they marvel at the child and, one by one, bring him their simple gifts. Parrado and Tebano are the first to make their offering, followed by Gila. Upon presenting her gift, Gila is asked to dance as part of her supplication. Acquiescing, the shepherds sing the *Canto de la Palomita* (Song of the Dove), as Gila, accompanied by the hermit, dances to this lively *ranchera*-style song. Each of the shepherds follows the lead of Parrado, Tebano, and Gila, presenting the following gifts to el Niño Dios: a basket of flowers, bed sheets, a rosary, an ox, cheese, a cock, spoons, linens, a bandola, a honeycomb, a hat, and a lamb. They each sing a few lines as they approach the nacimiento, prostrating themselves before the child. This is one of the places in the text where the performance expands or contracts depending on the location, weather, and time. For example, only the first four of five shepherds may pay tribute to el Niño Dios in order to shorten the performance.

At one point, Bartolo, the lazy shepherd, refuses to pay homage to el Niño Dios. While the other shepherds are busy making their offering, one of the devils sneaks out of the *infierno*, takes hold of Bartolo and lays him on the ground, standing over him so that he cannot rise. When Bartolo's turn arrives to present his gift, he refuses, saying he is too tired.

BARTOLO:

¿Qué quieres que yo le lleve?	What do you want me to take him?
Si antes le voy a pedir,	Instead, I will ask
que me quite estas flojeras,	that he take away this laziness,
que no me dejan bullir.	that does not allow me to move.

PARRADO AND TEBANO:
Antes que los reyes salgan,
tiraremos al llegar.

Before the Kings (stars) rise,
we will try to arrive.

BARTOLO:
Mejor llegaré esta noche,
que habrá mucho que cenar.

It will be better to arrive this
evening, when there is more to eat.

GILA:
Levanta, come, Bartolito,
mira que se hace muy tarde.

Get up, eat, Bartolo, see
that it's getting very late.

BARTOLO:
Déjate ahora de cariños,
anda y trae los tamales.

Drop the sweet talk,
go and get me the tamales.

ERMITAÑO:
Vamos, y verás Bartolo,
corre leche en los arroyos.

Let's go and you will see,
Bartolo, milk runs in the creeks.

BARTOLO:
Si quieres que te lo crea,
traeme un buen tarro de apoyos.

If you want me to believe you,
bring me a jug of cream.

The shepherds surround Bartolo, beckoning him to make his offering, while the devil, invisible to the shepherds, hovers over him, pinning him to the ground. Finally, after all the shepherds have taken their *ganchos*, using them as levers to pry Bartolo off the ground and out of his sleep, he arises and takes his turn in making an offering.

After Bartolo has finished, the shepherds line up, two by two, facing the *nacimiento,* and sing the *arrullamiento,* or lullaby. Then, in rows of twos, they line up and kiss the statue of el Niño Dios. The action in this part is primarily limited to the domain of the referential, but there is some interaction with the other domains. The previous part saw the end of the devils, except for this scene, in which Bartolo refuses to adore el Niño Dios. Although one of the devils is represented as being responsible for Bartolo's actions, it is totally within Bartolo's character to play the lazy shepherd. Second, the devil's role is passive; that is, he merely lies on top of Bartolo and does little else. Nevertheless, his presence is still an intrusion of the cosmological domain into the domain of the shepherds.

The presence of the archangel represents another intrusion of the cosmological domain into the referential. But again, like the devil holding down Bartolo, Michael no longer plays an active role but merely stands to the side of Mary and Joseph, as he does throughout most of the performance.

The Adoration by the Audience

When all the shepherds have finished paying homage to el Niño Dios, the audience is invited to do the same and to place a monetary offering in a basket held by Gila. Some may consider this part, with its emphasis on the adoration, to be the climax, but structurally it is not. There is little dramatic tension or crisis, and although the presence of el Niño Dios can be seen as another example of the cosmological in the referential, the fact that el Niño Dios is represented by a statue diminishes this action. Structurally, the presence of el Niño Dios does little to heighten the dramatic tension and serves primarily as an icon of one of the text's subjects.

In the final scene, the audience plays an active role in the performance for the third time, and their act of adoration represents another blurring of the distinction between ritual and drama. Moreover, it serves as a means of bringing the performance to an end as well as returning the dramatic action to the present.

In many ways, the dramatic structure of *Los Pastores* follows the pattern of breach, crisis, redressive action, and reintegration that Victor Turner (1974) has found in social and ritual dramas. The shepherds are in the fields tending their flock when Michael appears to announce the birth of the Messiah and thus brings about the first breach in the drama by allowing the cosmological to intrude into the realm of the referential. A second and more important breach occurs when Luzbel arrives and makes an all-out attempt to dissuade the shepherds from visiting Belén. The story does not reach a crisis until Cucharón is led into the *infierno*. It is here that the hermit intervenes and takes redressive action on the referential level, by rescuing Cucharón; Michael takes similar action and intervenes on the cosmological level by defeating Luzbel and sending him back to the dungeons of hell. With these redressive actions complete, the shepherds are free to continue their journey to Belén and pay homage to el Niño Dios. Although an analysis that features *Los Pastores* as a social drama substantiates the importance of the tension and crisis between the three domains, it tells little about the way these tensions are specifically coded in this event. This coding is in all likelihood related to the process of recognition and misrecognition.

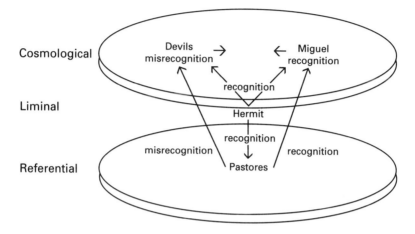

3.5. The dialectics of recognition and misrecognition.

STORY, STRUCTURE, AND THE FRICTION
OF MIS/RECOGNITION

In *Los Pastores,* narrative scheme and dramatized tension—those of story and structure—coalesce into a dramatized event guided by the friction between recognition and misrecognition. Luzbel greets the shepherds in the guise of a man of the cloth, thereby ensuring that they will not identify him as Lucifer; the shepherds recognize Michael as the archangel, a messenger from God, but fail to recognize the devils; Michael goes unrecognized by Luzbel as the one who delivered him into the abyss of hell; the hermit recognizes the devils and therefore gives chase with rosary in hand, cognizant of his ludic role (see figure 3.5).

But the tension between structure and story—that of dislocation and mis-recognition—not only informs the performance of *Los Pastores,* but becomes, in metaphorical fashion, the process of performance. Dislocation and misrecognition are not only aspects of drama, but—to use a phrase of James Fernandez (1986:43)—they have "become metaphor[s] predicated upon [it]." As a dramatized work, *Los Pastores* is informed by a constant tension between and ambiguity about the dislocation and misrecognition of this event as ritual/drama, devotion/entertainment, and present/historical time.

The tension between ritual and drama is exhibited in the opening scene, at the point where the director crawls on his knees carrying the statue of el Niño Dios to Mary and Joseph. This act, more ritualistic than dramatic, ambiguously pleads for recognition: Is this drama or ritual, performance or worship? In effect, the misrecognition of *Los Pastores* as ritual occurs through its recognition as drama; and its misrecognition as drama is facilitated by its recognition as ritual.

Further tension arises in the misrecognition of *Los Pastores* as diversion and not devotion. *Los Pastores* begins with the director giving a brief introduction to the audience, commenting on several points related to the dramatic tension of the performance, beginning with the contrast between *devoción* and *diversión* (devotion and diversion). While stating that people attend performances for diversion instead of devotion, he frames the performance as a ritual, as was made explicit during a performance at a local church when he offered the prayer intentions of the group while crawling on his knees carrying el Niño Dios from the *infierno* to the *nacimiento*. Although the director claims that people no longer attend the performance for religious reasons, he continues to interpret the performance as a religious event. He also states that the most important part of the entire drama is the end, when the shepherds and the audience *van a adorar* (go to adore) el Niño Dios. The director reinforces this tension by stating that the reason the performers maintain this event is that people, and especially children, no longer know the true meaning of Christmas. Implicit in his statement is the suggestion that through this event people will recognize the true meaning of Christmas and thereby thwart its misrecognition.

In addition, tension occurs between present and biblical time, the mechanism by which the audience is actively engaged in performance. By breaking the flow of the dramatized event, drawing the audience into present time, this device draws attention to its own making.[6]

Although as a dramatized event *Los Pastores* is the result of both story and structure, it has other poetic properties that are essential to the event as an aesthetic practice. They are the subject of chapter 4.

4

Poetic Performances: The Making of *Los Pastores*

The poetic and stylistic structures of *Los Pastores* inform the way poetry, music, dance, and song emerge in the dramatized event. As a folk drama, *Los Pastores* differs from other genres of *mexicano* expressive culture like proverbs, jokes, or tales in that it represents a complexly performed and elaborately rendered example of "cultural aesthetics in process" (Green 1981:422). Besides containing elements of story and structure that inform the performance of *Los Pastores,* the dramatized event is an assemblage of poetic conventions, impromptu speech, and aesthetic styles. These elements produce a richly textured, sonically poetic, and colorfully staged dramatized event. *Los Pastores,* as a communicative sign, is performed poetry: from text to enactment, the entire semiotic scene is one of heightened self-awareness. Like Jakobson's poetic functions (Jakobson 1960), the poetic forms in *Los Pastores* draw attention to themselves, scrambling the semantic meaning of the narrative through various genres and poetic functions. This chapter elaborates on and organizes the aesthetically salient features of *Los Pastores* into the various genres that render this event artistic. These features are verbal conventions, musical genres, movement and dance, and theatrics.

VERBAL CONVENTIONS

The verbal conventions found in *Los Pastores* consist of both formal and informal speech. Its formal conventions are related to the octosyllabic line and the *copla;* its informal verbal conventions are improvised during a performance and are not part of the written text, although they at times follow the poetic structures of formal conventions.

Formal Conventions

THE OCTOSYLLABIC LINE. The primary poetic structure of *Los Pastores* is the octosyllabic line. This strict formal feature is maintained by manipulating phonological and accentual rules to create a disciplined cadence of repetitive tone and sound from line to line. An eight-syllable line is maintained by changing the position of accents and manipulating vowels to create different phonological sounds. Therefore, although some lines may contain nine phonological syllables, the syllabic line is manipulated to maintain an eight-syllable form.

Spanish poetry does not have stressed and unstressed syllables, as does poetry written in English, but instead uses the accent that is a natural part of each word. Every Spanish word consists of accented and unaccented syllables referred to as tonic (accented) and atonic (unaccented) syllables, with normally only one tonic syllable per word. It is the position of the last accent in a line that determines the number of syllables in the line. The accent in a word can fall in one of three places:

Agudo	The accent falls on the last syllable of a word, as in *reunió, cené, mamá, papel, cortar.*
Grave	The accent falls on the second to last, or the penultimate syllable of a word. This is its most common position in Spanish and is not designated with a diacritical mark: *hermano, resultado, merchero.*
Esdrújulo	The accent falls on the third to last, or the antepenultimate syllable of a word: *célebre, régimen, bolígrafo* (Quilas 1986).

In prosodic analysis, if a line ends with an accent in the agudo position, an extra syllable is added to the line. If a line ends with an accent in the grave position, the number of syllables stays the same. And if a line ends with an accent in the esdrújulo position, a syllable is subtracted from the line.

_ _ _ _ _ _ _ _/   agudo = add one syllable to the line

_ _ _ _ _ _ _/_   grave = no change in syllables

_ _ _ _ _/_ _   esdrújulo = subtract one syllable from the line

The phonological syllabic structure of a line can also be changed by manipulating the vowels and sounds. This occurs through *sinalefa, sinéresis, diéresis,* or *hiato. Sinalefa,* or synalepha, occurs when two vowels, one at the end of a word and the other at the beginning of the next word, as in *se es-tan,* are joined to create one syllable: *sēes-tan.* Although these two words contain three phonological syllables, they are pronounced as two. *Sinéresis,* or syneresis, occurs when two vowels in one word are joined to form a diphthong and create one sound instead of two, as in *poesía.* This word should have four syllables, po-e-sí-a, but it is manipulated to sound like poe-sia. *Diéresis,* or diær-esis, is the opposite of *sinéresis:* a diphthong, as in *insaciable,* is split to form two sounds instead of one. Here the *i* and *a* can be split to form two sounds instead of one, in-sa-cï-a-ble. *Hiato,* or hiatus, is the opposite of *sinalefa:* two vowels in adjoining words, as in *mi hado,* are not run together but remain two distinct sounds. Here, instead of pronouncing the words as *mĩhado,* one would split them up to maintain their distinction, *mi-hado* (Quilas 1986).

The following analysis of a segment of the speech forms used by Luzbel and Lizardo is based on the preceding discussion of octosyllabic poetic structures. I first show the rhythm and meter of the poetic line and then the distribution of accents as a form of stylized speech. The first segment is from Luzbel's opening monologue.

	Syllabic Line	Phonological Line
1. Luz-bel-soy-luz-hay-en-**mí**	8	7
2. luz-en-mi-nom-bre-se-**vé**	8	7
3. y-con-la-luz-que-ba-**jé,**	8	7
4. to-dõel-a-bis-mõen-cen-**dí.**	8	7
5. Es-te-mon-tẽen-su-re-**ga**-zõa	8	7
6. que-jar-me-de-ter-mi-**nó**	8	7
7. al-ri-gor-de-mi-des-**ti**-no	8	8
8. por-no-te-ner-em-ba-**ra**-zo.	8	8
9. Por-so-ber-biõy-por-a-**troz**	8	7
10. por-un-va-no-pen-sa-**mien**-to	8	8
11. ba-jé-dẽa-quel-fir-ma-**men**-to	8	8
12. con-la-mal-di-ción-de-**Dios.**	8	7
13. Tiem-bla-Man-sión-ce-les-**tial**	8	7
14. tiem-bla-des-di-cha-do-**mun**-do	8	8
15. que-si-tũe-res-mi-ri **val**	8	7
16. yo-tam-bién-lo-soy-pro-**fun**-do	8	8
17. pa-rãha-cer-tẽe-**ter**-no-mal.	8	7
18. O-mi-ni-stros-de-los-**cie**-los	8	8
19. quẽha-bi-tais-en-e-sos-**se**-nos	8	8
20. bien-sa-béis-que-fũĩha-bi-**tan**-te	8	8
21. del-im-per-io-ce-les-**tial.**	8	7
22. Pe-ro-la-gra-cia-per-**dí**	8	7
23. me-fué-qui-ta-dõel-a-**sien**-to	8	8

24. don-de-di-cho-so-vi-**ví**-a,	8	8
25. go-zan-do-con-mil-con-**ten**-tos.	8	8
26. Ỹa-ho-ra-tris-te-de-**mí**	8	7
27. cuan-dõa-guar-da-bãel-con-**sue**-lo	8	7
28. mẽa-tor-men-ta-mas-el-**Cie**-lo	8	8
29. con-un-lo-co-fre-ne-**sí**.	8	7

Accented Line	Distribution of Accents
1. Ĺ _ _ Ĺ _ _ Ĺ (_)	1,4,7
2. Ĺ _ _ Ĺ _ _ Ĺ (_)	1,4,7
3. _ _ _ Ĺ _ _ Ĺ (_)	4,7
4. Ĺ _ _ Ĺ _ _ Ĺ (_)	1,4,7
5. Ĺ _ Ĺ _ Ĺ _ Ĺ _	1,3,5,7
6. _ Ĺ _ _ _ _ Ĺ (_)	2,7
7. _ _ Ĺ _ Ĺ _ Ĺ _	3,5,7
8. _ _ _ Ĺ _ _ Ĺ _	4,7
9. _ _ Ĺ _ _ _ Ĺ (_)	3,7
10. _ _ Ĺ _ _ _ Ĺ _	3,7
11. _ Ĺ _ _ Ĺ _ Ĺ _	2,5,7
12. _ _ _ _ Ĺ _ Ĺ (_)	5,7
13. Ĺ _ _ Ĺ _ _ Ĺ (_)	1,4,7
14. Ĺ _ _ _ Ĺ _ Ĺ _	1,5,7
15. _ _ _ Ĺ _ _ Ĺ (_)	4,7
16. _ _ Ĺ _ Ĺ _ Ĺ _	3,5,7
17. Ĺ _ Ĺ _ Ĺ _ _ _	1,3,5
18. _ _ Ĺ _ _ _ Ĺ _	3,7
19. _ _ Ĺ _ _ _ Ĺ _	3,7
20. _ _ Ĺ _ Ĺ _ Ĺ _	3,5,7
21. _ _ Ĺ _ _ _ Ĺ (_)	3,7
22. Ĺ _ _ Ĺ _ _ Ĺ (_)	1,4,7
23. _ _ _ Ĺ _ _ Ĺ _	4,7
24. Ĺ _ _ Ĺ _ _ Ĺ _	1,4,7
25. _ Ĺ _ _ Ĺ _ Ĺ _	2,5,7
26. _ Ĺ _ Ĺ _ _ Ĺ (_)	2,4,7
27. Ĺ _ _ Ĺ _ _ Ĺ _	1,4,7
28. _ _ Ĺ _ _ _ Ĺ _	3,7
29. _ _ Ĺ _ _ _ Ĺ (_)	3,7

The following example is spoken by Lizardo and has many of the same characteristics as those above.

		Syllabic Line	*Phonological Line*
1.	An-te-no-che-con-re-**ca**-do	8	8
2.	ba-jé-por-la-bre-ña-**so**-lo	8	8
3.	bus-can-dõa-Ta-ta-Bar-**to**-lo	8	8
4.	a-Na-bal-a-Gi-lãy-**Ba**-to	8	8
5.	Pe-ro-con-su-ri-gor-in-**gra**-to	9	9
6.	mẽhan-de-ja-dõen-lão-ca-**sión**	8	7
7.	el-ga-na-dõa-sũe-lec-**ción**	8	7
8.	Pe-ro-si-los-lle-gõãhal-**lar**	8	7
9.	el-pel-le-jõhan-de-lar-**gar**	8	7
10.	en-la-pun-ta-dẽun-chir-**rión**	8	7

	Accented Line	*Distribution of Accents*
1.	$\angle\_\angle\_\_\_\angle\_$	1,3,7
2.	$\_\angle\_\_\angle\_\angle\_$	2,5,7
3.	$\_\angle\_\angle\_\_\angle\_$	2,4,7
4.	$\_\_\angle\_\angle\_\angle\_$	3,5,7
5.	$\angle\_\_\_\_\_\angle\_\angle$	1,6,8
6.	$\_\_\angle\_\_\_\angle\,(\_)$	3,7
7.	$\_\_\angle\_\_\_\angle\,(\_)$	3,7
8.	$\angle\_\_\_\angle\_\angle\,(\_)$	1,5,7
9.	$\_\_\angle\_\_\_\angle\,(\_)$	3,7
10.	$\_\_\angle\_\_\_\angle\,(\_)$	3,7

Several rhythmic patterns can be now be detected in Luzbel's speech. First, the prosodic line consistently maintains an octosyllabic structure, even if the phonological line does not. Second, of the twenty-nine analyzed lines of Luzbel's speech, only six have accentual distributions that are not repeated (lines 5, 6, 12, 14, 17, 26). Therefore, twenty-three lines of this speech sample repeat their distribution of accents at least twice. Also, of the eight available accentual positions, three (position 6, 7, and 8) are consistent. That is, position 6 is never used, position 7 is used in every line but one, and position 8 is never used. Such repetition and pattern makes for a very rhythmic and stylized line. At the same time, the use of syllables to add to or subtract from the syllabic line allows for variety in the text.

The narrative recited by Lizardo, although not quite as repetitive as Luzbel's, is still fairly uniform. Of these lines, four have the same accentual distribution (lines 6, 7, 9, and 10). Here again the distribution of accents is fairly similar, with positions 6, 7, and 8 remaining consistent (position 6 used once, position 7 is used nine times, and position 8 is also used once).

THE COPLA. The octosyllabic line, already a highly rhythmic sound structure, is further patterned into several varieties of quatrains, known as *coplas*. The *Diccionario de la Lengua Española* defines the *copla* as a poetic composition itself composed of various forms: a *cuarteta de romance,* an octosyllabic quatrain whose rhyme scheme is ABCB; a *seguidilla,* a quatrain of alternating heptasyllabic and pentasyllabic lines whose rhyme scheme is ABCB; a *redondilla,* a quatrain of octosyllabic lines whose rhyme is ABBA; and other short combinations that are often characteristic of popular songs. The *copla* is a classic folk and literary form used in Spanish, Mexican, and Chicano narratives. For example, the Texas-Mexican corrido which dates from the mid-1800s to the 1930s—a genre whose influence in later Chicano narratives must not be underestimated—is said to be preceded by *coplas* and *décimas* (Paredes 1958a:139).[1]

The following octosyllabic lines are further patterned into *coplas* and performed by different characters in *Los Pastores.* I have not translated these verses since such an endeavor would fail to capture the poetic quality I am describing.

Cuartetas de Romance
Rhyme

PASTORES / CHORUS:

Ay, qué linda es la noche	A
Cuando Jesús nació;	B
y los ángeles cantaron	C
luego que ya amanecío.	B

ANGEL:

Pastores, que en las cabañas	A
aposentáis el ganado	B
Caminéis para Belén	C
que nació el Verbo humanado.	B

Redondilla
Rhyme

TEBANO:

Escucharon ya las voces	A
de aquellos ángeles bellos,	B

que parece que uno de ellos	B
veo venir por esos bosques.	A

GERARDO:

Por este tiempo, hermanitos,	A
como caen fuertes heladas.	B

CUCHARÓN:

Se entumen en las majadas	B
ovejas y corderitos.	A

To return to Luzbel's monologue, his speech is poeticized further by a series of quatrains, some of which are formal *coplas*, as well as *redondillas* and *cuartetas de romance*. The following text from his opening soliloquy provides a prime example of the poetic devices employed in this event.

	Rhyme	Form
LUZBEL:		
Luzbel soy; luz hay en mí	A	redondilla
luz en mi nombre se vé;	B	
y con la luz que bajé,	B	
todo el abismo encendí.	A	
De este monte en su regazo,	A	redondilla
a quejarme determino,	B	
al rigor de mi destino	B	
por no tener embarazo.	A	
Por soberbio y por atroz,	A	redondilla
por un vano pensamiento,	B	
bajé de aquel firmamento	B	
con la maldición de Dios.	A	
Tiembla, Mansión celestial,	A	This has the
tiembla, desdichado mundo	B	form of a
que si tú eres mi rival	A	quintilla
yo también lo soy profundo,	B	
para hacerte eterno mal.	A	
O ministros de los cielos	A	Imperfect cuar-
que habitáis en esos senos	A	teta
bien sabéis que fuí habitante	B	
del imperio celestial.	C	

Pero la gracia perdí	A	cuarteta de ro-
me fué quitado el asiento,	B	mance
donde dichoso vivia,	C	
gozando con mil contentos.	B	

Y ahora, triste de mí,	A	redondilla
cuando aguardaba el consuelo	B	
me atormenta más el Cielo	B	
con un loco frenesí.	A	

This example from Luzbel's speech, marked by rhyme and assonance, creates a performance that is both structured and poetic.

THE DÉCIMA. The *décima*, a ten-line octosyllabic narrative form, is also found in *Los Pastores*, although to a much lesser degree than the *copla*. The following are two examples of the *décima*.

	Rhyme
LIZARDO:	
Antenoche con recado	A
bajé por la breña solo	B
buscando a Tata Bartolo,	B
a Nabal, a Gila y Bato.	A
Pero, con su rigor ingrato,	A
me han dejado en la ocasión,	C
el ganado a su elección.	C
Pero si los llego a hallar,	D
el pellejo han de largar	D
en la punta de un chirrión.	C

This *décima* is known as an *espinela*, a lyrical narrative whose creation is attributed to Vicente Espinel, a sixteenth-century Spanish writer. The presence of such a formal genre among the folk is unexpected, "yet the décima for centuries has been an important folksong type among all peoples of Spanish culture" (Paredes 1966:154). In fact, Paredes credits the missionary activities of the church as a source of its diffusion in the Southwest.

The following *décima* is also found in *Los Pastores*.

	Rhyme
ANGEL:	
Levántate, fiera horrorosa,	A
y sepúltate en el abismo	B
donde castiga Dios mismo	B

tu malicia perniciosa.	A
Crújete cruel, serpiente venenosa,	A
que de la tierra al abismo	C
Dios te destierra	D
y con amor Soberano	C
le deja al linaje humano	C
armas para darte guerra.	D

This *décima* inverts the last five syllables, in a common variation of the *espinela.*

The musicality of the spoken line in *Los Pastores* is clearly one of the primary aesthetic characteristics of this drama. It consists of a highly regulated, patterned, and rhythmic speech style, whose primary unit is the octosyllabic line. The rhythm is repoeticized through the use of rhyme and assonance found in the formal patterns of the *copla,* especially those of the cuarteta de romance, the redondilla, and the décima. There is seldom, if any, a speech phrase that is not stylized by the use of rhyme and assonance in couplet or quatrain form, making *Los Pastores* a drama in verse form.

The performers, who have no formal training in Spanish prosody, continue to maintain the eight-syllable line in their enactment. Yet the rules of Spanish prosody, although unspoken, are not unknown, as is evident from the leader's comments to a young boy he was training: "Run your words together so that it makes it sound *smooth.*" This smoothness is the ability to project the rhythmic speech of the octosyllabic line.

The use of octosyllabic narrative forms—the *copla* and *décima*—has a long history in Spanish, Mexican, and Mexican-American verbal art (Limón 1992; McDowell 1975; Paredes 1958a, 1958b, 1966). This stylistic structure lends itself to a form that is phonologically disciplined and aurally harmonious. The form also blurs the distinction between music and speech, adding a sense of poetic ambiguity to the enactment of *Los Pastores.* That is, this style cannot be classified as true speech since it clearly shows a high degree of patterning and rhythm. At the *same* time, it is not like the singing that occurs at other times throughout the performance, which I discuss below.[2]

Informal Conventions

As mentioned earlier, the hermit is responsible for a good deal of the ludic quality of this drama, which he achieves primarily, although not entirely, through his skill as an impromptu verbal artist. This ability is apparent in his interactions with Luzbel and the other devils. I limit my analysis of informal verbal conventions to those utilized by the hermit, since for all practical purposes he is the only character whose verbal skills exceed what is called for in the written script. These conventions can be described as, first, a gloss on Luzbel's speech, and second, as forms of speechplay.

GLOSS. During his first monologue, Luzbel refers to his fall from heaven, as well as his fear of the Messiah. Off to the side, the hermit provides a running commentary on the monologue that shows his poetic and verbal artistry at work.

LUZBEL: ERMITAÑO:
Y ahora triste de mí,
cuando aguardaba el consuelo
me atormenta más el Cielo
con un loco frenesí.   ¡Ah! Todavía.
Porque airado pretendí,
sentarme en ese trono augusto: Pero te quitaron la silla.
pero no tuve ese gusto,
porque jamás a él subí.   ¿No? Porque dejaron escalera.

And now, unfortunate that I am,
while I waited for consolation,
the heavens torment me again,
with a wild frenzy.   Oh! Still at it!
Because angrily I pretended,
to sit in that august throne.   Because they took the chair away
But I did not have that pleasure,   from you.
because I never ascended to it.   No? Because they left a ladder.

Here is another example of this same convention.

LUZBEL: ERMITAÑO:
Mas ¿qué miro? lúcida esfera   ¡Otra vez!
que melodía en todo placentera;
qué es esto que se escucha
causándome temor y pena mucha?   ¿Por qué estas tan terco?

But, what do I see? A brilliant   Again!
sphere, what melody, pleasant
in every way, what is this that
I hear. Causing me much fear   Why are you so
and pain?   obstinate?

The hermit swinging his cane at the devils.

Although Luzbel's soliloquy is scripted as a monologue, the hermit, by extending, commenting on, and verbally interacting with Luzbel, transforms the focus of the narrative. As a result, he shifts the audience's attention from Luzbel to the interaction between him and the hermit.

The hermit also uses a succinct verbal form to respond to Luzbel. Throughout Luzbel's monologue, the hermit utters "¡Aha!" or "¡Ah!" This device, along with his longer interjections, changes the entire focus of Luzbel's monologue to one of dialogic speechplay.

SPEECHPLAY. Another convention used by the hermit is the pun. He puts a ludic twist on the words of Luzbel, and thereby fulfills his charter role in the drama: "to play with the devil." He does this in part by playfully converting the terms Luzbel uses to proper names:

LUZBEL:	ERMITAÑO:
De mi soberbia y pesar	
que Dios es Omnipotente	
Sabio, infinito y clemente	
nunca lo podré negar.	No, no vive aquí
	Clemente.

In spite of my pride,
that God is omnipotently wise,
infinite, and clement,   No, Clement does not live
I can never deny.   here.

Pues con dulces acentos
los celestes querubines muy
   contentos
hoy le cantan Victoria
al Creador del cielo y de la gloria.   No, no vino
                            Victoria.

With sweet melodies,
the heavenly cherubs very happy
today they sing victory
to the Creator of the heaven and of   No, Victoria
glory.   did not come.

Note that in almost every case the hermit employs the same octosyllabic form, which highlights his poetic and verbal ability and maintains the highly rhythmic and patterned structure of the performance.

Displaced Genres and Shifting Meaning

The significance of the hermit's informal verbal conventions becomes clearer when they are compared with the highly formalized conventions of the overall narrative. Hymes (1974:105) states that a shift in formal patterns, such as that invoked by the hermit's informal conventions, is a salient linguistic feature that calls forth a subsequent shift in meaning. In this situation, a shift in meaning is found in the dialectical interplay between the formal and informal poetic structures. This is evident in the two conventions of the hermit's verbal speech, those of gloss and speechplay. The first shift in meaning, already mentioned, occurs with the transformation of Luzbel's monologue into a dialogue. By commenting on Luzbel's speech and using phrases such as "¡Aha!" the hermit breaks the cohesiveness of the former's monologue. These continuous interjections and comments redirect attention from the sole figure of Luzbel to that of the hermit and Luzbel together. At the same time, the seriousness of Luzbel's soliloquy is interrupted by a humorous device that turns Luzbel's words on their head. This is the second change: a comic and ludic atmosphere is created through speechplay. The hermit turns the word "mercy" (*clemencia*) into a proper name, Clement, thereby poking fun at Luzbel's serious speech; and while Luzbel bemoans his pain and suffering, the hermit tells the audience he is a stubborn fool. These verbal inversions turn Luzbel's all too serious monologue into farce.

The verbal conventions used in *Los Pastores*, both formal and informal, are similar to those referred to earlier as displacement and misrecognition. The hermit displaces the absolute power of the singular voice by shifting Luzbel's monologue to a dialogue. Furthermore, by inverting the seriousness of the monologue with popular humor, the hermit encroaches on the power of Luzbel's words.

MUSICAL FORMS

The musicality of *Los Pastores* is intrinsically related to its formal and informal poetic forms, creating another rhythmic layer by fusing verbal and musical conventions. Although no musical instruments are used during the performance, the speech and singing of the shepherds, devils, and other characters imbues it with a musical quality. An ethnomusicological analysis is beyond the scope of this chapter, but a few comments are in order about the various musical and singing styles incorporated in this event.[3]

The shorter song forms are sung *coplas*, like the *redondillas* discussed in the earlier section of this chapter, which are sung by Gerardo and Cucharón. Another example of this form can be found in the *levantamiento de Bartolo*, or the scene in which Bartolo refuses to adore el Niño Dios and instead lies on the ground until he is lifted by all the shepherds.

PARRADO Y TEBANO:
Antes que los reyes salgan
tiraremos al llegar.

Before the kings come out
we will try to arrive.

BARTOLO:
Mejor llegaré esta noche,
que habrá mucho que cenar.

It will be better to arrive tonight,
there will be more food then.

GILA:
Levanta, come, Bartolito
mira que se hace muy tarde.

Get up and eat, Bartolo
it is getting very late.

BARTOLO:

Déjate ahora de cariños	Drop the sweet talk
anda y trae los tamales.	and go and bring the tamales.

ERMITAÑO:

Vamos y verás Bartolo	Let's go and you will see
corre leche en los arroyos.	milk is flowing in the creeks.

BARTOLO:

Si quieres que te lo crea	If you want me to believe
traeme un buen tarro de apoyos.	you, bring me a big mug of cream.

This scene continues with the other shepherds contributing their own *coplas*.

The songs of longer duration vary in style and tempo. In general, these songs have *coros*, or refrains, that are led by Tebano and Parrado, who act as song leaders for the shepherds. They have attained this position by virtue of the many years they have been participating in the performance (more than twenty-five each), their singing ability, and their gender. In this role, Parrado and Tebano sing the verses while the other shepherds follow with the *coro*.

Two of their songs can be considered *estribillos*, a refrain that uses ono-matopoeic syllables or vocalization and is meant to be an iconic representation of specific sounds. The first is an *arullo*, or lullaby, in which the following refrain is sung by the shepherds:

Quieres que te tape	Do you want me to cover you
con telas de mi amor,	with the cloth of my love.
quieres que vengas a mi pecho tú?	Do you want to be held to my breast?
Quieres que vaya al pesebre	Do you want me to go to the manger
y te ruru?	and lull you?
A la ruru, ruru, ruru.	A la ruru, ruru, ruru.

Here the "ruru, ruru, ruru" is an iconic sound image of the cooing one makes in rocking a baby to sleep.

Another example of the estribillo is found in the following song, called the *canto del pecador,* or the song of the sinner, sung by the shepherds:

Titireando de frío	Shivering from the cold
y llorando de dolor	and crying from pain
en los brazos de María	in the arms of Mary
se contempla al Salvador.	we contemplate the Savior.

The first word, *titireando,* is an iconic representation of shivering and is meant to imitate the sound of chattering teeth.

Another musical genre that is found in *Los Pastores* is the *alabanza,* or song of praise. Many of the songs performed by the shepherds seem to fall into this category since, in one form or another, they are praises to God or el Niño Dios. The following is a prime example of this genre.

CORO:

Gloria a Dios en las alturas	Glory to God in the Highest
y Paz al hombre en la tierra	and Peace to men on Earth
porque en el portal está	because in the entrance is
la Sagrada Omnipotencia.	the Sacred Omnipotence.

Although many of the songs in *Los Pastores* differ in tempo, they exhibit the copla form, rhyme and assonance, and to some extent the octosyllabic line of the traditional musical genre on which they are based. The musical structure and poetic conventions of these songs echo the highly formal style of the poetic structures of the narrative, creating a consistent auditory form that emphasizes the poetic function of *Los Pastores.*

MOVEMENT AND DANCE

Movement and dance do not play a significant role in this event, especially in comparison with the verbal and musical elements discussed above. For the most part, the characters stand in a line throughout the performance, moving only to walk or dance.

Walking

In their movement, both the shepherds and the devils are structurally bound by the staging area; that is, the pattern of their marching and walking is restricted by the boundaries of the stage. As seen in figure 4.1 the only space available for movement in any systematic fashion is the space that falls between the two rows of shepherds and between the *nacimiento* and the *infierno.* Therefore, all movement or dance occurs within these boundaries.

The movement of the shepherds takes place on several occasions and is meant to represent travel. In these instances, the shepherds have talked or sung about visiting the Messiah, and their subsequent marching is representa-

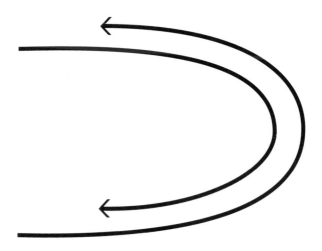

4.1. The primary flow of movement.

tive of the journey. Although their movement in these instances takes place within the context of singing, they are clearly not dancing, since they are miming the type of movement being referred to in the song. In this context, the shepherds follow either one of two patterns as they "travel" within the space of the staging area. The first pattern is circular: one line of shepherds circles around the other until the lines end up on the opposite side of the staging area from which they began (see figure 4.1).

In the second pattern of travel, they rotate around and out but remain on the same side of the staging areas from which they started (figure 4.2). It is the task of Tebano, as leader of the shepherds, to decide which pattern will be followed.

The movement of the devils, although it, too, follows a consistent pattern, is not meant to be iconic or representative of travel. At the end of the *concilio infernal*, and after Luzbel has been released from the chains of Michael the Archangel, the devils march around the stage as they sing, but follow the rhythm of what they are singing. The only other systematic movement undertaken by the devils occurs when Luzbel is tied up and lying at the feet of Michael the Archangel. With the shepherds singing, the devils form a line, gripping each other's hands, as they attempt to free Luzbel. They rock back and forth mimicking a tug of war. With their outstretched arms acting as a tether, they try to pry Luzbel free from Michael's hold, but without success. This is the only other time that patterned movement is used by the devils.

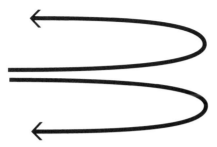

4.2. The secondary flow of movement.

Dance

Dance occurs even less than ritualized movement in this event. Only three people dance in the performance: Gila, the hermit, and Melicio. Gila's dance is meant to stand out from the other two. Just before she takes her gifts of adoration to el Niño Dios, she is asked by Bartolo, her father, to dance for the others. Parrado and Tebano begin a song about a *palomita* (beautiful dove), to which Gila dances in two circular or figure-eight designs. Her dance is rather simple: it consists of two or three steps followed by a small skip, a routine that is repeated until the end of the song. On almost all occasions the hermit joins in, dancing behind Gila or taking her hand as they move in a circular fashion. Upon completing her dance, Gila takes her turn in adoring el Niño Dios.

Besides dancing with Gila, the hermit, on occasion, takes his cane and dances around the floor while the shepherds are marching. The hermit, true to his humorous character, moves in a freer motion than that of the shepherds and steps in a sliding shuffle motion similar to the Texas-Mexican polka. On another occasion, the devils step out of the *infierno* and take the hermit by the arm, dancing with him until he realizes who they are and chases them away with his cane.

Melicio dances just before he goes to adore el Niño Dios. His (although the character is male, it is played by a woman) dance consists of a shuffle and skip, also similar to that of the Texas-Mexican polka. The song to which Melicio dances is the only one that can be characterized as a *ranchera,* a genre of song that grew out of the cattle society of the northern part of Greater México. The use of this genre for Melicio's dance is quite significant because of its gender association: as noted above, although played by a woman, the character is male, and a ranchera conveys the qualities of *lo ranchero* such as "manli-

ness, self-sufficiency, . . . or mexicanismo" (Peña 1985:11). So, of the two formal dances in the performance, the male character is restricted to a genre of
dance that exhibits male qualities.

The performers consider Gila's dance the primary dance event of the performance. I was told on several occasions that previous young women who
played this part "stole the show" with their footwork. Lamentably, many of
them added, this is no longer the case since the current performer does not
seem to put as much effort into this aspect of her performance, as was done
"in the past."

THEATRICS

Stage and costume construction are discussed under the rubric of theatrics.
These two elements are related to the objectification of the symbolic clusters
surrounding the ritual and dramatic aspects of this performance.

Stage

The stage is divided into two opposite poles (see figure 3.3), characteristic of
the binary markers of heaven and hell. At one end stands the *infierno*, a large,
enclosed area constructed of plywood panels that faces the *nacimiento* at the
other end. The *nacimiento* is a small manger that holds the statue of el Niño
Dios. The *infierno*, painted red and black, with drawings of dragons, demons,
and figures that are half animal and half demon, is the hellmouth, from which
Luzbel and the other devils emerge. The small manger, covered with blankets
and flanked by María and José, the angel, and Gila, is representative of the
holy and the sacred. Here lies another binary distinction: the *infierno* is
adorned with figurative icons whereas the *nacimiento* is flanked by real people,
who pose as icons of sacred characters. On most occasions when *Los Pastores*
is performed in people's homes, the hosting family will build an altar directly
behind the nacimiento to emphasize its sacredness, as well as its binary
quality.

The binary poles of the staging area frame the proscribed flow or movement of the drama. The director, in his opening ritual, crawls on his knees
from the *infierno* to the *nacimiento*. The shepherds always begin their routinized movement toward the *nacimiento* while the devils begin their movement
toward the *infierno*. Luzbel is chained at the feet of Michael the Archangel
directly in front of the *nacimiento,* and the audience, like the shepherds, adore

The devils brandishing their swords as they make their exit.

the statue of the child in front of the *nacimiento*. The home altar could be placed anywhere, but it usually stands behind the *nacimiento*. Likewise, the devils use the protection of the *infierno* to hide their *bote,* or urinal bucket. Therefore, the association of pollution, metaphysically in the presence of the devils, and socially and physically in the presence of urine, is connected with the *infierno*, whereas the *nacimiento* is associated with the sacred and the holy.

Gender markers are also present in these representations. In Mexican-American folk culture, the construction and maintenance of altars is associated with the work of women, as is religion in general (Turner 1982).[4] The *nacimiento*, too, is associated with the work of women, whereas the *infierno* is connected with men's work. Because of its size and weight, it has to be carried on a truck, by men capable of lifting it. It is a place where men, both shepherds and devils, gather and have a few shots of whiskey before the performance, a place where men urinate, and a place that is off limits to women performers and audience members.

There is also a binary demarcation in the space between the hellmouth and the *nacimiento*. The shepherds move about on the side of the stage that is closest to the *nacimiento,* as does the angel. The devils' movements are close to the *infierno*. These boundaries are crossed now and then, when members of one group intersect the domain or structural world of the other. For example, such an intrusion occurs when Luzbel, in disguise, speaks to the shepherds, or when Cucharón, lost in the darkness, wanders into the *infierno*. True to his liminal domain, the hermit moves freely across the entire staging area.

Costume

I have already described the costumes used by members of the troupe. Here I show how these costumes generally follow the same symbolic structure created by the binary oppositions of the stage setting.

The costumes worn by the devils leave no doubt as to the identity of the characters wearing them. They resemble medieval "demons with human feet and hands, wild hair, and animal faces and ears; demons with monstrous, hideous bodies, lizard skin, ape-like heads, and paws" (Russell 1984:131). Their opposites in the drama are the angel and Gila, whose costumes are primarily white. Mary wears blue and white, as in the traditional pictures of her, while Joseph is dressed in religious garb. The colors used in the costumes of these characters associate them with either the *infierno* or the *nacimiento,* which form binary poles, as they do in the Christian cosmology of heaven and hell.

The shepherds appear to depart from this pattern. The colors they wear have no connection with either the *infierno* or the *nacimiento.* Thus it seems that the shepherds' costumes differentiate them in the same manner as the dramatic structure: they are neither devils, angels, nor the hermit. The distinction is not that clear-cut, however. Both the shepherds and devils use a cape with their names inscribed on the back, the only difference being the color.

The hermit's costume resonates with that of the dramatic structure and distinguishes him as neither devil, angel, nor shepherd. He does not use the same type of *gancho* as the shepherds, nor does he use a cape and hat as they do. His costume is more bleak, cast in colors of browns and grays. His use of the mask is also significant. First, it marks him as an elderly person; second, no other human character uses a mask, further inscribing the liminal role he plays in the drama.

The costumes used in *Los Pastores* emphasize the boundaries associated with the structural domains of the drama. As such, the poetics of costuming forms an artistic homology that accents the tension and generic organization of the dramatized event. But generic organization and homologous artistic forms are not limited to literary readings alone. As Hanks (1987) and others have demonstrated, genres derive their organizational ability from the interplay between textual structures and social life, making dramatic form and narrative displacements open to readings of history and the cultural poetics

The hermit, ca. 1965. (Courtesy, the Institute of Texan Cultures, San Antonio, Texas)

of representation. To reiterate, the dramatized event is influenced by its historical development and multiple places of performance. This relationship between artistic performance and history, or more specifically, between performance and context, expands the dramatized event to include the politics of cultural representation as it emerges in the dramatic event. These are some of the issues and relationships explored in part two.

PART II

History, Place, and the Politics of Performance

Play the terrific march of these trumpets and drums,
because if this God, who was born here, dies, men
will be entirely conquered.
All of you go out into the world,
war against men, war, war!
— LUZBEL, *LOS PASTORES*

Like work, science and all social activities of man, art too is a product of
social development, of man becoming man through his work.
— LUKÁCS, *INTRODUCTION TO A MONOGRAPH ON
AESTHETICS*

To insist that these practices are different is not some form of reservation,
marking off an "aesthetic" sphere, but a social indication of the actual
modes and functions of different practices.
— WILLIAMS, *THE SOCIOLOGY OF CULTURE*

5

Historical Poetics and Cultural Practice: The Dislocation of South Texas *Mexicanos*

As the holy season of Advent approaches, one cannot fail to notice among the inhabitants of the Mexican ranches and towns of the lower Rio Grande, Texas, a degree of bustle and unwonted activity . . . which indicates that the normal . . . apathy of life has been seriously disturbed" (Bourke 1893:89). So begins the account of *Los Pastores* by Captain John G. Bourke, one of the earliest writers in Texas to pen an essay on the subject. While Bourke found the performances "crudely constructed" with "ludicrous incongruities," a critical examination of his various writings, as well as the writings of those who follow him, reveals a number of tropic formulations or discursive styles that serve to fashion a place for South Texas *mexicanos* that is not only "crude" and "ludicrous" but marginal to the emerging socioeconomic structure.

Bourke's discourses, like other discussions about Mexicans in South Texas during his time, cannot be fully understood unless they are seen in the context of the changing political, cultural, and economic order of that period. These discourses serve as a means of fashioning a social place, and concomitantly, a social identity, for *mexicanos,* and any effort to understand the historical practice and contemporary meaning of *Los Pastores* cannot be separated from the way both performers and event have been narratively inscribed through such representations. These inscriptions are based on particular, historically emergent, socially constituted narrative structures that I refer to as historical poetics, after Greenblatt (1980).[1] Therefore the social history of *Los Pastores* I want to write concerns the way its cultural practice and performance has been "inscribed" in the larger discourse of social formation in South Texas. Accordingly, in this chapter I trace the shifting and changing historical poetics that constitute *Los Pastores* as well as inform the broader social environment in which it is performed. In doing so, I interpret the complex textual assemblage of its cultural history among *mexicanos* and Anglos as it shifts with the political and social terrain of South Texas.

Between 1850 and 1900 the poetics was informed by war and an emerging exploitation; during the 1920s and 1930s, it became a poetics of isolation and marginalization; and beginning in the 1940s, it turned into a poetics informed by the preservation of this *mexicano* cultural form for touristic consumption. These transformations did not occur in a vacuum but were accompanied by particular strategies and narratives that clear the cultural space through which the practice of social dislocation occurs. A poetics of dislocation gives narrative texture to forms of exploitation that are coterminous with the geographic and social subordination of *mexicanos* in South Texas. By dislocation I mean displacement, in the sense suggested by Stallybrass and White (1986:196): namely, a "particular kind . . . of transcoding mechanism" that displays competing claims on power, identity, and meaning. Furthermore, the counterside of dislocation is relocation, meaning the way these same transcoding mechanisms reinscribe identities and meanings, shifting them from one domain to another. Through this process, members of the *mexicano* community, and their social place in the economic and political world of South Texas, have been dislocated by forces related to racial and class experience in the United States.

THE MEXICAN-ANGLO WORLD, 1800–1890

The history of the Texas-México border between 1800 and 1910 is one of crisis, tension, and conflict. Those involved were Spaniards, Mexicans, a number of Native Indian groups, and Anglo-American settlers. However, the greatest tension and conflict, both in terms of demographic numbers and social power, arose between the local Mexican population and the incoming Anglo-American settlers.[2]

México gained its independence from Spain in 1821, and like many postcolonial governments, it was forced to search for a political and national identity through factionalized parties. The main source of strife was political ideology: some wanted power to be concentrated at the center, whereas others hoped to see México develop into a cohesive federalist nation composed of fairly autonomous states. For several years the balance of power teetered in one direction and then the other, until in 1824 a constitution was written establishing the United States of México as a federalist republic.

It was during the struggle for independence that Moses Austin petitioned the Spanish Crown for permission to settle in Coahuila y Tejas, but he died before achieving his goal. The newly established Mexican government then agreed to extend colonization rights to his son Stephen F. Austin. Many of Austin's early frontiersmen, as well as those who soon followed, saw opportunity in this new land, but they found the presence of Tejanos (Texas-Mexicans) an unwanted sight:

> The immigrants, then, did not arrive in Texas with open minds concerning the native Tejanos: their two-hundred-year experience with "different" peoples had so shaped their psyche that their immediate reaction was negative rather than positive. . . . They had retained impressions acquired before their arrival in the state then reapplied and transposed those racial attitudes upon the native casta. (De León 1982:11)

Arriving in Coahuila y Tejas in 1821, Austin and his fellow settlers soon began learning what it meant to live under Mexican rule. By 1827, 12,000 Anglo-Americans had entered México and were living in Texas, outnumbering the Mexicans in the province by almost two to one. And by 1835, Mexican citizens in Texas were 7,800 to 30,000 Anglo-Americans. These numbers alarmed Mexican officials, who, in an effort to curb the growing immigration from the United States, passed an emancipation proclamation in 1829 forbidding slavery. Since slavery was not practiced in México, this law was aimed specifically at the U.S. citizens in the Mexican province of Texas.

This move intensified the friction that was already present between the province and the central government owing to the distance between them. Texas had been appended to the state of Coahuila for governmental purposes, but the citizens of Coahuila y Tejas, both Mexican and Anglo-American, were discouraged by the inefficiency of the central government, and by the distance they had to travel to reach government and appellate court offices for their state, which were situated in Saltillo. In 1833 Austin traveled to México City to try to persuade President Santa Anna to allow Texas to become an independent Mexican state. Santa Anna refused, but he did agree to allow citizens of the province more latitude in conducting their affairs. Accordingly, he revised the tariff laws, repealed the anti-immigration law, and permitted trial by jury (Long 1990:53).

Tensions between Anglo-Americans in Texas and the Mexican government came to a head when Santa Anna abrogated the Constitution of 1824. In response, both Mexicans and Anglo-Americans in Tejas called for independence.

A key Mexican figure in this dispute was Lorenzo de Zavala, one of the writers of the 1824 Constitution and a former minister to France, who had relocated to the province of Tejas. De Zavala, in fact, became the first vice president of the Republic of Texas, serving with David Burnet as president.

In an effort to suppress the federalist movement in Texas, Santa Anna led his forces north, making his move on San Antonio de Béxar in the now famous battle of the Alamo. Late in February 1836, three hundred men, organized into a small militia, gathered to defend this one-time Franciscan mission against Santa Anna's forces. But on March 6 the Mexicans, greatly outnumbering those in the Alamo, made their final siege, taking the Alamo and leaving no prisoners.

This proved to be a decisive point in rallying support for Texas independence. Soon afterward, as Texas nationalist legend has inscribed in all Texas school children's repertoire of populist history, the battle cry of "Remember the Alamo!" led the Texan forces at the battle of San Jacinto. And on April 21, Sam Houston's troops engaged San Anna's forces by surprise at the battle of San Jacinto, capturing the Mexican leader several days later on his retreat south.

It is important to remember that the dispute in Texas stemmed from the pressure by both Mexicans and Anglo-Americans for a federalist government in México. Mexicans in the province had also tired of Santa Anna's exploits and of having to conduct their political affairs with distant provincial and national capitals, in Coahuila and México City. Note, too, that despite his unilateral control of Mexican affairs and politics, and his egotistical and personal ambitions, Santa Anna's actions can be viewed as an effort to control an internal uprising in his own country.

Texas gained its independence under the Treaty of Velasco, signed May 4, 1836. This treaty put a temporary end to the fighting between the Anglo-Americans and the Mexican government and established the Nueces River as the official border between Texas and México (Weber 1973). After independence, however, the local *mexicano* population rapidly declined, and anti-Mexican sentiment increased. Although the fighting had stopped, the hostility between the growing Anglo-American population and *mexicanos* intensified.

In the ensuing years, the United States was inspired by the notion of Manifest Destiny, which became the justification for seeking to expand its territorial holdings in the West and Southwest.[3] On January 13, 1846, President James Polk sent General Zachary Taylor across the Nueces River to the Rio Grande in defiance of the earlier border agreement. As noted above, the tensions between the Mexicans and Anglo-Americans in Texas never fully subsided after the Texas Revolution, and on May 11, 1846, the United States declared war on México out of a desire to expand U.S. territory and develop American economic interests. The war ended with the signing of the Treaty of Guadalupe-Hidalgo on February 2, 1848, which established the Rio Grande as the new border between the two countries and ceded still other lands in northern México to the United States. This included the states of California, New Mexico, Texas, Nevada, and parts of Colorado, Arizona, and Utah. *Mexicanos* living in these areas had the option of becoming U.S. citizens or returning to México. Land grants and property were to be respected, as well as the Mexican culture and language. Although the treaty formally ended U.S. aggression in México, it did not take long for new conflicts to erupt between Mexicans in the United States and the Anglo-Americans. The control and ownership of land were a critical part of this conflict:

> Immediately after the war with Mexico, a greedy land grab ensued which alienated the Mexican community in Texas for good. . . . The authorities declared "vacant" all communal and municipal lands distributed earlier. The General Law of 1852 validated some original Spanish land grants but many claims were lost simply for the lack of representation before the commission as required by law. The "vacant" lands were then sold to Anglos at very low prices. (Richmond 1980:3)

As a result, by the 1890s, South Texas found itself in the midst of a dramatic social and economic transformation. From the time it was settled, this area was cattle country, known for its large haciendas and cattle ranches. Many *mexicano* elites of this time were landowners whose interest in land stemmed from the Mexican *hacendado* tradition: "The Mexican elite," continues Montejano, "saw land as a family patrimony, as the basis for preserving a traditional lifestyle" (1987:51).

After the war, more Anglo-American settlers arrived with different attitudes toward the land. "The Anglo elite saw land mainly as an investment, as a basis for the business of ranching" (Montejano 1987:51). The famous King Ranch is the epitome of a mercantile cattle industry that was in large part responsible for the subsequent erosion of the *mexicano* ranching elite and its underlying social and economic formation. Subsequently, *mexicano* ownership of South Texas ranches decreased from 34 percent of the population in 1850 to 16 percent in 1900. In this same period, the Anglo-owned ranches increased from 2 percent in 1850 to 31 percent in 1900 (Montejano 1987:73).

The shift in ranch ownership from *mexicano* to Anglo control was accompanied by other changes in economic structure. By the 1890s, the locus for the organization of production was changing from an established cattle industry to commercial farming.

> "Home-seekers" from the north bought the land after first being enticed by attractive brochures and free visits sponsored by land developers; many of these land developers soon became the nucleus in structuring the local banking and financial system. Mexicans served as the labor force for the agricultural infrastructure—irrigation canals, railroad lines and cleared lands which made agricultural development possible. From the beginning the availability of a cheap source of potential farm labor was advertised by land developers as a major attraction to farmers. (Miller and Maril, in Hansen 1981:50)

The economic shift from cattle to industrial farming on the border between Texas and México created the need for a cheap labor force to work the fields. The Anglo elite controlled this new industry with the strong arm of the Texas Rangers, while *mexicanos* provided the labor. As a result, "a clear racial-cultural stratification and subordination began to emerge, as a new wave of Anglo-American entrepreneurs and farming interests established a political and economic hegemony over the native population" (Limón 1983a:216). Under these conditions, narratives concerning *Los Pastores* cannot be read neutrally but must be interpreted as part of the same culturally mediated principles of organization that inform the social displacement of the local *mexicano* population.[4]

This is the political and economic environment that Captain John G. Bourke found when he arrived in Texas, and that Limón (1994) has characterized as conditions of war. They were conditions that his narrative representations of *mexicanos* helped reproduce.

THE POETICS OF DISLOCATION IN THE ERA OF WAR

Captain John G. Bourke is perhaps better known for his writings on Brigadier General George Crook, as well as for his participation in the Indian wars in the United States. He also gained significant recognition as an ethnologist, folklorist, and scholar, becoming an early president of the American Folk-lore Society in 1896. Bourke's initial association with Mexicans occurred during his first duty station at Fort Craig, New Mexico, soon after he graduated from the military academy at West Point, in 1869. His ethnological studies on *mexicano* folklore did not begin until the spring of 1891, when he was sent to Fort Ringgold in Rio Grande City, Texas (Bourke 1893, 1894a, 1894b, 1895).

A controversy arose during Bourke's stay at Fort Ringgold that pitted him against the local *mexicano* population, and eventually, a contingent of Texas officials. It had to do with his attempts at capturing Catarino Garza, a Texas-Mexican revolutionist who had organized military campaigns against the Mexican dictator Porfirio Díaz from the Texas side of the border. In pursuing Garza, Bourke "regarded himself and his men at war with a military force, and he ordered his soldiers to kill any armed *Garzistas* they encountered" (Porter 1986:87). Considering these to be extreme measures, local U.S. Marshals decided to withdraw their support of Bourke's efforts and at times aided the *Garzistas* themselves. Bourke nevertheless persisted in his military efforts, which culminated in a series of legal battles when charges were brought against him for unlawful arrest, false imprisonment, and assault after a raid on a local ranch in La Grulla (Porter 1986:288–90). In 1893 Bourke was offered an opportunity to leave Texas for a detail with the Latin-American Department of the World's Columbian Exposition in Chicago, which he accepted.

Bourke's anthropology was shaped by the classical cultural evolutionary tenets of his time, and he spent his Texas days, when not involved in military exploits, collecting ethnological data from his local *mexicano* informants. One can envision him coming in from his raids on local ranches, where he was wont to kill any armed Mexican, gathering his field notes and heading off to interview María Antonia Cavazo de Garza, a local *curandera* (healer)—his main informant—on her healing practices (Bourke 1894b). Bourke's writing covered a variety of topics, including material on language usage, foodways, and "superstitions" of Mexicans in South Texas (Bourke 1893, 1894b, 1895). He wrote a number of articles on *mexicano* folklore in this vein, including one of the first essays about *Los Pastores* in Texas, "The Miracle Play of the Rio Grande," for the *Journal of American Folk-lore* in 1893.

In writing for *Scribner's* Magazine in 1894, Bourke "compared the Rio Grande to the Nile, in the facts [*sic*] that, like its African prototype, the fierce River of the North had its origin in snow-clad sierras far away in Colorado" (Bourke 1894a:590–91). In addition, Bourke compared the Apache, Comanche, and other tribes of the Southwest to the "wild tribes of Central Africa [that] kept the forces of civilization at bay" (Bourke 1894a:591). But, a few pages later Bourke goes even further. He displaces his own ethnographic narrative: instead of taking the wild Comanche and Apache savages as the subjects of his prose, he juxtaposes *mexicanos* with the Congo.

> Through the centre of this unknown region, fully as large as New Eng-
> land, courses the Rio Grande, which can more correctly be compared to
> the Congo than to the Nile the moment that the degraded, turbulent, igno-
> rant, and superstitious character of its population comes under examina-
> tion. To the Congo, therefore, I compare it, and I am confident that all
> who peruse these lines to a conclusion will concur in the correctness of
> the comparison. (Bourke 1894a:594)

Here, Bourke equates the entire South Texas region with the Congo. This
shift of geographic location from the Nile to the Congo emphasizes his perception of *mexicanos* as closer to what he perceives as the "degraded" land of
Central Africa than to the Egyptian site of early civilization. This narrative
displacement from the Nile to the Congo resonates with his other displacement of seeing Mexicans, not Apaches, as responsible for keeping the forces
of "civilization at bay." Relocating South Texas and its native Mexican inhabitants in a New World Congo implicates Bourke in the economic and geographic displacement of *mexicanos* that Barrera (1979) refers to as internal co-
lonialism. As a military officer, Bourke is a critical actor in this social and
economic drama. And his own scholarly endeavors, those related to investiga-
tions of Mexican healing rites, foods, and "superstitions," are part of this same
process: they exoticize the local *mexicano* population, thereby socially distanc-
ing and narratively displacing it. By portraying the more exotic elements of
mexicano expressive culture and narratively relocating them in the Congo,
Bourke is playing the role of colonial agent.

In a fine display of their own poetic counterdislocation, the local population
produced their own caricature of Bourke. According to his own, seemingly
naive admission, the character of Lucifer in *Los Pastores* dressed as a cavalry
officer (Bourke 1893:90), and when Bourke was asked to lend his uniform for
this purpose and offered one of the infantry instead, "the offer was declined"
(Bourke 1894a:609). The performers, and perhaps others, it seems, found their
Lucifer in the guise of a cavalry Captain named Bourke.[5]

Before exploring further the significance of these narratives, I want to contrast them with those of one of Bourke's rather different, yet quite compatible,
contemporaries. Father Pierre F. Parisot was an Oblate missionary who spent
more than thirty years working in the Southwest. His book *The Reminiscences
of a Texas Missionary* narrates his departure from France in 1852 and his jour-
neys as a missionary in Texas and México. Even after spending more than
thirty years in the Southwest, Parisot viewed Mexicans as a "nomadic" lot
coming from the "wilds of the neighboring States of Mexico" (1899:107).

At one point in his memoirs, where he reflects on his travels through México, Parisot describes a version of *Los Pastores,* but it is not one he has seen in performances in México. Rather, he inserts descriptions written by Cordelia Fish Brodbent for the Texas *Gulf Messenger.* After spending ten pages recording her words, Parisot (1899:164–65) concludes:

> The Pastores were originally intended by the Holy Friars to impress upon the minds of the rude untutored Indians the truth of the principal mysteries of religion, but in the course of time, the religious drama passed through the unscrupulous hands of ignorant men and degenerated into a worldly show, now restricted to Mexican jacales or the opera house.

For Parisot, the "passing" of *Los Pastores* from religious hands to those of the "unscrupulous" and "ignorant" represents more than the diffusion of tradition. It is a shift in domain that attempts to relocate the social place of its *mexicano* actors. The shift from "untutored Indians" to Mexicans reflects Parisot's hierarchical order, which interprets *mexicanos* as lower, and therefore more degenerate, than the Indian population. In a flash of unrestricted racism, the passage of *Los Pastores* to the local *mexicano* population represents, for Parisot, a far worse demise than its original impression in the minds of "untutored Indians." For at least with the Indians the friars maintained control, but with its degenerative passing to the Mexican jacales, control, like the salvageable elements of this dramatic form, is lost.

Both Bourke's and Parisot's narratives on *Los Pastores* reveal the presence of early discursive strategies that function as "strategies of containment" (Jameson 1981) or narrative inscriptions concerning the *mexicano* population. In this sense, the emergence of popular culture is seen not as a social phenomenon rooted solely in the maintenance of traditional cultural forms; rather, and more important, it derives from the restructuring of the social order, whereby particular cultural practices are dislocated, differentially valued, and associated with specific social classes. As Bourke (1894a:606) claims, in speaking about the Mexicans' willingness to "amalgamate" or assimilate, "there are on the river some few representatives of a higher stage of evolution; but in general terms, the Rio Grande Mexican resists to-day, as he has always resisted, the encroachments of the Gringo." These encroachments were followed not by amalgamation, but by exploitation: "The handsome residences of merchant millionaires, cattle kings and 'real estate princes' were replacing the old adobe houses and jacales, with Mexicans 'being gradually driven out of the place'" (Montejano 1987:90).

The narrative practices of Bourke and Parisot reveal a similar kind of discourse based on a poetics of dislocation whose practice both resonates with, and informs, the shifting perceptions of *mexicanos* and their place in the social formation of South Texas. These shifting poetics have a dual character. First, there is the attempt to dislocate *mexicanos* from their geographic terrain. Bourke does this by relocating them to the Congo, while Parisot's reference to *mexicanos* as "nomadic" accomplishes the same task. Second, these shifts aim at creating perceptions of social and hierarchical displacements. Besides relocating *mexicanos* to the Congo, they are also inscribed as degenerate, ignorant, superstitious, and nomadic. Such narratives construct a *mexicano* identity as one that is "uncivilized" and yet pervious to colonization—a subaltern class in need of displacement. The poetics of dislocation, as exhibited in the writings of Bourke and Parisot, selectively fashion a discourse of South Texas *mexicanos* that facilitates their social exploitation in the present, while shaping future perceptions of exploitability.[6]

DON LEANDRO GRANADO AND THE POETICS OF ISOLATION

Don Leandro Granado learned how to perform *Los Pastores* in his hometown of Irapuato, Guanajuato, México. The exact reason for Don Leandro's departure is unknown, but he arrived in San Antonio, Texas, in 1894 with few financial resources and, once there, found little hope of securing them in the anti-Mexican social climate of South Texas.[7] Mexicans at this point were still suffering from the violence of the Texas Rangers, social and economic upheaval, and from a political system responsible for their social and economic demise.

As already mentioned, Don Leandro supported himself by selling *raspas y melcocha* (snow cones and taffy) from a cart he pushed through the streets of San Antonio's West Side. And it was here, in 1913, that he began organizing performances of *Los Pastores*. As he states in a letter written to Father Carmelo Tranchese, the local parish priest who plays an important role in the history of *Los Pastores* in San Antonio, "En mexico comense aser pastor en 1884 y en este ciudad [San Antonio] aser pastor en el 1913 y desde entonses comense (a) escrivir este libro" (In México I began to be and perform a shepherd in 1884 and in this city I began to be and perform a shepherd in 1913 and since then, I began to write this book).[8] The *libro* of Don Leandro is a ledger in which he wrote, from memory, the text of *Los Pastores* as he had learned it in México.

Don Leandro Granado as Luzbel, ca. 1945. (Courtesy, the Institute of Texan Cultures, San Antonio, Texas)

Memory played a critical role for Don Leandro. I elaborate on this point later, but here it is sufficient to point out that it is Don Leandro's memory that bridges the performative gap between Irapuato, México, and San Antonio, Texas. Thus, the memory of *Los Pastores* in México and its subsequent performance in San Antonio become a powerful form of cultural meaning. In the words of Victor Turner (1986:36), whose work speaks to many of the performative issues discussed in this study, "It is only when we bring into relation with the preoccupying present experience the cumulative results of similar or at least relevant . . . past experiences . . . that the kind of relational structure we call 'meaning' emerges." Through the performance of *Los Pas-*

tores, the past articulates meaning in the present. For Don Leandro, the writing of the ledger, the gathering and training of performers, the rehearsals, and the performances themselves (which at that time lasted up to seven hours or more) were an active and performative process of meaning construction. Memory did not serve as a reproduction of the past for Don Leandro but as an active process of re-membering: drawing together members of the *barrio* for the communal task of performing *Los Pastores.* One can envision him, pushing his cart through the hot, dusty, streets around San Antonio's West Side, spinning with local patrons yarns that connected them, their traditional past, and their present social concerns through the mode of performance. As this experience makes clear, "ritual and its progeny, notably the performance arts, derive from the subjunctive, liminal, reflexive, exploratory heart of social dramas, where the structures of group experience (Erlebnis) are replicated, dismembered, *re-membered,* refashioned, and mutely or vocally made meaningful" (Turner 1986:43, emphasis added).

The narrative practices of previous generations succeeded in influencing those writing in the early 1900s. For example, Dorothy Hirschfield (1928:904), in an essay about *Los Pastores* for *Theatre Arts Monthly,* states, "The play contains the Mexican peon as he exists in the Southwest—ignorant, primitive, beauty-loving, a devout and childlike mystic." A few years later, the newsletter of the City Federation of Women's Clubs, edited by the wife of a prominent statesman, Mrs. Preston H. Dial, contains an article entitled, "Christmas in Our Little Mexico." The author, Loleta Hagy (1933:5), describes the *mexicano* population as a "pathetic yet dignified . . . little group of foreigners, doomed to live in poverty, and to hard work all their life." And although "this foreign colony that has settled within the city limits . . . love(s) to gamble . . . [they are] charming people, these Mexicans, when you know them" (Hagy 1933:5–6).

The earlier narratives of dislocation have shifted, giving way to metaphors of isolation and marginalization. These writers, echoing Bourke's "Congo-esque" formation, still see Mexicans as ignorant and primitive, but they are now "childlike," "mystical," and, while "charming," they remain a "foreign colony." These texts figure a social place for *mexicanos* on the periphery and, when contrasted with those of the late 1800s, offer an insight into the changing status and marginalizing practices that *mexicanos* faced. Bourke, Parisot, and those of their time could discursively dismiss the *mexicano* population, geographically connecting them to the "wilds" of México or the "Congo," so as to reconfigure the geographic territory of South Texas for the dominant. But the 1920s were different. *Mexicanos* were no longer confined to the rural areas but were now a needed presence in the developing industrial economy of South Texas. This region was well on its way to industrialization and required a stable, disciplined labor force, one that was teachable like "children," "hard working," and easy or "charming" to manage. These marginalizing narratives serve to implicate the necessary proletarianization of the *mexicano* population. The difference between the narratives of the 1920s and their precursors signals a change in practice—social and geographic displacement was followed by economic marginalization and social isolation.[9]

Informed by their own narrative and ideological practices, local writers were unable to see the efforts of Don Leandro at this historical juncture. Instead, they explained the presence of *Los Pastores* as the work of the early Spanish missionaries in the area, as in an article for the *San Antonio Express* on Sunday, December 18, 1921, written by Eugene Sugranes, CMF (1921):

> Now when the Pastores was brought to Texas by Father Margil in the early part of the 18th Century, quite naturally the play underwent a remarkable change. . . . [It] has to some degree lost a great deal of its original purity and pristine glory and splendor. May we not indulge in the fondest hope that some gifted playwright hailing from our wonderful Southland in God's good time will arise and rewrite the play and accommodate it to the present local conditions of our great, fast-growing metropolis.

And, in the view of Helen Raley (1924), another writer for the local press, not only Don Leandro but the Spanish missionaries as well were bypassed in an effort to find an even more suitable literary pedigree in Lope de Vega.

Like most narratives, there is some truth in both Sugrane's and Raley's claim. It would be difficult, if not impossible, however, to find any direct literary link between Lope de Vega and Don Leandro's text; or in the continuous performance of *Los Pastores* from the era of Margil to that of Sugranes. Furthermore, there is the slight historical contradiction between these discourses and the presence of Don Leandro himself—while the memory of Don Leandro is enough to constitute the local performance troupe, the poetics of dislocation finds his historical presence beyond the realm of narrative possibility.

LOS PASTORES AND THE EMERGENCE OF MODERNITY

Father Carmelo Tranchese, born and educated in Italy, arrived in San Antonio in 1932 at the age of fifty and, witnessing the poor social and economic plight of his parishioners, immediately began to work on alleviating the conditions he witnessed in this West Side *barrio*. Within months, Tranchese had established food relief agencies and played a significant role in founding the Catholic Relief Association. Several years later, he established the Guadalupe Community Center, which provided health care and educational programs for residents in the area. Perhaps his most renowned accomplishment was his work with the San Antonio Housing Authority Board of Commissioners, through which he was able to lobby federal and local officials for the construction of public housing units in San Antonio's West Side (R. García 1991). Indicative of his reputation and accomplishment was a *Saturday Evening Post* feature story on him entitled, "The Rumpled Angel of the Slums" (Perry 1948).[10] Like many of his religious contemporaries, Tranchese was a liberal in matters of social and public policy, but a conservative in matters of ecclesiology; it is not surprising that while Tranchese was busy lobbying for social programs, he was also involved in warding off the evils of secularization within the church by promoting "traditional" religious practices like *Los Pastores*.[11]

But Tranchese's relationship with Don Leandro and his attitude toward *Los Pastores* reveals a noticed discrepancy from his otherwise altruistic and admirable practices. When asked why he attended all the rehearsals of *Los Pastores* he quipped: "If I don't go, they don't go" (Perry 1948:47). And yet, by 1948, performances of *Los Pastores* had been in existence at his church for almost forty years. Perhaps the best indicator of Tranchese's attitude toward *Los Pastores* comes from his Foreword to the text of *Los Pastores* that he translated and published. Because it is brief, and its importance as a cultural document is significant, I quote it in its entirety.

> We have attempted one of the most difficult jobs in trying to re-write *Los Pastores* of Don Leandro. Leandro Granado came from Mexico some 40 years ago, and brought with him "un Cuaderno" a copy of this old Mexican play. It was incomplete. Here he tried to finish it by writing from memory what he had seen and played when he was a boy in his native Mexico. But the memory is unreliable. The result of his effort was an amalgam of songs and dialogues, without unity and without dramatic interest. The scenes are mixed up and out of place. For instance, the pastores start out by talking about the birth of Christ. Then they receive the message of the Angel, which is an anachronism. Then the manuscript is written in very bad orthography. For instance, Hunibersario in the Preface, has no place in the Spanish Dictionary. He meant: "Aniversario"—Anniversary—etc.
>
> In this work we have tried to amend the orthography, and to arrange the scenes in chronological order, so as to give the play some kind of unity

of action. However, we have kept all the movements, scenes, words, songs, etc. intact.

The fame of the play lies in the fact that when it is enacted very few understand what it is all about. The actors do not make any efforts to make themselves understood by the hundreds of spectators who attend the beginning of the play. We say the beginning, because the spectators are anxious to say that they have seen the play. But generally, they do not wait for the end thereof. It is too long and too complicated. So they quit. But the actors go on because for them it is an act of worship, a "devoción," they call it.

A full performance of the Pastores will last from three to five hours. It is too much. There are many "incidents"—or dialogues which are not necessary. We have cut those out. For instance, the play starts with the "Posadas"—or looking for shelter. The Posadas have been condensed into a special work, with music and all. They are given during the Novena of the Nativity—which starts on December 16th and lasts until December 24th., when the Pastores follow.

It is customary that the first performance be given at the Church, in a hall, or better, in a yard. Then it continues to be given at the home of each performer, who are 24, including the Director or prompter. Besides there are extra performances given at the homes of some prominent citizens. . . . Thus the "cycle" of the Pastores will last from December 24th to about February 2nd. and, at times, to March 19th, the feast of St. Joseph.

This work, undertaken in the interest of the traditional Latin-American Culture, is affectionately dedicated to all the Citizens of San Antonio, who love old traditions, and to the lovers of traditional art, wherever they may be.

July 4th., 1948—3 o'clock (Tranchese 1949)

A cursory examination of this text expresses another version, thinly veiled, of the poetics of dislocation. In the guise of preservation, Tranchese's efforts at creating a "realist" text serve to undermine Don Leandro's text "without unity." This is seen in a number of places, beginning in the first paragraph, when he states, "Memory is unreliable." For Tranchese, memory is unreliable because it produces a text without order, unity, or proper orthography. To remember is to produce, in chronological order, a text that develops a "unity of action." Tranchese is displacing Don Leandro's mythic-sacred text of the shepherds for a realist text of the nativity. This displacement of *Los Pastores's* narrative paradigms undermines the mythic aura of the text in favor of a realist rendition that preserves its doctrinal content. This is a critical point, for in attempting to ward off the perils of the modern world, Tranchese preserves

Los Pastores as a "traditional" practice; but in rearranging the text in realist fashion, he displaces its narrative paradigms in favor of a realism this is itself rooted in the modern dichotomy between the sacred and the secular. Tranchese's secular humanism led to a distinguished career of social activism; but his religious sensibilities, while informing his secular ideals, created a separate social space in which devotion was a religious matter, not one performed in the street.

The narrative paradigms on which *Los Pastores* is founded are hinted at in another text that reveals a very different kind of discourse. In 1949, at the age of seventy-five, Don Leandro wrote a letter to Tranchese entrusting him with his ledger and text of *Los Pastores*. That letter, translated literally so as not to change the grammatical and "orthodox errors" that concerned Tranchese, follows:[12]

> San Antonio, Texas January of 1949
> A Little bit of History
>
> Mr. Leandro Granado
> Native of the city of Urapuato Guanajuato, Mexico I came to this city of San Antonio, Texas the 27 of February, 1894 In Mexico I began to be and perform a shepherd in 1884 and in this city I began to be and perform a shepherd in 1913 and since then, I began to write this book taking the representation to many homes and continuing making (performing) them every year and this year, 1949, with the favor and Grace of God on the 27 of February I will complete 75 years and considering that I will no longer be able to make (perform) pastores, certainly and in spite of my desire. . . . and seeing that the Father Carmel has very good intentions of continuing the practice of this representation of the shepherds with all my goodwill and all my affection I present my book of the pastorela to him so that he does not let this traditional devotion be lost and when he dies or he moves that he leave a copy for his successor so that this representation continues at the church of Our Lady of Guadalupe in San Antonio Texas and that they pray to God for he that wrote these poorly written lines.
>
> > Leandro Granado
> > 415 Elvira St.
> > San Antonio, Texas
>
> note
>   This is a comprobation that I Leandro Granado grant the right of this book to the Reverend Father Carmel Tranchese (Granado 1949).

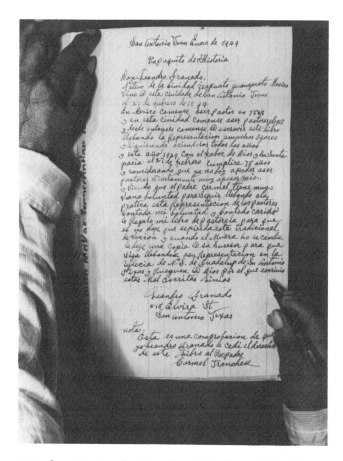

Letter from Don Leandro Granado to Father Carmelo Tranchese bequeathing him his *libro,* or book, in which he wrote the text of *Los Pastores,* 1949. (Courtesy, the Institute of Texan Cultures, San Antonio, Texas)

The "initial givens" of *Los Pastores,* as glossed from this letter of Don Leandro, are clearly spelled out: "In Mexico I began to be and perform a shepherd" (*En mexico comense aser pastor*). For him, performance was the representation, production, and reproduction, not of the realist story of the nativity, but of a *devoción,* a devotion. It is exactly this point that Tranchese misreads when he states: "But the actors go on because for them it is an act of worship, a 'devoción', they call it." Tranchese misreads the significance of devotion because of his own religious constraints that understand ritual as orthodox practice. For

Don Leandro and his performers, *devoción* encodes a vastly underestimated and powerfully salient realm of experience. "Aser [*sic*] pastores," is not about mimetically representing the past, but acting in the present; it is about experiencing the myth in all its cosmological, integrative, symbolic significance. Performing *Los Pastores* is not merely the enactment of a preexisting script of the nativity, but of making and fashioning a devotion that engages the troupe's own social world. For Don Leandro, such conditions were the very fabric of performance; to *aser pastores* is the active process of engaging the myth—to encounter the sacred aura of its telling—as it resonates with one's social experience; to *aser pastores* is to be a shepherd, to fight off the devil, to bear gifts to the Christ Child. This is why memory, and not mimesis, is essential for Don Leandro. It is not the correct and realistic representation that interested him, but the juxtaposition of memory and performance, creating a disjointed performative discourse of good and evil that refractively represents, and actively engages, his social world.

For Tranchese, memory is mimesis. It is a realist attempt to capture the chronology, retelling the event, but doing so without recognizing the way myth encapsulates the social world of those who engage it. To displace the myth, to secularize it, is to disengage the narrative from ritual, displacing it to the realm of drama.[13]

Tranchese's effort is a sign of loss. His translation and rearrangement serve to differentiate him and the English readers for whom this translation exists from the social and cultural world of those who perform *Los Pastores*. The mythical experience of the event must be decoded, its meaning belonging to another age. Only by translating it into a text "with unity" is *Los Pastores* accessible to the modern world. Tranchese's work begins a twofold process. First, his interest in preservation was quickly adopted by others, especially those attempting to establish San Antonio as a site of touristic interest, including its authentication by the San Antonio Conservation Society; second, his effort to preserve *Los Pastores* was an attempt at its institutionalization. Don Leandro and his pastores had been associated with Guadalupe Church before Tranchese's arrival, but Tranchese's efforts solidified that relationship, forging its continuation until the present.

MEMORY, PLACE, AND MODERNITY

Beginning in the 1940s, a series of books began to appear that promoted San Antonio as a tourist site, featuring the Alamo, the historical missions, and *Los*

Pastores. One of the earliest books in this genre, *San Antonio: City in the Sun,* by Green Peyton [Wertenbaker], contains the following notes on the book jacket:

> As one who knows the city thoroughly, Mr. Peyton has been able to interpret it in terms of its history and the significance of its present-day activities. The book presents a rounded and living picture of San Antonio, and captures the peculiar kind of glamour, compounded by Southern gaiety, Latin violence, and rugged Texas individualism, which for more than a century has made San Antonio one of the most distinctive cities in the United States. It will serve as an invaluable guide for the tourist and as delightful and informative reading for the armchair traveler. (Peyton 1946)

Included in Peyton's book is a chapter on Tranchese entitled "Father of the Slums" along with a brief mention of *Los Pastores.* Peyton's prose, a mixture of journalistic factuality and fictive imagination, attempts to lure the unknowing reader to this city, where the historical and the exotic meet. His comments on *Los Pastores,* for example, portray it as "more earthy than religious, [and] enlivened with a good many broadly comic touches. [It was] developed," Peyton (1946:160) claims, "by the Indians of Mexico from a blend of Catholic liturgy with pagan legends."

A few years later, Albert Curtis published *Fabulous San Antonio,* another text aimed at the prospective, Anglo, tourist. The book begins with a series of black-and-white photographs of key tourist sites (the missions, local military parades, different plazas in the city) followed by chapter one, entitled, "A Century of Pleasure." Curtis's text illustrates the same kind of touristic romanticism found in Peyton, as seen in his introduction to *Los Pastores:*

> Want to see one of San Antonio's picturesque Christmas plays? Alright, then, pretend that you are with me in San Antonio, on Christmas Eve, and that we are en route to *"Los Pastores"* theatre, where we shall see the *Los Pastores* or shepherds' version of the Spanish-language nativity play. We board a Guadalupe Street bus, ride into the always pictorial Mexican quarter, and after a dozen streets reach Our Lady of Guadalupe Church, in whose electric-lighted sideyard, the best of these bizarrely-costumed Christmas plays is annually given. (Curtis 1955:157)

These texts attest to the emerging moment of modernity, where situated next to the modern technological world are relics of its past and present conquests. Such a moment celebrates with rare intensity and almost blind allegiance, the dislocation of its object: the *mexicano*. The discourse on *Los Pastores*, not only preserved as a ritual practice from the other, unsecularized (and premodern) side of the border, engages the world beyond as a sign, as Dean MacCannell puts it "of displaced forms . . . elements dislodged from their original natural, historical and cultural contexts [that] fit together with other such displaced or modernized things and people" (1976:13).

While this discourse of preservation was developing under the influences of modern tourism, the San Antonio Conservation Society began sponsoring performances of *Los Pastores* at San José Mission in 1945. One discourse propagated by the San Antonio Conservation Society was that the origin of *Los Pastores* in San Antonio stemmed from the early Franciscan missionary, Antonio Margil, whose story was previously elaborated by Sugranes in 1921 (lending special historical, not to mention romantic, affect to its sponsored performance at San José Mission):

> The origin of *Los Pastores* is lost in time. The drama was brought to the New World by early Spanish missionaries in an attempt to convert the Indians to Christianity. It is said that Father Antonio Margil, who founded Mission San José, performed the play for Indians here in San Antonio 255 years ago. (Inkley 1976)

But such a discourse belies the historical record it seeks to preserve: the earliest known references to *Los Pastores* in San Antonio come from its performance at San Fernando Cathedral, not the mission. In fact, an account given by Enrique Esparza, who was born in San Antonio around 1828, seemingly contradicts, if not undermines, any evidence of an early eighteenth- or nineteenth-century performance at the missions. After recalling that, on occasion, the "tame Indians" from San José Mission attended ritual services at San Fernando Cathedral, he states, "Then we would join in fiestas around San Fernando. One time we rode from the Alamo in an ox-cart to the Cathedral to see the Pastores" (Driggs and King 1936:219).[14] It was the cathedral, it appears, that housed the earliest performances of *Los Pastores* in San Antonio, among the *mexicano* population, not the local missions that provided for the "tamed Indians."

The discourse supported by the San Antonio Conservation Society takes on marked significance when coupled with the performance itself. The presentation of *Los Pastores* at the mission is more than a new venue of performance, as demonstrated in chapter 7. Furthermore, narrative displacements are not neutral—shifts and displacements from one domain to another reveal

Los Pastores, with Don Leandro Granado to the far right, ca. 1950. (Courtesy, the Institute of Texan Cultures, San Antonio, Texas)

competing claims to meaning and power.[15] As a result, the meaning of *aser pastores* that Don Leandro articulated so cogently has been displaced; the initial givens of this event, the mythic narrative that powerfully integrates those who participate, has been relocated to a site where participation is observation, devotion is entertainment, and *mexicanos* are objectified as the contemporary practitioners of native Indian traditions. Relocating this event to the mission is an act that allows the performance to fall, once again, before the scrutiny of the dominant.

The mission performance reproduces the historical poetics of Bourke and Parisot a century before that provided a discursive counterpart to the geographic and social displacement of *mexicanos* in South Texas. The mission performance features *mexicanos* performing beneath the shadows of the rising bell tower, dressed in medieval-styled costumes, reciting a text composed of Spanish golden age poetry, for an audience of outsiders. As such, the historical mystique of the old mission is used to add another layer of realism to Tranchese's text, undermining further the "initial givens" of Don Leandro's performance. The performance of *Los Pastores* at the mission for a tourist audience—one that displaces this event geographically (from the *barrio*), linguistically (it is now translated into English), and socially (it is commercialized)—is the active process of erasure, of dis-membering, of presenting the artifactual form in place of the social relations that constitute it.

In analyzing the historical poetics of *Los Pastores,* and their resonance with the social dislocation of *mexicanos* in South Texas, I attempt to portray a dynamic relationship between popular cultural practice and changing social relations. Narrative shifts cannot be read neutrally but must be seen as part of the social scheme in which they occur, what I have identified in this case as the poetics of dislocation. This analysis reveals that at critical moments in the social history of South Texas, Anglo-American discourses concerning the practice of performing *Los Pastores* add narrative credence to the social, geographic, and economic dislocation of *mexicanos.* In the late 1900s it was a discourse informed by war and economic exploitation; during the 1920s and 1930s, it was one of social isolation and marginalization. And, beginning in the 1940s, a poetics expressed through the idiom of cultural preservation and tourism emerged. In each of these moments, aspects of the social place of *mexicanos* are fashioned by dominant perceptions of popular cultural practices. Such fashioning has worked to render elements of the *mexicano* community as marginal, premodern relics of another age. The significance of this cannot be overlooked, for what takes place is a modernist version of previous attempts at dislocating *mexicanos* from the soil of South Texas. As the ensuing chapters demonstrate, shifts in locations of performance, like narrative displacements, are critical to the reproduction of meaning and power.

6

Memory, Place, and Contextualization: Performance and the Centering of *Los Pastores*

Nomás otro tragito mas. Es para la garganta!" (Just another shot more, it's for the throat!) I am told as the flask filled with *Presidente* (a very smooth Mexican brandy) is handed to me. It's almost four in the afternoon, and already several cans of beer, and more *Presidente* than this *garganta* would even need, have helped hone my ethnographic skills as I stand over with the men, waiting to document their rehearsals. At that moment, the assistant director, stepping into our closed circle where the usual banter of *chingaderas* (verbal screwing around) has occupied its prescribed amount of rehearsal time, says: "The best way for you to learn about the pastorela is to perform it."[1] So I did.

For the next five months (and the following performance season as well), I spent every weekend either rehearsing or performing with the troupe. As a performer, I came to experience, first-hand, not only my lines, the internal rhythm of the poetics, and the stories from previous years' events, but also what it means to go before an audience in three different venues, and to be on display. Although the dramatized text remained relatively the same, I came to realize that our enactments in the *barrio*-home, church, and mission were not. My suspicions were validated when, during one of our conversations, Vicente Manuel claimed: "Yo, anytime, prefiero darlas en casas" (I, anytime, prefer to give them [*Los Pastores*] in homes). His insights, coupled with my own performative experience, led me to understand how the performance of *Los Pastores* in distinct locations constituted three kinds of events.

In this chapter I explore how performances in three venues, each a distinct domain of social intercourse, produce varying claims on the meaning of *Los Pastores*. Although one can expect no two performances to be the same, the difference between these three venues is related to the way performance, as an emergent, processual event, produces distinct domains of experience that map different semantic fields. By comparing and contrasting the different venues, one finds that a number of elements contribute to the various meanings associated with this event. The most salient are: how *Los Pastores* is contextualized or grounded by the sponsoring agents in each venue, a process Hanks (1989) refers to as centering; the social location of sponsors in relation to the performers; and the way popular and historical memory is embedded in the physical and geographic spaces of performance, a process I refer to as memory-place.[2] Because the same performers tend to keep coming back, I take the features of centering, social location, and memory-place as the changing aspects that give shape, meaning, and texture to each domain. The relationship between these three aspects of performance is grounded in the performance events themselves, as well as in the discursive practices that inform them.

Tonight is our first *barrio* performance! I recall Pablo's voice, strong and quick with excitement, as he described performing at various locations in the different *barrios* of the West Side, including the Cielito Lindo, a local cantina. You never knew who or what would be there. But you could always count on one thing: that *esos pinches perros* (those goddamn dogs) would start barking every time the devils donned their masks.

Riding the bus to our place of performance, I am not sure what to expect, the quiet whispers of some and shrill laughter of others create an air of nervous anticipation. *¡Andale vieja!* (On with it, old lady) Pablo quips as he grinds whatever gears are left and we pull up to the house where tonight's event will take place.

The devils are busy setting up the *infierno,* the hellmouth, where they hang out, drink, and put on their costumes (in fear that *esos pinches perros* will see them and begin barking once again until they are chased down the street). A few children, looks like five of them, are gaping at the 10-foot-square *infierno* painted with devil pictures and beasts on three sides, leaving only the red curtain-door unadorned. I follow Juan to where Vicente Manuel, now in his early seventies, is standing. He has been performing in *Los Pastores* for more than forty years. "Este infierno (This hellmouth). It's getting so old, I need to repaint it. Fix all the hinges. And mira (look), we barely have any room here. When I came out last week, pensé que había más lugar (I thought there was more room). But, we'll make it, con la ayuda del Niño Dios (with the help of the Christ Child). It will be fine."[3]

As the early evening wind momentarily calms, Vicente Manuel passes around a flask of *Presidente,* and when it comes around to me I take two big swigs. Immediately, the anxieties of performing sink deep. My emotions begin to stir, triggered by the anticipation of the gathered crowd and their quiet murmurs every time I engage them eye-to-eye. The stars are beginning to appear, flickering like many of the Christmas lights I saw as we approached the house. If we were closer to the hub of the city, they would be hidden behind a screen of city glare and fog. But here, only a few miles from downtown, the pot-holed streets and closely lined houses form a dense mass of people and sound, not the brightness of glittered street scenes. The stars are now fully visible.

I walk over to a row of chairs that mark one end of the rectangular performance area. "Hola, señoras, buenas noches" (hello, ladies, good evening) I say as I try to get a feel for who is present. "¿Ustedes viven aquí?" (Do you live here?). "No, nos invitó la señora, Margie. Ella vive en la esquina. Y yo vivo aquí cerquita" (No, Margie, invited us. She [pointing to her left] lives over on the corner. And I live here nearby). We chat a few minutes more, and just before I leave to make my way into the house, the woman who lives on the corner says how nice it is to see a young man take an interest in the pastorela. "Ya los jóvenes no quieren participar" (the young people don't want to participate any more), she says, with a sigh.

Inside I find Margie. At least I believe her to be Margie. She is busy in the kitchen making sure everything is going as planned. She has her mother, a woman who is quite heavy and appears much older than Margie, watching over all the pots and pans while Margie busies herself with other matters. The house smells musty and damp, but the fumes from the open-flamed heaters are more malodorous than the dampness. The smells and sights trigger a memory: frequent winter visits to my grandparents' house just beyond the tracks from here and on the other side of the interstate. Their house was equally damp and warmed by the same gas heaters, ones my mother used to warn me not to get too close to. The smell of water and coffee grinds boiling on the stove is the only thing missing. . . . Margie interrupts my reminiscence, "Teresita, go and make sure *que toda la gente está lista. Ya vamos a comenzar* [that all the people are ready. We are going to begin] and tell your *papá* to put some more wood in *las barrillas* [in the barrels], *si no, se hace mucho frío*" (if not, it gets too cold). Just as I get ready to move outdoors, I overhear Margie tell one of the women inside that she and two neighbors spent six hours working on the altar. Are they the two women I met earlier? I make a mental note to go back and check. As I go out the door, I look to a spot on the driveway, opposite the *infierno,* and find Margie's altar. It is filled with candles, ribbons, a picture of the Virgin de Guadalupe, and several other saints that, though familiar, I cannot name. I remind myself to recall the difference in color between the altar and the *infierno:* one, adorned in mostly pastel blues, with white and splashes of Christmas red; the other, dark and dominant, painted in blacks and reds. In front of the altar are four chairs, for Joseph, María, the archangel Michael, and the shepherdess Gila. Dividing the four chairs into two equal sections is the small wooden manger where the statue of el Niño Dios will soon be placed. From the corner of my eye I see Teresita moving in my direction. She stops and calls to her brother: "¡Javier! ¡Javier! ¡Te quiere papá! [Daddy wants you]. And you better behave yourself and quit running around, we're going to start soon."

When we finally start, Margie welcomes and thanks everyone for coming and helping, especially the pastores. "Hace dos años que hice una promesa al Niño Dios. Si él curara mi mamá, yo prometería tener una pastorela en mi casa. Pues, la salud de mi mamá se mejoró, y me siento felíz que ya llegó este día" (It has been two years since I made a vow to the Christ Child. If he cured my mother, I promised to hold a *pastorela* in my house. Well, my mother's health improved, and I feel happy that today has arrived). People clap. Then, after a few more words she invites Vicente Manuel, as a leader of *Los Pastores*, to speak. "Buenas noches damas y caballeros" (Good evening ladies and gentlemen), he begins, as he always does. He tells why he believes *Los Pastores* is so important and explains that this event has been shortened from seven-and-a-half hours to three. "La gente ya no viene por devoción, sino por diversión. Pero lo hacemos porque hay que enseñar los jóvenes que la navidad es importante, no porque viene Santa Clos, ni por los regalos. La importancia es el Niño Dios [People no longer come for devotion, but for entertainment. But, we perform this because we need to teach the young ones that Christmas is important, not because Santa Claus comes, nor for the presents. The importance is the Christ Child]. We need to keep el Niño Dios in Christmas. It's not the presents or the stores, *las malls* [the malls]. It's el Niño Dios!" Finally, he concludes with a warning to the parents, "Por favor! Madres y padres de niños, no dejen que sus hijos corran cerca del infierno cuando estamos trabajando. Los diablos usan verdaderas espadas con filo y punta. Cuando estamos trabajando no podemos ver con las máscaras. Cuiden a sus hijos" (Please! Mothers and fathers, do not let your children run near the hellmouth when we are working. The devils use real swords that are sharp and have a point. When we are working, we cannot see because of our masks. Be careful with your children).

Then, with the jingle of the bells from the staffs of the shepherds, a hush comes over the crowd of fifty to sixty people who have gathered, as Vicente Manuel, in an act of devotion, crawls on his knees carrying the statue of el Niño Dios from outside the doorway of the *infierno* to the altar. Even the children stop running to take a closer peek, as do the neighborhood men who have been hovering by the barrels of burning wood, having a few beers just in case the fire does not keep them warm enough. We begin, "Qué hermosa noche! . . . Todo es calma y tranquilidad" (What a beautiful evening! . . . Everything is calm and tranquil).

Throughout the first half of the performance, I cannot help but feel surprised by the informality of the event. Some of the shepherds turn and speak with the audience, family members, or other shepherds. And the whispers of the audience, though less noticeable than before we started, never stop.

Immediately following a scene in which Luzbel meets with all his devils, the performers have an intermission. At this time, Margie and other *madrinas* (ritual godmothers), friends who have made little ribbons with small trinkets, pin these items to our cloaks. Often, dollar bills are also used as pennants by these *madrinas,* as well as by other members of the audience. Audience members select their favorite performer for this honor. Invariably, the Ermitaño, or hermit, is chosen more than the rest of us because of his antics. His character has special comedic license to taunt and poke fun at Luzbel and the other devils. This, along with his spry dancing and prancing as he runs to and fro, giving chase to the devils with his cane, makes for some humorous scenes. Humor is also injected into the middle of one of Luzbel's eloquent and formal monologues when the Ermitaño turns Luzbel's words over in his own spontaneous way.

LUZBEL:	ERMITAÑO:
Mas ¿qué miro? lúcida esfera	¡Otra vez!
que melodía en todo placentera;	
qué es esto que se escucha	
causándome temor y pena mucha?	¿Por qué estas tan terco?
But, what do I see? A brilliant sphere,	Again!
what melody, pleasant in every way;	
	Why are you so obstinate?
what is this that I hear?	
Causing me much fear and pain?	

Whereas Luzbel delivers his lines in a serious and reflective mood, the *Ermitaño,* in an aside to the audience, mocks Luzbel's seriousness and in word and gesture, calls him an obstinate fool for not realizing that *el Niño Dios* has been born.[4]

We begin performing again. From here to the end of the performance, the narrative consists of the Archangel Michael doing battle with Luzbel, whom he defeats and enchains, banishing him to the dungeons of hell. Our journey to Bethlehem is completed without further interruptions. After we arrive, we present our gifts to el Niño Dios. But at the moment that Bartolo, one of the shepherds, begins to approach the manger where the statue of el Niño Dios is kept, he writhes to one side in pain. Rushing to his side, we assist him to a chair. The leader of the shepherds, after attending to Bartolo and seeing that he is not seriously ill although unable to continue performing, collects Bartolo's offering and proceeds to present it to el Niño Dios, reciting the lines assigned to the stricken shepherd. This occurrence demonstrates one of the internal dynamics of *Los Pastores:* at various moments in the performance, aspects of devotion or entertainment are emphasized, allowing a broad range of interpretations and meanings to emerge, depending on the particular scene and action.

Our gifts now delivered, the audience is invited to offer gifts themselves. As we stand singing on either flank of el Niño Dios, people from the audience kiss the statue and place whatever monetary offering they can afford in a small white basket held by Gila, the shepherdess of the group.

As soon as we finish, Margie dashes inside to make sure all the last-minute arrangements have been taken care of, and the local women, along with some of the women from our troupe, prepare to serve the food. As guests of honor, we are served first. Tonight we are having *mole poblano,* a thick sauce made from chocolate, chili, peanuts, and other spices served over chicken, with rice and beans. The smells are wonderful. Many of the neighborhood families have brought over a number of side dishes or desserts, and the *fiesta* begins. Moving outside with the other men from the troupe, we are joined by Roberto, Margie's husband, and other men. We all comment on the food, and after several more servings, the usual banter begins.[5]

After about an hour the crowd thins, the devils begin dismantling the *infierno,* and those of us who came on the bus begin making our way back to it. Some of the women are still talking to Margie, and as we head out she thanks us once again. The ride back is quieter. People are tired, and for some, their third plate of mole and who knows how much drink have finally settled in. The teen-aged women in the back quietly laugh, recalling incidents from the school dance the night before.

A week later we are ready to depart for a performance at Christ the Redeemer Church. Only a few blocks from our rehearsal site of Guadalupe Church, we arrive, Pablo once again cursing the bus to a halt, with more than half an hour to spare. Proceeding onto the church grounds, I see the devils have already set up their hideout, enjoying inconspicuous shots of *Presidente* for their *gargantas,* and quickly make my way toward them. Seeing the burgeoning crowd of over one hundred and a steady flow still arriving, I could use some pre-performance elixir to strengthen my *garganta.*

Standing with my cohorts as people continue to arrive—there must be close to two hundred people by now—I marvel at the size of the audience. And it is still twenty minutes before we are scheduled to begin. Soon, a man of about fifty makes his way toward us and spying Vicente Manuel, engages him in conversation. This white-collared gentleman, I am told, is the local pastor. He has been here only a few years and is well known for his caring personality and warmth and is much respected by the local people. Another gentleman, about the same age but more withered, tanned, and with harsher lines around his face and neck, joins the priest and Vicente Manuel. He is the president of the Men's Club, the church organization that has done the work to make this performance possible. "Hemos tenido la pastorela aquí por quince años. Y siempre hay mucha gente" (We have had the pastorela here for fifteen years. And we always have a large crowd). His smile reveals his pride in accomplishing such a task.

I walk to where three of the shepherds are standing, noticing the long shadows of the church bell tower cutting the performance area in two. Jaime, sensing that I am impressed by the number of people gathered, tells me it is not unusual for this many people to be in attendance on a day like this: "Hace 70 degrees, yo lo predije" (It is 70 degrees, I predicted it).

From the corner of my eye I see Vicente Manuel make his way to the center of the staging area, where he tries to get the crowd to quiet down. "¡Por favor! . . . ¡Por favor!" (Please! . . . Please!). After several minutes the audience is quiet enough, and he turns to the priest, who, after welcoming everyone, proceeds to give a brief theological explication of the performance. He concludes by saying: "Y quiero dar la gracias a los miembros de *Los Pastores* por este ejemplo de fe, sacrificio, y servicio a nuestra iglesia" (I want to thank the members of *Los Pastores* for bringing this example of faith, sacrifice, and service to our church). Upon finishing, the president of the Men's Club takes his turn at welcoming the audience, thanking the troupe for returning once again this year, and concludes by inviting everyone to gather in the church hall at the end of the event where *tamales* (meat surrounded by cornmeal dough, then wrapped in a corn husk and cooked), *frijoles* (beans), rice, beans, and hot chocolate will be sold. Vicente Manuel's introduction contains the usual parts, only this time he beckons all to silence so people can hear.

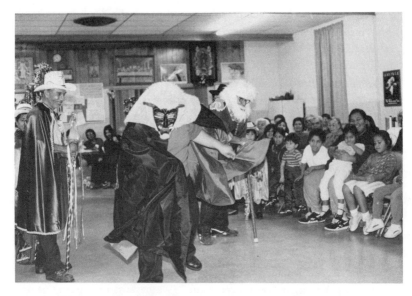

A devil and hermit exchanging barbs.

Then, with more than usual solemnity, Vicente Manuel begins his rite of carrying *el Niño Dios* the length of the performance area from the *infierno* to the manger. The crowd is hushed. Only the gravel scraping beneath Vicente Manuel's knees can be heard amidst the throng of nearly three hundred people. The performance has begun.

Influenced by our leader's example, our opening canticle is sung with more seriousness and solemnity than the week before. Words are recited more loudly, postures are more erect, and gestures more exaggerated. After thirty minutes, however, I sense the crowd unwinding, relaxing to the performance: children are running and playing once again, and the noise level has increased. As if taking our cue from them, we begin performing in a more relaxed manner. And solemnity gives way to joviality as the Hermit, sensing an apt moment to show off his verbal skills, has the crowd in an uproar as he prances around Luzbel mocking his solemn tone.

Later in the performance I am startled when Michael the Archangel, upon banishing Luzbel to the dungeons of hell, receives a vigorous round of applause. Goodness has won! Evil defeated!

We continue performing until the conclusion, when silence returns as the crowd watches us make our individual offerings to el Niño Dios. The solemnity continues as the audience joins in the adoration, but because of the large numbers, it takes nearly twenty minutes to complete. After repeating our final song at least ten times, the last person makes the adoration and we conclude to an emptying churchyard.

Immediately, a number of women from the audience surround us, asking questions, congratulating us, and eyeing the comical hermit. I make my way to the hall, hungry and tired from standing, where I sit with other members of the troupe. We occupy two neat rows of tables as if we were assigned seats, commenting on the day's achievements. With the memory of the *barrio* performance just a week old, I am struck by the lack of interaction between our troupe and the local people. Here we sit, off to the side of the hall, exchanging stories and glances, fatigued from the stress of the performance, basically alone. The president of the Men's Club has joined us, as well as the pastor, but considering the number of people present, conversation between the troupe and others who have stayed to eat is relatively scant.

One of the last to finish, slowly savoring every bite, I make my way outside to an empty churchyard. Hearing the bells announce the beginning of the late service, I find the bus where my cohorts have settled in, resting from an emotionally charged afternoon. The ride home is quiet and short.

Our next performance, the following weekend, is at San José Mission and is sponsored by the San Antonio Conservation Society. On the bus trip to the Mission, Vicente Manuel is encouraging everyone to speak loudly, to enunciate, and to "perform." This is the first time that he has placed so much emphasis on our skill. Our weekly rehearsals consisted solely of learning our parts and the few dance steps needed. Never had there been any discussion of performative techniques outside of how to walk or to stomp one's staff in unison with the others.

The bus is pulling into the parking lot of the mission, but this was not the relaxed ride of a week before—the women are hurriedly passing mirrors around the bus to check their makeup, and brushing and tying their hair with colorful ribbons, all in an uncharacteristically quiet manner. As we slowly, almost reluctantly, leave the bus, the troupe meanders to an area directly in front of the church where the performance will take place. I follow the men over to the *infierno* where the devils have just completed their arrangements. There is more drinking, although this time it is to calm one's nerves. I shoot back a double.

The performance space is larger and more spread out than the week before. A podium has been set up for the master of ceremonies, a well-known Mexican radio announcer who has been retained by the San Antonio Conservation

Society and employed over the years to provide translation and commentary. He speaks over a microphone, translating the text into English as we perform in Spanish. Along one side of the performance area are a number of white, plastic, folding chairs where people have already begun to sit. Most, I realize, have come equipped with cameras. Beyond the chairs are a number of food booths. Even from here I can read the signs indicating that *tamales, buñuelos* (fried dough covered with sugar), *frijoles,* hot cocoa, and cold drinks are being sold.

As the performance begins, Vicente Manuel again gives his introductory speech, this time followed by the introductory speech of the emcee. When we start to perform, the immediate disjuncture between our voices, which are not amplified, and that of the emcee, whose is, becomes apparent. It is difficult to keep our rhythm with the emcee's voice ringing in our ears; and some of us are not sure if we should speak or wait for the translation to be completed. The leader motions us to keep on.

At intermission, I have my first chance to mingle with the audience. It occurs to me that here, my costumed appearance is attracting more attention as I make my way through the audience than it did the week before at the *barrio* performance. The reason sinks in: these are mostly tourists. Their cameras poised, they shoot us "on stage" and "off," especially the devils.

At one point, I walk up to a Mrs. Sacks. Her name tag identifies her as a member of the San Antonio Conservation Society. She wears a "Mexican" festive dress that is brightly colored with embroidered flowers, animal figures, and other ornately designed stitchery. Then, I notice all the women from the conservation society are dressed in similarly colorful garb; this must be a festive occasion for them.

Mrs. Sacks smiles at me and asks, "And how many years have you been in *Los Pastores?*" I start to explain that I am conducting field research on *Los Pastores* when she interrupts, "Excuse me, Oh Mary!, Mary! Can you come take a picture of me with this young man! And Kathy, come join us, please." Mary, it turns out, is a photographer for the *San Antonio Light,* the daily paper.

The remainder of the evening is uneventful. Luzbel is again defeated and my fellow shepherds and I make our way to Bethlehem. Intrusions by the emcee continue all evening. At several points in his monologue, he encourages audience members to buy food from the booths, since "we must support *Los Pastores* and not let it die. This is the reason the conservation society sponsors this event! Please, support *Los Pastores* and buy something from the vendors!" The oddity of this statement strikes me. Never has there been any discussion by members of the troupe about quitting *Los Pastores* for lack of money. In fact, money is never discussed. Besides, we do not receive money for performing, it is all done freely. How can something collapse fiscally if there are no finances involved? I store that one away for a later date.

Upon finishing the performance, we talk for a few minutes with each other, complaining about the intrusions of the emcee's voice and the difficulty of performing under those conditions. After purchasing something to drink or eat from the booths (as performers we are given free tickets for our food), we gather our belongings, stopping for an occasional camera flash, and make our way back to the bus. Once on board, a flurry of jokes involving both men and women begin, and the younger members of the troupe sit in back singing a chorus piece from the drama. The relaxed atmosphere on the ride home is distinctively different from the trip there.

DOMAINS OF PERFORMANCE

The three venues of the *barrio*-home, church, and mission constitute three distinct domains produced from the various elements of centering; social location of performers, hosts, and audience; and the memory-place of these three locations. A variety of other structures or markers of performance could be drawn upon; however, I take these three to be critical factors that capture salient forms of meaning construction: respectively, contextualizing discourses, subjective identities, and the social and physical markers of each place.[6] These three aspects are not concrete attributes of performance, but shifting semantic elements that draw upon the emergent process of performance in each domain.

Centering is a critical element in the production of each performance and refers, in this case, to the way hosts contextualize or ground *Los Pastores* in the various domains. These centering discourses represent the understandings and ideological underpinnings of *Los Pastores* for hosts, framing the performance through these narratives. As such, centering discourses provide important information that allows the audience to interpret this event in specific ways, even though such information could never provide for all interpretative cases. By necessity, the comparative analysis of these three venues draws on the related concepts of recentering and decentering, revealing a fluid process whereby particular discourses shift from one domain to another for the purpose of recontextualizing or recentering an event.

Social location refers to the way social identities of performers, hosts, and audience members are drawn upon as semantic resources. As a result, in some domains, meanings and cultural knowledge specific to the event go unmarked because the ethnic identity of those gathered, one aspect of social location, is implicitly taken for granted. In one domain, however, this is not the case, and a variety of meanings emerge. Another aspect of social location that goes unmarked except for the domain of the mission is class. In the *barrio* and church events, both performers and audience members are from the same socioeconomic class. Granted, a few visitors could be found, adorned and mannered in distinctively other forms of class attire and practice, but they are few and do not represent a majority or near majority of those present.

The other factor that influences the meaning of *Los Pastores* is memory-place, which refers to the way semiotic features in each venue interact with, and give credence to, centering discourses and social location, thereby allowing the physical and semantic markers embedded in these spaces to contribute to a range of meanings. Performances occur in significant, socially produced places that cannot be ignored: the *barrio*-home, church, and one of the historic missions. As such, each of these places, as social spaces, is a product of past experiences and the emergent event. Memory-place is my attempt to render such places and their meanings as manifestations of relations made through performance with the structural coordinates embodied in each physical location.[7] These three elements—centering, social location, and memory-place—point to a combination of indexical signs, framing devices, ideology, and subjective identities that empirically shape the meaning of *Los Pastores* as it emerges in performance in three distinct venues.

The *Barrio*-Home Domain

CENTERING. In the *barrio*, the introduction by the host inevitably references the commemorative aspects of *Los Pastores*. "We celebrate *Los Pastores* because it is our tradition!" Or, "Cuando era jovencita [I was a young girl], I would see the pastores down the street, y desde entonces quería tenerlos a mi casa [and since then I wanted to bring them to my house]." Statements like this assert a claim over the past as a way of staking out one's present right over the event. In this process, tradition is the thread that weaves history to practice. Without tradition, the past is an amalgam of experiences without unity; a practice that has lost its lineage to the present. Centering the *barrio*-home performance through tradition legitimates this venue as its proper place of performance, authenticating both the event and place.[8] Centering through tradition not only situates *Los Pastores* within this household, but makes it available to any member who identifies with this cultural body. It anchors the meaning and history of the event to a cultural and ethnic lineage, making it available to any person of the community.

At other times, *Los Pastores* is introduced as a dyadic ritual event, or as a fulfillment to a *promesa* or ritual promise. "Hace dos años que hice una promesa al Niño Dios. Si él curara mi mamá, yo prometería tener una pastorela en mi casa. Pues, la salud de mi mamá se mejoró, y me siento feliz que ya llegó este día" (It has been two years since I made a vow to the Christ Child. If he cured my mother, I promised to hold a pastorela in my house. Well, my mother's health improved, and I feel happy that today has arrived). Centering the *barrio* performance as a ritual event builds upon and expands the means of legitimizing this domain. Ritual is a collective affair, not private. By framing *Los Pastores* as ritual, hosts are working on two semantic planes. First, they are repaying el Niño Dios for a ritual favor granted them. In this capacity, the event serves as a means of fulfilling a ritual obligation. The second aspect is related. In my two years of performing with the troupe, only women framed the event as a ritual discourse. Although men were present, many times at the women's side, it was women who spoke of *Los Pastores* as a *promesa*. Taking my lead from the work of Turner and Seriff (1987:457) on women's home altars, I suggest that framing *Los Pastores* as ritual in the *barrio* is a "testament to intimacy." Turner and Seriff speak of intimacy as it relates to gifting and reciprocity in the building of home altars. For my purposes, intimacy is expressed in the ritual bartering or negotiation between the hosts and el Niño Dios. The hosts agree to fulfill a particular duty, normally some form of devotion, if el Niño Dios provides some special favor for them, usually related to the health of one's family member. This negotiation is one that involves a dyadic relationship between hosts and el Niño Dios. By centering *Los Pastores* in this way, the intimate relationship that forms the core of ritual negotiation is made public through a personal narrative, inviting audience members to participate and engage the event more intimately. Such narratives build a sense of empathy for the hosts; but more important, they serve as narrative indexes to one's own life experiences. It allows those listening to recall their own personal events of sickness, death, or other moments of human passage. Suffice it to say that these narratives function as performative discourses that incorporate, draw in, and gather those present into one social body by building on human experiences that affect everyone. Their success is evident in the social conviviality that emerges. This kind of public ritual is essential for the development of a collective memory and the propagation of a social group.

SOCIAL LOCATION. The social location of hosts and audience is entwined with the centering of the event through tradition and ritual. The hosts and audience are overwhelmingly from the same geographic locale: the *barrio*. Neighbors often live on the same street or within walking distance; those not from this area are usually friends from work or other social groups, such as church organizations or senior citizens groups.

The discourse of tradition melds with the ethnicity of those present: with few exceptions, everyone present is of Mexican origin. This is not to say that everyone is fluent in Spanish, especially the younger people, or that everyone has seen, or is familiar with, *Los Pastores*. It is to say, however, that knowledge of the language and cultural traditions is implicit. When those members feign or express ignorance of such information, especially the young, it is interpreted as a lack of experience or education in the norms and values of the community (*bien educado*), and not a marker of one's existential belonging.

But all are not the same; there still exists a hierarchy of gender and age. The cleavages between male and female roles experienced in daily practice are evident in this emergent social domain. Women are found cooking and preparing food, maintaining ritual practices such as keeping home altars, and generally confining themselves to domestic chores. Men are outside, directing neighbors, filling barrels with wood, and offering little assistance in the domestic work of hosting. Even the aspect of formally welcoming guests is usually undertaken by the women.[9]

But these differences are themselves a critical aspect of role negotiation and semantic meaning. The fact that it is women who mostly center *Los Pastores* in the *barrio*-home domain cannot be ignored. Not only do their voices resonate with the emerging collective sentiment of the group, but this sentiment provides the women with salient forms of meaning-making. As noted above, their narratives function to produce a certain intimacy among those present. This is critical for the women, since it enables them to step forward in a public moment and take charge, shaping and centering the public meaning of this event and its resonance with the personal experiences of those present. Women's public and private voices have been documented in other areas (Abu-Lughod 1986; Briggs 1992; Goodwin 1980), but the nexus of personal narrative, home altars, and dyadic ritual provides a particularly important idiom through which these women shape meaning in the *barrio*-home domain.

Elders, both men and women, are given special attention. They are deferred to in matters of organization and traditional practice: where and how to make a home altar, or where to locate the infierno. But even here, the gender roles found in their children are reproduced. Elder women are indoors helping their women kin-folk; elder men are outside, keeping watch and interacting with their male progeny.

MEMORY-PLACE. Memory-place helps shape the semantic topography of this domain in two respects. First, this place is a home and thus facilitates the construction of a familial atmosphere in which informality and a heightened sense of social conviviality emerges. This influences *Los Pastores* by creating boundaries of performance that are less defined, more fluid, and at times, quite informal. The beginning and ending of the performance are clearly marked (by the introductions and adoration), but in between performers can be found speaking to themselves and audience members while still in character and "on stage." During intermission, or when characters are not "on," they can be found interacting with members of the household or guests with intimacy and familiarity.

The informality of the home is also reflected in the way guests, performers, and hosts can be found intermingling and sharing space. There are no boundaries between indoors and outdoors; everyone is treated as if they were *en casa,* or at home. Those present know and understand the social organization and rules governing social interaction; furthermore, the space is usually small, bounded by other houses, fences, and familiar sounds of the surrounding *barrio*. The economic means and resources available to the hosting family, like those of almost everyone present, are limited—fostering a sense of cooperation between performers, guests, and hosts—marking this event with a communal ethos.

The Church Domain

CENTERING. Like the *barrio,* the church domain makes commemorative claims on *Los Pastores* but does so with a different kind of discourse. The religious needs of church members are the primary means of framing this event, and the church's access goes unquestioned since *Los Pastores* stems from the Christian tradition of religious drama and reenacts the Christian scene of the nativity. The discourse invoked here is not that of history or cultural practice, but religious tradition. *Los Pastores* is introduced as ritual, and efforts are made to emphasize its religious content. Furthermore, an effort is made to highlight the religious commitment of those who perform it. Although in practice there may be no long-term association between the troupe and the church in which

Troupe and audience members peering at the approaching devils.

the performance takes place (except for the church in which the performers practice and have their first and last performance), the discourse of ritual allows any church to claim *Los Pastores* as its own form of religious expression.

The ritual centering at the church is different from that of the *barrio*. While this discourse still functions as a means of legitimation, its focus is no longer the personal devotion expressed through ritual bartering. That is, the ritual discourse of the home invites others to witness the intimate relationship between the host and el Niño Dios, an intimacy that is then extended to all the members present. The church is different. The discourse of ritual that centers this event is communal; it is the propagation of a Christmas ritual that is accessible to any person who participates in the religious ideology and practice of the Catholic Church. The impetus of the event is the Christian celebration of the nativity. Although a number of people in the audience may have personal and intimate religious sentiments that inform their participation in this event, the public church discourse is that of the Christian nativity, not the personal narratives espoused at the home. This makes for an event that is open and amenable to any church group, since performance in this domain is not bound by family or geographic constraints, but by the Catholic body at large.

SOCIAL LOCATION. The ethnic identity and class affiliation of those present at the church are the same as those of the performers: Mexican American and working class. Not surprisingly, one aspect of their social location is accentuated in this domain: their shared religious belief. The religious discourse that centers this event speaks to a common understanding of mutual belief. Beyond ethnic identity and class position, a shared sense of Catholic belief constitutes another layer of identity among those present.

Like the home, gender also contributes to the way *Los Pastores* is centered and interpreted in this domain. The one difference, however, is that where the home exhibits a strict domestic-public dichotomy between men and women, that is not the case here. Men also participate as leaders and organizers, playing a more central role than seen in the home performance. The result, too, is different. Absent from this domain is the central way women figure this event, their use of personal narratives, dyadic ritual, and altar making; the result is a less personal and intimate initial frame of performance. Instead, a more diffuse appeal to the Catholic tradition, albeit one rendered in a cultural frame, contextualizes this domain of performance in ways that are more general and doctrinaire.

The other social actors who sometimes participate are clergy. Their status as keepers of religious orthodoxy and official members of the institutional church provides them with a base of authority and stature that is not held by anyone else. In their presence, both performers and audience members defer to them in matters of decision making (where to perform, how to arrange space, when to begin) and religious practice.

MEMORY-PLACE. Memory-place is an important element in the church domain that influences the structure of the performance. First, since this is a public space in which the norms of etiquette that govern society at large are more strictly followed, the timing of the event is much more critical. If the performance is supposed to begin at four in the afternoon, it begins quite near that hour. Second, the more public atmosphere, along with the ritual frame, creates a more formal event, with less interaction between performers and audience. Unless people know one another from other contexts, a social distance between these two groups is more evident, indicative of a less cohesive social group.

Furthermore, there is the physical site itself. *Los Pastores* is performed either inside the church, a church hall, or outdoors on church property. The physical features present, especially when performed in the church proper, create a

Shepherds and audience members in one of the church domains.

more intensive religious ambiance. Although it may be a familiar site, the formality of the church and the religious architecture, either within the church or as it hovers in the background, emphasizes the ritual aspects of the event.

Another issue is the memory of religious practice that is associated with this place. For members of this church, the church building is the site where previous religious events have been experienced. The place itself contributes to the religiosity of the event, making it difficult not to be influenced by the surrounding smells of votive candles, incense, statues of Mary and Jesus, shadows of crosses overlapping the area of performance, bells signaling the passing hours. All these create an aura of religious experience not found in the other domains.

The Mission Domain

CENTERING. The domain of the mission contains a number of centering elements. For one, the event is publicized well in advance through radio spots, newspaper articles, and broadside flyers. These announcements center *Los Pastores* at the mission in two ways. First, they make this event available to a group of people who are unfamiliar with it, gearing the publicity to the large tourist population visiting the city at this time of year. Second, these advertisements portray *Los Pastores* as an authentic Mexican Christmas celebration, instituted by the Friars who founded the missions. This discourse recenters the event from one in which people participate in their own religious and cultural history to one in which tourists and other outsiders who attend experience *Los Pastores* as spectators.

The use of an emcee functions as another centering element. His presence formalizes the event, providing a frame that marks the event as entertainment; he verbally interacts with the audience, welcoming them, serving as the official voice of the sponsors. He mentions throughout the event the importance of supporting *Los Pastores* so as to preserve it from cultural extinction. This narrative recenters the performance from one that is flourishing within the *mexicano* community to one on the verge of fading away.

SOCIAL LOCATION. The social location of hosts, audience, and performers is quite varied. This performance is hosted by members of the San Antonio Conservation Society. Their sponsorship of this public performance is only one of the many activities they support throughout the year. Their roster reveals the membership of the organization to be non-Latino, affluent, and mostly women. It is a private group and those interested in joining must be nominated by a current member. There is a probationary period before new affiliates are accepted as full members. Judging from their list of members, none live in the *barrio* or in the area of the sponsoring church, and there is a clear ethnic and class difference between the members of the Conservation Society and the troupe.[10]

It is more difficult to know the social location of the audience members. The emphasis on attracting a tourist audience and the need to provide translation throughout the performance suggests that those in attendance are also non-Mexican. The explanatory comments that are offered beyond the mere translation of the performed text signal a need to explain elements of religious and cultural knowledge to an audience unfamiliar with such practices.

The sponsorship by the San Antonio Conservation Society and the participation of tourists constitute a domain that is quite different from the other two. The presence of the emcee signals not only a linguistic divide between hosts, audience, and performers, but also a cultural and class difference. In neither the home nor the church domain is the issue of class and culture a factor, whereas here it is a critical element in the construction of the semantic field. In this domain, the distinctive features of class and cultural dominance—notably, the positioning of one group above another through various social and economic practices—are reproduced. *Los Pastores* is tendered for the tourists, not in conjunction with them; the event is witnessed and experienced as spectacle and touristic entertainment, not as a practice that emerges from the personal and historical experience of those gathered.

MEMORY-PLACE. The historical significance and physical features of the mission, coupled with a discourse on cultural preservation, provide for a tightly constructed semantic field. The mission compound consists of a large area of land enclosed by high, hand-made, stone walls. Rooms containing artifacts in museum exhibits and an old granary are found adjacent to the walls, but the mission church is by far the largest physical structure in the compound. Outsiders and tourists experience this event within the mystique and among the historical architectural artifacts of the Spanish Colonial period in Texas. These elements contribute symbolic and historical evidence that supports claims of the authenticity of *Los Pastores*. In this place, the performance of *Los Pastores* in Spanish prosody, with original costuming, and with working-class Mexican-American performers is the experience of "real" culture.[11]

But such a place yields a rather different meaning from the other two domains. *Los Pastores* is now a spectacle, and not part of one's cultural or historical practice. The ritual elements of the event may be commented upon by the emcee and witnessed by the audience, but it is ritual as observed, not one participated in by those in attendance. The selling of food as separate items in booths situated around the mission grounds, the large open area with spotlights focusing on the performance area, and the aura cast by the architectural features of the mission mark this domain with a sense of spectatorship.

THE SHIFTING DOMAINS OF PERFORMANCE

The differences exhibited in the three domains of the *barrio*, church, and mission exhibit shifts in meaning as *Los Pastores* is recentered from one site to another. These differences are, following Stallybrass and White (1986), displacements, or dislocations, that signal "shifts" and "gaps" in the meaning of this event. Such displacements are not neutral but are discontinuities that reveal competitive claims over social identity, the emergent social meaning, and social power (Bauman and Briggs 1990:76).

The discontinuities between the *barrio* performance and the church, though slight, are enough to provide for substantially different semantic fields. The *barrio* is produced from elements of traditional discourse, familial relations, and a memory-place that represents quotidian concerns and experiences. Although performances here exhibit a more heightened sense of the everyday (for example, through the festive meals and seasonal timing of the event), they are grounded in the social relations that govern everyday practice. The sounds and smells are familiar; the space, while rearranged, is common; the work that prepares food, space, and welcomes guests is the same as that performed on other days. The experience of *Los Pastores* in the home constitutes an event of shared social meaning, identity, and everyday experience.

The discourse of ritual in this domain serves to reinforce the familiar through intimacy. Religious invocation is invariably about personal matters: the health of an elder, child, other family relative, or other concerns that affect those present. This discourse, as noted above, serves as an invitation to intimacy. It provides a social frame that allows others to recall similar events in their own lives and thus unites the group through a performative event common to their experience.

The church, on the other hand, while containing some similarities to the *barrio,* is quite distinctive. Its emphasis on ritual, highlighted by the memory-place of religious iconography and architecture, provides for a semantic field based on religious experience and the collective, universal, religious body. The displacement from the *barrio* to the church domain reveals a shift in meaning produced from elements of religious ideology and a memory-place of the sacred. *Los Pastores* is recentered as one of religious experience; the event is interpreted and propagated as a cultural way of celebrating a Mexican, Catholic, Christmas enactment.

The meaning shifts from the familial and social to the institutional. This new domain is no longer a family-supported event, but one sponsored by a church; it is open to any member of the institution, including those from neighboring parishes. This domain extends the social body from one that is familialy and geographically centered to one that is potentially available to any member of the wider Catholic community. As a result, any person of Catholic persuasion, regardless of cultural knowledge, can viably claim *Los Pastores* as part of his or her tradition. This displaces the cultural authority and knowledge from the hosts and performers to the priests or other Catholic officials who claim control over the event in its newly reconstituted, official, domain.

The discontinuities between the *barrio* or church and mission are the most significant. The mission performance, advertised as a tourist event, produced with translation and commentary, sponsored by a private organization of mostly non-Mexican women from a distinctly higher social class, displaces both the familial and religious sentiments of the home and church.

The semantic shift between the mission and the other two domains is most evident in the way the memory-place of this venue is used to recenter *Los Pastores* for a tourist audience. San Antonio's missions were founded in the eighteenth century by Franciscan missionaries, in the service of the Spanish Crown, for the purpose of "civilizing" the native Indians of Texas. To this end, the mission compound was composed of agricultural fields, work areas for the teaching of technological skills, and the mission church, where worship and religious doctrine was provided. These three facets of mission life—agriculture, technology, and Christian ideology—worked as a means of taming the local tribes by displacing their cultural knowledge and beliefs.

The historical practices of the colonial church are reproduced in the preserved walls, buildings, and narrative discourse of the mission. The San Antonio missions, now the property of the National Park Service, have been restored to depict the lifestyle and activities of their day. As such, they constitute a place of discipline, labor, and indoctrination. Relocating *Los Pastores* from the *barrio* and church to the mission resonates with the historical practice of this place by reproducing a form of power that stems from the colonial gaze.

The performance of *Los Pastores* for a tourist audience is really about social control. The familial experience of the *barrio* is displaced in favor of an event that exhibits a cultural and class division between performers, hosts, and the audience. The cultural knowledge vested in the performers who reproduce this practice is displaced by an emcee, as his voice now constitutes an authoritative discourse that is projected over the voices of the performers through his position as the official spokesperson of the San Antonio Conservation Society. Furthermore, his voice subsumes that of the performers, reshaping it and speaking with social, cultural, and political authority (see Bakhtin 1981:343).

The texture of social relations that govern everyday practice is reproduced in the three domains in which *Los Pastores* is performed; distinctions based on gender, age, cultural knowledge, class position, and authority are replicated. These distinctions are not of equal weight, however. In the *barrio,* cleavages of gender and age demarcate lines of difference but do so within the realm of shared social meaning and conviviality. It is not that these differences are irrelevant, or that social rankings based on gender and age are benign. On the contrary, they are real forces that lead to conflict and crisis in many families, except here the social interaction that emerges in performance—one that I explore at length in chapter 7 and that I see as articulated through the idiom of gifting—holds these disparate forces in abeyance even as they continue to structure this event.

The kinds of social cleavages that are found in the home are replicated in the church. Only now, the presence of clergy and secular leaders affiliated with the church organizations, because of their institutional links, assert more authority and control over the event. Although the issue of class is negligible in the church domain, since the secular leaders are of the same social location as the participants and performers, the issue of power and influence, what Bourdieu (1977:183) refers to as "symbolic capital," is not. Secular leaders, as a result of their affiliation with the institutional church, have a certain amount of status and influence and receive recognition even if, in comparison with the clergy, they have very little decision-making authority. The presence of these leaders and the sponsorship of *Los Pastores* by their organizations provide for a different frame for understanding this event, since the familiar and personal centerings of the home have given way to the more diffuse and, at times, bureaucratic structures that govern the social relations that emerge in this domain.

The mission, quite distinctly, exhibits the sharpest divisions between performers, hosts, and audience members. This cleavage is the result, in part, of ethnic, class, and social distance. However, differences here are based less on everyday forms of social interaction and more on their absences. That is, the texture of social relations at the mission results from the touristic centerings and physical surroundings of this domain. Language, religious sentiment, and cultural knowledge are displaced from everyday practice and put on display as a form of social entertainment; intimacy is transformed into spectacle.

I have suggested above that the *barrio*-home domain and the kinds of social cleavages that demarcate it exhibit a form of social solidarity that is not present in the other two domains. The point here is that forms of difference, be they gender, age, or other aspects of one's social location not discussed in this chapter, are not negated through some mystical form of communitas; on the contrary, these differences are themselves the vehicles through which performers and audience members negotiate the immediate task of rendering the moment meaningful. At the evening's close, family members, friends, neighbors, and work cohorts continue to engage each other as they always have, except now the experience of social conviviality that emerged in the performance of *Los Pastores* exists as a "model of" (Geertz 1973) social intercourse that can lead to new forms of social interaction.

But why does this happen in the *barrio* and not in the other two domains? What is it about this place, and the form of social relations that emerge in performance here, that is distinct from the other two places of performance? This problem and the solution that I propose are the subject of chapter 7.

7

Gifting and Performance: Toward a Production-Centered Theory of Expressive Culture

A cold *Especial*, any beer that happens to be on "special" at the ice house at the end of the street, passes my way as talk about the recent past ensues. "¿Y sabes qué? [And you know what?]. Una vez [one time], we went out to this ranchito [small ranch] . . . you know, way out Highway 181. It was cold, and drizzling, y a toda madre [one hell of a day]. And once we started performing, ya sabes [you know], we can't stop hasta que terminamos la pastorela [until we finish the pastorela]. It was so cold we kept pistiando [drinking] to stay warm, and after we finished, y Daniel counted el dinero [the money] from the adoración (adoration), tuvimos diecisiete centavos! Seventeen cents! lo crees [could you believe it]. ¿Y sabes? [And you know], we'd go back again tomorrow—if they asked."

A few weeks later, in the midst of discussing our performance for the local conservation society, Vicente Manuel claims: "Las señoras [the women] from the Conservation Society, they want us to give two performances en la misión [at the mission]. Pero nomás querían darnos ciento cincuenta dólares [But they only want to give us $150]. They give us a hundred dollars for one time, and they want to give us $150 for two. I told them, 'No Ma'am! It's not worth all our work.'"

In my field notes I scribbled the apparent contradiction between these two positions. How is it that at one place, marked by the most inclement winter weather one could find in South Texas, collecting seventeen cents is not an issue; and on another occasion money is the reason for not performing a second time.

A few days later, during one of our conversations, Vicente Manuel began to discuss the differences between performing *Los Pastores* in the three venues of the *barrio*-home, church, and mission. In comparing the *barrio* performance with the mission he claimed: "Yo, anytime, prefiero darlas en casas. . . . Ellos

. . . son muy comercial, pa' mí" (I, anytime, prefer to give them in homes. . . . They [performances in the mission] . . . are too commercial, for me).

THE GIFTING OF PERFORMANCE: PERFORMATIVE ASPECTS

My discussion with Vicente Manuel, coupled with earlier comments concerning the amount of money collected at two different performance locations, serves as the problematic of this chapter, expanding the previous discussion of centering discourses, social location, and memory-place to include that of social relations. A comparison of these three domains reveals the structure of their boundaries and shows how the physical and symbolic forms indicate the kinds of social relations that emerge in each of them. More specifically, I demonstrate how performances in the different domains emerge from distinct social formations.

Cultural performances are spatially bounded events that transform everyday spaces into places of heightened social significance. This is the difference Vicente Manual refers to when he states that he prefers to give performances in homes rather than the mission, which he finds too commercial. Vicente Manuel's concern exemplifies Raymond Williams's notion of a "structure of feeling" (Williams 1977). For Williams, a structure of feeling is precisely the kind of pressure, often personalized, that articulates one's discomfort and dissatisfaction with an emerging, yet undeveloped, social form. Like much of what Williams brings to cultural theory, a structure of feeling is concerned with social forces that are "actively lived and felt" and marked by a particular "set" of "relations" (Williams 1977:132). The words of Vicente Manuel echo those of Williams: although he would rather perform *Los Pastores* in "las casas," because "hay más devoción que en la misión" (because there is more devotion than in the mission), performing at the mission serves as a means of pride, accomplishment, and special recognition. The sense of identification found in the *barrio*, evoked through some greater sense of "devoción," coupled with the unwillingness to negate the attention received from the more "comercial" mission performance, is the kind of lived tension, a structure of feeling emergent in performance, that cannot be dismissed.

But how is this tension the product of a particular "set" of relations? What are the parameters of these relationships? Or more specifically, how is the structure of these relations connected to the distinct places of performance? Before moving to these questions, I would like to emphasize that *performance* is itself a term that captures particular forms of social relations. In a formulation of the different foci performance-centered analyses have taken, Richard Bauman (1986a) articulates three general perspectives: performance as practice; cultural performance; and the poetics of oral performance. It is his framing of "performance as practice" as "centrally informed by the Marxian notion of praxis" (Bauman 1986a:132) that informs this analysis.[1] Marx, in the *Economic and Philosophic Manuscripts of 1844* (1964:110), at times equates labor with free activity or praxis, and elsewhere in the same work, with alienation and estrangement. The distinction between labor as free activity and labor as an act of alienation is critical in my attempt to reground performance to praxis. My position is to return to a notion of labor employed by Marx in this early document, albeit with the condition that such a move bears further ethnographic scrutiny. Labor, life activity, can be both the free action associated with praxis and the alienated activity of human misery. It is exactly this kind of tension, one caused by the fluid boundaries between labor as praxis / alienation, that informs Williams's notion of "structure of feeling." The boundaries between these two experiences exist, but human activity melds and flows between them, leaving no tracks except for that lingering sense of something gone awry.[2]

At this point, and for reasons that will be clear below, I refer to the productive aspects of human activity found in performance as the "labor of performance." By focusing on performance as labor, I seek to highlight how *Los Pastores*, both as text and event, is produced by the sensual activity of performers and audience. Actors do not merely "enact" a text, nor do audience members "receive" a performance: the performance event is produced by, and emerges from, the human activity that stems from the event itself.[3] I take seriously Bauman's comment that the "structure of the performance event[s] is a product" (Bauman 1986b:4) and as such, want to explore the "structure" of that product as the result of human activity or labor.

THE GIFTING OF PERFORMANCE: GIFTING ASPECTS

In his review essay, "Western Marxism and Folklore: A Critical Introduction," José Limón (1983b:49–50) provocatively suggests that gift-giving, not as the semantic content of folklore but as "process, production, and aesthetic form," evokes "the inherent oppositional quality of all folklore." At this point, I want to engage Limón's comments more directly and concur that gift-giving is indeed critical to any oppositional quality inherent in folklore.[4] My emphasis, however, is that an understanding of gift-giving, following Marilyn Strathern

(1988), can only function heuristically when contrasted with its paired Western discourse, commodity-exchange. In this way, the distillation of difference between gift-exchange and commodity-exchange allows us to perceive the qualitative difference between two social forms and the social relations that produce them, thereby bringing to material perception Williams's structure of feeling. As Mauss and others have shown, gift- and commodity-exchange are not bounded "things" and routinized "events" but are themselves categories for understanding particular sets of relations (Mauss [1925] 1990; Sahlins 1972; Strathern 1988). And, by understanding the way social relations are reproduced and affirmed through performance, a better understanding of the lived tension between *devoción* and *comercial* can be attained. The heuristic conflation of *devoción* and *comercial* with the more political-economic discursive forms of gift- and commodity-exchange is not without precedent; there is a long trajectory in anthropological literature that explores gift-exchange and its relation to the production of commodities (Abrahams 1981; Appadurai 1986; Godelier 1977; Mauss [1925] 1990; Sahlins 1972; Strathern 1988; Taussig 1980). This chapter adds to this literature by considering how performance events function as forms of social and aesthetic exchange that are themselves produced from various logics of social interaction.

The primary distinction between gift- and commodity-exchange exists in the way social relations are organized around the objects of exchange. In gift-exchange, the gift offered functions as a means of establishing or maintaining social relations, thereby fostering and highlighting the "human value" involved in such an exchange (Strathern 1988:90). Even so, this does not mean that those involved in such exchanges are free from coercion. Strathern (1988:161) continues: "It is hardly admissible to decide that this particular transaction results in alienation, while that particular one does not. One cannot tell by inspection." Commodity-exchange, according to Godelier (1977:156), is the process whereby the "very essence of the value disappears in its mode of appearance," thereby embedding the human value inherent in all forms of commodities back into the commodity as a natural characteristic of the object itself.

But what about "performance?" How is artistic expression, and in this case, folk drama, related to gift- and commodity-exchange? Or, again, how is it that the performance of *Los Pastores* in two places can be understood as the emergence of difference found in gift- and commodity-exchange. At this point, the insights of Lewis Hyde's *The Gift* (1983), set alongside Limón's remarks noted above, offer a way of bridging this interpretive juncture. Hyde (1983:155) claims that the primary arena of art is not the exchange of commodities, but that of gift exchange, which he claims is critically linked to a process based on "relationship, bonding, 'shaping into one.'" Building on the earlier works of Mauss ([1925] 1990), Van Gennep (1960), and the more recent work of Weiner (1976), Hyde speaks of a "threshold gift" that "marks the time of, or acts as the actual agent of, individual transformation" (Hyde 1983:41). But gift-exchange, if indeed it is linked to a process that fosters or maintains social relations, is not a one-way process; it fosters a notion of gratitude, born from the gift itself that in order to be complete must be reciprocated.[5]

Ideally, performance, as an artistic form of human behavior, is seen as a product of labor that is not abstracted from social relations but constitutive of them. If performance is understood as a gift-exchange based on the labor of performance, it is not because it embodies some higher, mystical under-standing of human interaction, but because the human activity from which it is produced is founded on a process that accentuates the social relations that constitute it. That is, the emergent social relations of performance create and sustain bonds of what George Simmel refers to as "sociability" (Wolff 1950).[6] And, like most gifts, the gift produced through the labor of performance must be reciprocated. It is here that Hyde extends Mauss's classic work by delineat-ing the notion of the "labor of gratitude." For Hyde, the "labor of gratitude" is the process through which a gift is given in recognition of the original gift itself. Through this process, the labor of gratitude completes the cycle of obli-gation inherent in gift exchange. This is clearly related to Bauman's emphasis on a performer's responsibility to an audience and the evaluation an audience levies on performers. This interaction of performative responsibility and eval-uation takes place within a shared sense of communicative interaction that is fundamental for social life. The gifting of performance, therefore, is the recip-rocal process of performance and gratitude that engages performers and audi-ence in a cyclical event founded on shared communication, social solidarity, and mutual obligation.

GIFTING AND THE *BARRIO* PERFORMANCE

With the three domains of performance in mind, I can now proceed to dem-onstrate how these three venues, sites where particular sets of social relations are enacted, constitute distinct social formations evoked through the gifting of performance.

The *barrio* performance, where there is *más devoción,* exhibits a number of qualities that are characteristic of gift-exchange. First, there is the rationale

Madrinas presenting troupe members with loaves of bread and pinning ribbons and dollar bills on the costumes of performers.

for performing at someone's home. Invariably, the main reason for hosting *Los Pastores* is to fulfill a ritual vow or *promesa* made to the Virgin or el Niño Dios. The cosmological dynamics of a *promesa* are based on an exchange of favors, bartered between humans and deities, that require each side to fulfill the terms of the promise through certain practices. These practices usually involve healing or special favors on the part of deities, followed by obligatory rituals on the side of humans. In essence, the practice involves the giving of self in a cycle of exchange based on ritual gifting.

Second, this place of performance is closely connected with the transformative qualities associated with a threshold gift. The audience, as noted before, consists of family members, neighbors, and invited friends. There is a sense of shared responsibility in hosting such an event: friends and family are involved in preparing the house, arranging the "stage" for the performance, setting up chairs, constructing temporary shelter against inclement weather, building a home altar, and preparing festive foods.[7]

Throughout the performance, it is not unusual to find family members inside the house preparing and serving different foods and beverages. This activity of preparation and sharing of tasks is equated with the "labor of gratitude." Whereas Hyde (1983) understands such gratitude as occurring at a different temporal point in relation to the gift, that is, after the gift is given, here it is coterminous with the performance itself. Performance events operate on their own cycle of gift-giving and reciprocity, further distinguishing them from the more common forms of commodity exchange that center on the commodity itself. It is important to underscore the notion of labor used by Hyde (1983:51) as "something dictated by the course of life rather than by society, something that is often urgent but that nevertheless has its own interior rhythm, something bound up with feeling, more interior, than work." It is clear from Hyde's definition that the labor of gratitude builds on a notion of labor that not only accomplishes work, but also fosters sociability. Like the relationships established by gifts, the labor involved in reciprocity fosters social relations. As Mary Douglas (1990:x) states, "The theory of the gift is the theory of human solidarity." In the *barrio*, even before the performance begins, particular networks of social and political obligation are already in place that coalesce in moments and places of performance.[8] Through performance, obligation and solidarity, though never a certitude, emerge.

Finally, there is no set fee for a performance. The only monetary exchange involves the *madrinas* pinning dollar bills on the gowns of the performers and the ritual offering at the end. *Madrinas* are sponsors, like Margie and the other women, who during the brief intermission, pin ribbons, buttons, and dollar bills on the cloaks of the performers. Recipients of these gifts are usually chosen for their displayed competence. Furthermore, the money placed in Gila's basket at the end of the performance is also interpreted as a ritual offering. Recall that the collection of seventeen cents was never seen as a reason to avoid returning in subsequent years. These offerings, however, are not taken as payment but as return gifts whose monetary value is insignificant.

The labor involved in preparation is the work that brings the gift of actual performance to fruition, and the labor of gratitude is the work that reciprocates, completing the transformation. These two aspects of labor constitute a single event that foregrounds the social relations constitutive of performance. The performance of *Los Pastores* in this place is a transformative gift both because it claims to bring to life another meaning of Christmas, and because the social relations that emerge in the dialectic between the labor of performance and the labor of gratitude create and sustain bonds that are based on sociability: people sharing food, talk, space, and labor, created through their mutual involvement in performance.[9]

GIFTING AND THE MISSION PERFORMANCE

The mission is quite different. First, there is no ritual vow that speaks to the rationale of the event as performed here. It is a secular event, free of ritual obligation on the part of those who sponsor it. And, because the event is staged for a largely tourist audience, the cosmological dynamics, beyond that of the narrative of the nativity, are not present. As a result, the ritual aspects of *Los Pastores* are displaced in favor of spectacle.

This process cannot be separated from the issue of the fee. The San Antonio Conservation Society, by paying for the performance beforehand, fulfills its obligation of reciprocity through a wage, thereby negating the necessity of a return gift. Instead of an event produced from the performance of gifting, *Los Pastores* at the mission is an event to be witnessed; it is an event whose meaning is the event itself, to be displayed for and witnessed by a tourist audience. The event is a spectacle to be seen, a commodity to be consumed, not a process of mutual interaction. That which is exchanged is not the dialectic of labor and gift as found in the *barrio* performance, but the witnessing of an "authentic experience": from the mystique of the historical mission to Luzbel ranting and raving in Spanish prosody, the mission event is constituted not as gift, but as a spectacle of the past experienced in the present. As Dean MacCannell (1976:23) claims:

> Modern culture may be divided and marketed after the fashion of a commodity, but the economic and social structure of these bits of modernity is quite different from that of the old industrial commodity. The value of such things as programs, trips, courses, reports, articles, shows, conferences, parades, opinions, events, sights, spectacles, scenes and situations of modernity is not determined by the amount of labor required for their production. Their value is a function of the quality and quantity of *experience* they promise.

What happens to the dialectic between the labor of performance and the labor of gratitude in the mission location? The performers, while treating this like any other performance, implicitly sense that something is different.[10] One of the leaders, on several occasions, confided that he felt he was not being dealt with fairly. Although the performers have maintained a long-standing relationship with the San Antonio Conservation Society, the leader felt they were being paid too little and therefore, being used in some way. What the leader felt, in the categories I have set up to analyze this issue, was that the troupe's labor of performance was not being reciprocated through the labor of gratitude. The amount paid, one hundred dollars, was not enough to compensate for their effort. In other words, *Los Pastores* was being bought as a commodity instead of being reciprocated through a mutual gift of labor. In effect, no amount of money could replace the labor of gratitude that was present in the *barrio* location. Where seventeen cents would suffice in one location, one hundred dollars would not in another.

The uneasy feeling of the leader was not without contradiction, however. He felt, as did other members of the troupe, that the invitation to perform at the mission validated and authenticated their efforts by gaining recognition and legitimation from the agents of the local conservation society. This point is crucial, for it again highlights the sense of ambiguity and discomfort associated with structures of feeling. The troupe, although it did not articulate the difference between these two sites as one based on the disjuncture between gifting and commodity exchange, "feel" the distinction as one of uncertainty.

There are other elements that differentiate the *barrio* from the mission performance, one of which is the lack of interaction or contact between the performers and audience members. Most spectators stand at a distance listening only to the emcee and not the performers. Indicative of the social distance experienced at the mission are the booths at which food and drink are sold to the public. Although food in the *barrio* is made by family members and shared by all, in the mission it is sold for a profit. Here, as in the *barrio*, food is an important marker of social practice and outlines the boundaries of gifting and symbolic action. "The rituals enact the form of social relations," Douglas (1966:128) states, "and in giving these relations visible expression they enable people to know their own society. The rituals work upon the body politic through the symbolic medium of the physical body."

Sharing food signifies a set of practices that make visible the form of social relations in a group, further distinguishing the mission from the *barrio* place of performance. In the mission, what is used to sustain the body, food, is sold as a commodity, item by item, and the sense of meal is disjointed; in the *barrio*, food is shared as a complete meal and given freely to all who attend the event. In the mission, food is marked by separation, itemization, and dislocation. Furthermore, the master of ceremonies repeatedly asks the audience to support this event by purchasing food from the vendors; however, none of this money goes to the performers, and although some of the money may be used to supplement the fee paid to the church, income from the vendors certainly exceeds the amount given. From paid fee to food vendors, *Los Pastores* in the mission is marked as a place of commodity exchange.[11]

Finally, the use of an emcee cannot be dismissed. His amplified English-language rendition projected over the Spanish poetic text, spoken by *mexicano* actors before a tourist audience, is most disruptive. This sole voice of the emcee constitutes what Bakhtin (1981:343) refers to as an "authoritative" voice, one that speaks with political authority, shaping all other discourses to itself. In this context, what is being heard is no longer *Los Pastores*, but a text reshaped to the needs of a tourist audience.

In this location, Spanish prosody, voiced song, masked performers, ritual elements, and the entire performance is marked (and marketed) as an opportunity to experience an "authentic" Mexican folk drama. This authenticity, the "promotion of local color" as Davydd Greenwood (1989) refers to it, is produced from both real and fictive claims that attempt to distance *Los Pastores* from the modern world. First, *Los Pastores* is introduced as a survival of Mexican culture that was first introduced by the early Texas missionaries. Second, its sacred content and emphasis on the "true" meaning of Christmas situates it against the mass commercialization of the season. And its performance at the foot of San José Mission, a national historical monument, envelops the entire event in a mist of romantic historicism. These elements offer an "experience" of the past in the present. But such renderings, however real or fictive, displace the performative and processual aspects of interaction that are the social character of folklore, and instead promote a certain distance associated with commodity experience.

GIFTING AND THE CHURCH PERFORMANCE

The church domain contains many of the elements of the *barrio* and mission, but in ways that are unique to this site. First, the ritual aspects of the church, while sharing the religious idiom of the *barrio* event, are not based on gifting. The ritual bartering and gift exchange that are essential to the *barrio* domain are absent; the social solidarity forged through the labor of gifting in the *barrio*, as related to the intimacy of ritual participation, has been displaced. The ritual aspects of *Los Pastores* exhibited in the church domain are not personal or familial, but institutional. Members participate and interact on the basis of their church affiliation, not their personal relationships with each other. As a result, the dialectic of gifting and reciprocity is not one that structures the interaction of the church domain. Unlike the *barrio*, this domain is not dependent on the performance of gifting, but on the institutional structures that provide the resources—personnel, leadership, and financial means to supply advertising and the meal—for its actuation.

At the same time, the payment of a fee that marks the mission is not found at the domain of the church. As in the *barrio,* there is no fee or monetary consideration for performing at a church. The hosting church may make a donation to the sponsoring one, but this is optional and not a prerequisite for performance. Except for the money collected during the adoration, the issue is not discussed in the church domain.

Food is another characteristic that distinguishes the church from the *barrio* and mission. Although the church domain does not sell food in disjointed fashion, item by item, neither does it feed everyone freely. When food is served, it is prepared by a church organization or volunteers and is sold as a complete dinner plate. The preparation of food, though done as a gesture of goodwill, does not stem from the economic resources of those who prepare it nor is it seen as part of a gift of gratitude for the event. Instead, it is seen as service to the church.

Moreover, the solidarity that marks the *barrio* domain is not the same at the church venue. The gift-giving that fosters intimacy and sociability in the *barrio* is displaced; instead, the relations created are based on a form of the consumption of religious experience. Because of its size and institutional links, the church domain does not constitute an experience of sociability based on gifting and gratitude; such a structure is too tenuous, fleeting, and difficult to replicate for institutional needs. Acquaintances are seen and neighbors acknowledged, but in the end, the kind of human interaction that builds and fosters sociability, an interaction based on the performance of gifting, is absent. Still, the church domain, because of the overlapping elements of social location, provides for a semantic field that is not quite as discordant as the mission.

But how about performers? How do they reflect this tension? Unfortunately, they are almost entirely silent on this issue. Vicente Manuel had no trouble contrasting the *barrio* with the mission, but the church is different. The social control of ecclesial ideology inhibits, almost entirely, the kind of emic critique leveled against the mission. Even so, the discordant experience of the church, the structure of feeling it produces, emerges between the cracks of religious hegemony. Recall Vicente Manuel's claim that people no longer come for "devoción" but "diversión." Although he says this in general about all performances, its salience is more acute at the church. This is the religious site par excellence; its centering discourse and memory-place leave no doubt as to its ritual intent. But what does it mean to say that devotion is displaced by diversion? One thought is that the terms of structural configuration that constitutes devotion have swayed, giving way to another set of practices that, though similar, are inconsistent with those of devotion. The centering discourse of the church domain is no doubt about ritual. But the experience at the core of ritual, which results, as Turner (1982:75) claims, in an "increase in . . . social or plural reflexivity, the ways in which a group tries to scrutinize, portray, understand, and then act on itself," has shifted. The reciprocal relations that constitute the gifting of performance have been displaced and objectified by the discourse of el Niño Dios. Those who attend, one might say, are no longer engaged in a process of sociability, but have objectified such an experience in the statue of el Niño Dios. This recenters the locus of ritual action from a project of social engagement to one of personal relations with el Niño Dios. The difference between the church and *barrio* domain is significant: in the *barrio* event, the ritual centering of *Los Pastores* invariably takes on the tone of the hosts through stories of personal faith and commitment to el Niño Dios. Personal narratives function as a device that allows the audience to engage the hosts with empathy as well as reflect on their own life stories. This process fosters a level of sociability born from the collective experience of one's human condition. These personal narratives are absent from the church domain, being replaced by a discourse centered entirely on el Niño Dios. The personal and intimate focus of the event is replaced by a focus on the inanimate statue. An event that produces a type of social experience by forging a sense of sociability is replaced by one that objectifies social experience instead of creating it.

THE SOCIAL CHARACTER OF PERFORMANCE

This chapter has demonstrated that the binary concepts of gift- and commodity-exchange provide a model that disaggregates the formation of social relationships from the aesthetic or poetic elements of performance discussed in part one. By heuristically focusing on gift-giving and reciprocity, I have been able to explain how emergent social relations of performance differ from one venue to the next. These differences, in turn, indicate how the semantic field of each domain provides for different, yet narrowly distributed, cultural meanings. Such theorizing sheds light on every act of performance, and I offer it here as a critical elaboration on the growing and extensive literature on performance theory in anthropology and folklore studies. In their most recent articulation of this approach, Bauman and Briggs (1990:60–61) correctly state that performance "provides a frame that invites critical reflec-

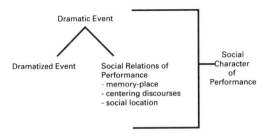

7.1. The social character of performance.

tion on communicative processes . . . open[ing] up a wide range of vantage points on how language can be structured and what role it plays in social life." Reflecting on the dramatic event as the interaction between relations of performance and the variable roles of communication, or the dramatized event, reveals how each event is stamped with its own social character (see figure 7.1).

The social character of the *barrio* performance mediated by the gifting of performance is one of participation and communal production. In many ways, the social character of performance, that of participation and sociability, reproduces the strategies of daily life: networks of familial and neighborhood support systems that provide economic resources are replicated in this event. Like most cultural performances, the social relations founded on the gifting of performance serve as a "model of" social behavior, representing strategies of social interaction that are commonly utilized; once enacted, relations based on the gifting of performance serve as a "model for" influencing future behavior (Geertz 1973:93). In effect, the social relations that emerge from aesthetic productions are not only based upon the poetics of everyday behavior, but like other metaphorical engagements, they potentiate a domain of unexperienced, yet culturally mediated, practice.

The performance of *Los Pastores* at the mission is quite different. The centering discourse of preservation and the effort spent on translating the drama into English signify the emphasis placed on the dramatized text. In this domain, *Los Pastores* is experienced not as a socially shared event, but as a cultural experience for a tourist audience; it is the objectification of Mexican folklore, open to public scrutiny, for outsiders. Absent are the reciprocal relations of gifting found in the *barrio*. Instead, the social character of the mission emerges from a form of interaction associated with commodity-exchange.

Tourists attend to experience the "local color" that is promised, void of the social interactions and obligations of human activity from which it is produced. This differs dramatically from the social character advanced by Don Leandro discussed in chapter 5. For him, to "aser pastores" was to be and to perform as a shepherd, a process that connotes his critical understanding of cultural performances as the product of active engagement and participation.

Like the barrio-home performance, this domain also provides a glimpse at the social relations that govern daily experience, except that here a class practice is replicated whereby "traditional" and "authentic" Mexican expressive cultural forms are put on display for the benefit of others. In effect, the historical poetics of dislocation (discussed in chapter 5) produce what Ortner (1990:63) calls a "cultural schema," structured and structuring practices that inform behavior. The mission performance embodies a cultural schema of authority that preserves Los Pastores as a form, event, and expression of Mexican culture, displaced from the social content, character, and experience from which it emerges. This domain serves as an important example of how inhabitants of the modern world display the "quaint," "ethnic," and "cultural other" to be pored over by the touristic gaze; it is a place where social distance and class practice are reproduced, providing a model for prospective forms of disjuncture instead of informing potential relations of solidarity between those present. And, if it were not for the performers' comments about preferring the barrio-home domain over the mission (a structure of feeling that things are not well), the encompassing hegemony of touristic consumption that imbues this domain would go unchallenged.

The social character of the church performance is similar to that of the mission, although it is grounded in religious experience and not tourism. The semantic field of the church is mediated by the worship of el Niño Dios, and this mediation constitutes a double displacement from the barrio-home performance. First, the significance of the event is not the gifting of performance but the dramatized story, which creates a shift in the way social relations are constituted. In the barrio-home domain, sociability emerges from the social relations related to the gifting of performance. In the church domain, relationships of gifting and reciprocity are nearly absent. That is, the solidarity that does emerge is mediated, and idealized, in the common religious sentiment expressed in ritual discourse. Those present are informed by their religious preoccupation with el Niño Dios, and the resulting religious experience is based on ritual and worship, not the social interaction that informs and builds solidarity. The inherent value of sociability is displaced and embedded back into the statue of el Niño Dios as a natural characteristic of this object of worship. The ritual discourse of the church domain differs from that of the *barrio*-home by its objective focus on el Niño Dios, not the revelation and personal disclosure that stems from the public expression of ritual bartering that draws others into intimacy.

A PRODUCTION-CENTERED THEORY OF EXPRESSIVE CULTURE

A number of theorists have provided processual definitions of folklore based on ideas such as "face-to-face" interactions (Abrahams 1972a); the production of "hand-made objects" (Jones 1975); competence and evaluation in performative skills (Bauman 1977); and socially shared production (Limón 1983b). Each of these approaches is concerned with the investment of human activity and its recognition through some form of reciprocal, culturally mediated, action. This is the twin dynamic between labor and gratitude that I refer to as the gifting of performance.

As this chapter demonstrates, the same dramatized event is structured by various forms of social interaction, and therefore it is vital to see expressive practice as a mode of social and aesthetic production. In the three domains described above, the dramatized event of *Los Pastores* is much the same whereas the dramatic event and the social relations and social character that emerge from it are quite distinct.

The conjoining of the social character of performance and the poetics of performance is what I term a production-centered approach to expressive culture (see figure 7.2). In examining production, I have found that the "social" and the "poetic" emerge from, and within, specific modes of social interaction, and thereby provide performance events with particular meanings. As already mentioned, the three domains of performance elevate certain features and articulations of its making, resulting in distinct productive processes. It is not by accident that each of these domains reproduce at the level of performance a set of social relations endemic to its place in the larger social order. As a result, the meaning of *Los Pastores* in three distinct venues is precipitated by the dominant form of symbolic production, or structuring principle, that informs each domain. It is precisely for this reason that gift- and commodity-exchange are crucial in this analysis, for they demonstrate how the social character of performance emerges from specific structuring principles: where gifting is dominant, a social mode of production emerges; where commo-

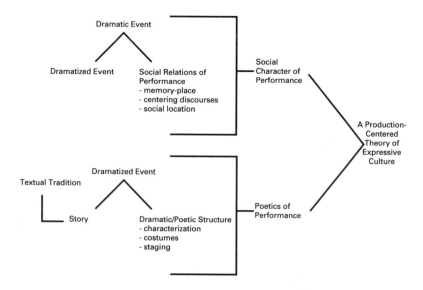

7.2. Elements of a production-centered theory of expressive culture.

dity-exchange is prevalent, the mode of production is informed by consumer relations; in other words, the product, not the process, informs the event.

This approach demonstrates that communicative processes are structured by particular sets of social relationships that may or may not be indexed by the analysis of poetic forms and functions. A production-centered analysis indicates that performance events are rooted in the daily negotiation of meaning and power, a process essential for the production of culture. Sociability and commercialism or diversion, my gloss of Vicente Manuel's *devoción* and *comercial*, are indices to forms of negotiation and appropriation in the sociocultural sphere that signal the realm of ideology since modes of aesthetic production are not neutrally structured domains but are connected to the beliefs and practices of particular groups. As Raymond Williams (1981:27) notes, there are "close connections between the formal and conscious beliefs of a class . . . and the cultural productions associated with it."

The notion of ideology, and its concomitant, consciousness, especially in relation to the production of culture, brings up the question of hegemony. Although there are various elaborations on the concept of hegemony, my use is informed by the Gramscian view, further articulated by Williams (1977:110), that hegemony is a "lived system of meaning and values . . . which has also to be seen as the lived dominance and subordination of particular classes." As explained in my discussion of his "structure of feeling," Williams (1977:112) sees the "lived experience" of dominance as a set of "relationships" that must be continuously "renewed, recreated, defended" as well as "resisted, limited, [and] altered." Hegemony is a process of imposition, coercion, consent, negotiation, and acquiescence in the maintenance of and resistance to particular social formations.

Modes of aesthetic production structured as relations of sociability and diversion provide vital insight into the uneven tensions of hegemonic relations. Although for analytical purposes I have stamped each of the three domains of performance with particular social characters, these domains are not entirely coherent wholes, as the performers' reserved enthusiasm for the mission domain exemplifies. And yet, Vicente Manuel's recognition of the inherent contradiction between performances structured as *devoción* or *comercial* cannot be dismissed; in fact, it serves as a necessary reminder to the lived experience and relational forms of the hegemonic. Under a production-centered theory of expressive culture, the inherent tension and struggle that exist between *devoción* and *comercial,* and the social relations of each of these principles of aesthetic production, reveal the conflictive forces and relations that attempt to define and, on occasion, displace forms of expressive practice along group or class lines. By focusing on the production of *Los Pastores* in three domains, and not the final product, I have indicated the form and shape of social relations, those between devotion and diversion, that emerge from this event. Attention to form is critical, as the centering discourses of each domain also reveal, because any effort to define *Los Pastores* through its semantic content is always open to further recenterings. As a result, the meaning of expressive cultural practices cannot be found solely in their symbolic elaborations: even the most politically salient messages can be recentered (re-righted or re-lefted) and made to speak for the other side.

Hermann Rebel (1989a:132) claims that the "quest for experienced cultural hegemony does not begin with what people say or what theatrics we can observe them perform but with the deducible structured irreconcilables of their social relations." As one who takes theatrics, as well as hegemonized social relations, seriously, I tentatively agree with Rebel (1989b:351) that "cultural hegemony has to begin with a precise analysis of social formations." I also believe, however, that such formations can be found in the structuring principles that a production-centered theory of expressive culture articulates. As I have shown, what is contested is not the "said" of folklore, but the "mode of saying" (Limón 1983b). The significance of *Los Pastores* lies not in its historical or cultural tenacity, but in the forms of social relations and practices—

those between devotion and diversion—that emerge and are negotiated through it. As Stuart Hall (1981:235) claims, "What matters is the state of play in cultural relations . . . the class struggle in and over culture."

PERFORMANCE AND RESISTANCE

Vicente Manuel's distinction between devotion and diversion also connotes a hesitancy and preference for one domain over another. This unsettledness— or structured feeling of unease—is an essential aspect of cultural negotiation and resistance. First, it is clear that the domain of the mission, and to a lesser extent that of the church, contributes to a performance that displaces the social relations of sociability that mark *Los Pastores* in the *barrio*. A different mode of aesthetic production indicates that the shift from one domain to another constitutes a change in social interaction that renders these domains uniquely distinct. Second, the mission and church domains exhibit a kind of social practice that ventures to control the knowledge that emanates from them, as exemplified by Tranchese's task of editing the text and the contemporary arrangement of the mission event. In contrast, the *barrio*-home event exhibits a kind of vernacular social arrangement that, although still embodying certain contradictions (such as age and gender discrepancies), continues to provide a space that is organized around a different set of social interactions. The difference between these three domains reveals a real break and struggle over the production of culture.

But are these differences considerable enough to warrant classifying them as forms of resistance? Limón's comments are instructive in this case. If, as he claims—and I believe him to be correct on this point—capitalism, and the commodification of social relations that are instrumental to it, has "induced folklore's decline, not by attacking the expression itself but by dissolving, fragmenting, and atomizing its nutritive social context" (Limón 1983b:40), then the continuation and production of these sites, structured along lines of sociability and solidarity, *are* a form of resistance. In like manner, those places of performance that displace one social formation for another, as the church and mission do, cannot be dismissed. I propose, and here I again refer to Williams's (1977:114) words, that the signs of sociability that structure the *barrio* domain are both sufficiently "independent" and "original"—that is, distinct from the institutional and commercial structures of status quo relations—and that their maintenance and continuation must be recognized as a form of resistance. As Richard Bernstein (1983:228) reminds us, we need to "seize upon those experiences and struggles in which there are still glimmerings of solidarity." Cultural resistance is not a totalizing affair, but one based on particular struggles and negotiations waged on turf that, in the grander scheme of things, may appear to be of little consequence. But this negotiation cannot be ignored. Producing a place in which one's collective identity is forged to a principle of solidarity affects, quite significantly, the social construction of reality. The purpose of such activity is to control one's world and oppose those who may have other plans.

8

Between Devotion and Diversion: *Los Pastores*
and the Modern World

After having been away from San Antonio for several
years, I returned in December 1993 to visit with the performers and witness what changes had taken place. Besides the loss of several members due to age and illness,
most of the performers were still involved. The director was still present, despite recent health problems, and was intent on completing two more seasons
and thus on reaching his goal of performing for fifty years. Those I knew as
adolescents were now young adults, and along with age came the realization
that youthful dreams were sometimes only that. Most were still living with
their families, either by intent or necessity, attempting to balance the needs
of maintaining a job with a steady income—no easy task in the tenuous economy of the day—and a desire to "take a few courses" at the local college. But
these changes were conveyed without despair, only the resolution that "así es
la vida."

Several of the younger members, however, were seeking alternatives to
the lives of the neighborhood. One had recently returned from military duty,
anxious to convert his experiences into a successful job; another was in her
senior year of college and looking forward to completing such a significant
threshold for herself and her family.

Perhaps the most striking change I saw during this visit, one confirmed
through my discussions with several of the performers, was a slight decrease
in both performances and attendance at home and church events. Although I
was not able to attend the mission event, I was told that more than a thousand
people came to it. Lest my discussion be misinterpreted, let me clearly state
that I do not believe these changes reflect the demise of *Los Pastores*: the performers, especially now that a growing number of young people are involved,
are quite definite about continuing in the future. Furthermore, events like
this often go through cycles of popularity and decline, and most members see
this as the current situation. There is, however, a sense in which the increased

violence of the city has affected home events. In one instance, a drive-by shooting a few blocks from where a scheduled home performance was to take place led to its cancellation. But this was an isolated incident and not the norm.

During a conversation with two troupe members, an older male and his granddaughter, the following views to my query about the changing significance of Los Pastores were supplied. The young woman said:

> I think it comes with education, education about our culture, education about our heritage, about your roots, and once the family unit starts emphasizing that . . . then I think Los Pastores will be stronger. . . . We need our traditions to be noticed here in America and here in our nation. I mean, we can't lose them along the way, you know. Striving to go forward, yes; I mean, technology brings us forward and everything, but we can't lose where we came from, it's very important, and that's why I stay, too. Like I said, it comes with education. We have to preserve what's ours. Yes, go forward and be a united nation, but also don't forget where you came from.

Her grandfather then interjected: "Yeah, the best part of the pastorela is that it's during the Christmas season. We put Christ back in Christmas."

The comments of these two actors, separated by more than forty years in age, demonstrates how Los Pastores continues to serve as a signifying event. There is no doubt that folk religious practices, affected by the forces of diversion or secularization, have waned over the decades. In spite of its initial perception, this woman has not displaced a devotional or religious view of the world with a secular one; instead she has replaced a religiously informed metanarrative with one of collective cultural identity. Here the emphasis on preserving what is "ours" shows that the continuation of Los Pastores functions as an event keyed to the present needs of social and cultural identity making. And, it does so without pretense to romance, on the understanding that even when "technology brings us forward," a group must strive to remain fixed to a particular set of social and cultural markers that allow one "to be noticed here in America." Although it is correct that most claims to such identities reinvent certain aspects of the past for their use in the present, it is also clear that the extended presence of Los Pastores in this community serves as a cultural practice that integrates its members as a collective unit. The emphasis of this young woman, quickly recentered by her grandfather, represents a collective symbolic affirmation, albeit in an idiom of cultural unity. This reading cannot be dismissed and is evidence that Los Pastores posits a "Utopian power as the symbolic affirmation of a specific historical and class form of a collective unity" (Jameson 1981:291). But the positing of such a reading is not, as Fredric Jameson (1981:292) warns, an attempt "to conjure such divisions away by an appeal to some higher (and imaginary) principle of collective and social unity," at least not by the young woman. The transference of *Los Pastores* from one discourse of collectivity to another lends critical weight to the social hermeneutic of this cultural practice since to maintain a collective interpretation is to insist on a restored collective life. To insist on a restored collective life is to understand or articulate its dissolution and fragmentation, not at the level of the abstract but at the point of aesthetic production. As shown in part one, *Los Pastores* is constituted from both text and enactment, and any effort to articulate a textual or performative social engagement must be grounded in both. This moves the discussion to the level of textual desire and enacted devotion.

TEXTUAL DESIRE

As a text, *Los Pastores* is open to a number of readings and interpretations on the basis of its polysemic symbols, iconic signs, and multiple voices. To propose a singular textual reading in unequivocal terms is impossible. But the structural elements that shape its meanings are more circumscript, as Roland Barthes (1987:3) claims when he states that "A literary science cannot be a science of the *content* of works . . . but a science of the *condition* of content, that is to say of forms." The poetic forms that produce the structural and narrative tension of the dramatized text are rendered from a process of dislocation and misrecognition. Recall the tension between the various symbolic domains—the cosmological, liminal, and referential—that are at the core of the dramatized action. Dislocation and misrecognition are the formal, structural devices that constitute the condition of *Los Pastores*'s making, the mechanism by which the human experience on which it is based is expressed in public drama. Gananath Obeyesekere (1990:57) refers to this as the "work of culture," the process whereby symbolic forms, under the psychoanalytic principle of substitutability, are distanced from the deep motivational springs that produce them.

Let me suggest at this point that desire serves as the textual motivation of *Los Pastores*. The work of culture, that complex, cognitive, historical, and symbolic process, is the mechanism by which desire, what Randy Martin (1985) refers to as "the absent cause in human social agency," is enscripted upon multiple signifiers that are historically and culturally contingent and made public. Northrop Frye (1957:105) agrees with Obeyesekere on this point when he states that civilization is "the process of making total human form out of nature . . . impelled by the force . . . called desire." For Frye, as for Obeyesekere and Martin, desire is the motivating force that conditions the work of culture.

But to say that desire motivates *Los Pastores* is to still speak of a mechanism that underpins this event. The inner content of desire, its articulation with its site of textual production, needs to be specified. Here I turn to Frye (1957:106) once again, as he provides a solution when he claims that the "conception of a garden develops the conception of 'weed.'" That is, the textual articulation of desire can only be known by its opposite, its "obstacle" to restoration, that is itself revealed in the work of culture.

The presence of textual obstacles in *Los Pastores* registers a site of friction where various meanings are competing for saliency, displacing one for the other. By isolating the textual friction and tension in the dramatized event, I hope to indicate both the content of these obstacles, and of desire, expressed in the text of *Los Pastores*. Again, I turn to Frye (1957:136), who states that displacement is a process by which particular textual and formal problems are solved, like those involved in the movement from myth to romance. This intratextual friction and realignment reveal disjunctures in form whose displacements are indicators of the content of desire.[1]

The case of textual desire concerns the cosmological tension between the shepherds and the devils. Luzbel, Satan, and the other devils attempt to displace the journey of the shepherds, keeping them from arriving in Bethlehem and encountering el Niño Dios. This cosmological struggle, mediated by the Archangel Michael, concerns the shepherd's desire for the sacred and the devils as its obstacle. Expressed in a religious and Christian idiom, the shepherds and devils form an axis of struggle between the arrival of truth or light and the forces of darkness. As the text states:

> Hail, Sunrise, who was born
> giving light to darkness,
> Our Hope begins—
> to all the world—new light
> to all the world—new light.

The language of lightness and darkness stems from the Christian doctrine of the Incarnation that interprets the Messiah as the light of the world. His pres-

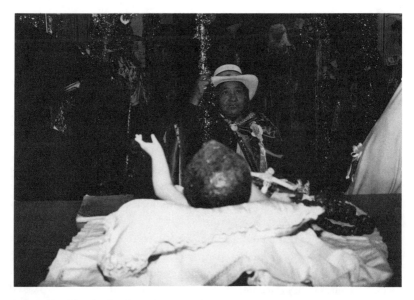

Bato, one of the shepherds, making an adoration to el Niño Dios.

ence destroys the darkness of evil, opening the heavens for all to experience. The desire of the shepherds is to encounter el Niño Dios in the sacred city of Bethlehem, while desire's obstacle is found in Luzbel, Satan, and the other devils. The devils revel in darkness and celebrate in the forces that signify the limitations of the human condition: the sins of greed, gluttony, and deceit. The devils' disguised intrusions into the affairs of the shepherds are attempts to thwart the sacred journey; their tactics and tauntings reveal the cosmological tension between the restoration of truth and light and the practices of darkness. The textual meaning of *Los Pastores,* the content that informs the various symbolic displacements, is that of the Christian hope for salvation and restoration, it is the renunciation of evil, and arrival in the sacred city that ends in adoration and devotion.

ENACTED DEVOTION

On the performative level, the dramatized event reveals an intratextual dialogue through which desire and its obstacles are enacted. This is most evident in the final scene, where a kiss and an offering of money fuse both desire and obstacle into one dramatic frame. Taken as symbolic markers, el Niño Dios and money signal the desire for the restoration of wholeness found in the devotion of the shepherds, alongside its obstacle, the money-form. This final frame, enacted at every performance, juxtaposes the utopian city of Bethlehem, where shepherds, after overcoming the agents of evil, end their apocalyptic journey in devotion, with money, what Weber (1946:331) refers to as the most "abstract" and "impersonal" aspect of human life.

El Niño Dios, the objectification of unity and wholeness, finds its obstacle in the money-form. But the money-form is itself a signifier for a particular configuration of social relations. According to Marx (1967), the abstraction of human labor from the product of one's labor is concomitantly related to the differentiation of use-value from exchange-value that leads to the objectification of value in the money-form. The final performative frame contrasts the desire for restored wholeness expressed through religious devotion with that of the alienation of human labor epitomized in the money-form. As Berger (1967:9) aptly notes, "Viewed from inside Western civilization . . . the original 'carrier' of secularization is the modern economic process, that is, the dynamic of industrial capitalism." Whether seen as a rupture from divine unity or from social process, the obstacle to social restoration represented in the discourse of Christian salvation in general, and *Los Pastores* in particular, is that of alienation.

The significance of *Los Pastores* as a dramatized event is likened to that of a critical modernism in performative vernacular form.[2] The final frame signifies a struggle between the desire for devotion and its binary opposite, social alienation; it reveals a tension between unity and disunity, between wholeness and fragmentation, between el Niño Dios and the money-form. The textual meaning of *Los Pastores,* expressed through the structural tension between desire and its obstacles, is the human desire for completeness, expressed and experienced through ritual enactment, against the all too real encroachments of the social world experienced as alienation and fragmentation.

Although the utopian desire for wholeness and completeness is rendered from a collective view of the world, it is a view that refuses to sentimentalize the collective for ideological ends. Althusser's definition of ideology is instructive on this point. For him, ideology is "a 'Representation' of the Imaginary relationship of individuals to their real conditions of existence" (Althusser 1971:162). For Althusser, one's relationship to the real is always imaginary, always represented, always textual. As such, it allows subjects to conceive, imagine, or dramatize, as in this case, one's relationship to desire. This imaginary relationship expresses, according to Althusser (1965:233–34), "a will, a hope, or a nostalgia, rather than describing a reality." But the performed text of *Los*

Pastores is different. It juxtaposes desire with its contemporary obstacle. As a result, its performance is "alter-ideological"—as Ramón Saldívar (1990:213) suggests of other Chicano narratives—since it "produce(s) clashes or textual aporias that demarcate the limits of ideology itself." *Los Pastores* contrasts the desire for collective restoration with the money-form, revealing the tension between a vision of solidarity and its dissolution by a system of impersonalization and abstraction. As my informant claimed, "Striving to go forward, yes; I mean technology brings us forward and everything, but we can't loose where we came from."

A desire for collective restoration serves as the social hermeneutic of the textual and enacted aspects of *Los Pastores*. This resonates with the social experience of its practitioners, providing a glimpse of the complex, yet real, relationship between the Utopian impulses of religious practices and cultural productions alongside the putative forces of social dissolution. *Los Pastores*, however, is also rooted in the social relations and structures that contextualize it. In other words, it is also a dramatic event framed by a complex network of social actors that contribute to its meaning. This frame does not negate the role of ritual symbols but dialectically and materially connects them to the social conditions and emergent social relations that are constituted in the dramatic event, a connection apparent in the movement from devotion to diversion.

FROM DEVOTION TO DIVERSION

Although troupe members have insisted that performing *Los Pastores* is an act of devotional self-fashioning, others, more specifically, the dominant Others, have thought otherwise. The tradition of performing *Los Pastores* in South Texas, one that began in the mid-eighteenth century, reveals how Anglo-American writers have interpreted this event while fashioning a place for its *mexicano* actors. The cultural poetics of dislocation, discussed in chapter 5, forged a perception of South Texas *mexicanos* as foreigners in their native land, relegating them to a marginal place in the emerging Anglo-American hegemony. Discourses of displacement, evidenced in the work of Bourke and Parisot; of marginalization, found in the texts of Hershfield and Sugranes; and the propensity to reorder exhibited by the work of Tranchese, sustain particular cultural and social perceptions of *mexicanos* as subaltern to the Anglo-American status quo.

In his insightful and critical book, *With His Pistol in His Hand*, Américo Paredes (1958a) writes that Anglo-Americans stole land from Mexicans even while they made them out as bandits. This double image-making, what Michael Taussig (1993:66) describes as the "colonial mirror of production," is precisely the kind of endeavor these early chroniclers of *Los Pastores* were engaged in. By making Mexicans out as bandits, Anglo-American writers inscribed them to a place on the margins of what was essentially their own social territory, and in so doing, legitimated their own exploitive practices.

The poetics of Bourke's writing, while influenced by former historical and intellectual legacies, produce an ideology that resonates with the later efforts of Tranchese and the San Antonio Conservation Society. Bourke's writings and actions are themselves part of an American nationalist modernism that emerged between 1870 and 1905 and procured a transformation in "the dominant system of cultural values" (Kammen 1991:162). This transformation, however, required the displacement of indigenous peoples, Mexicans included, so as to reconstitute them not as active agents of Americanism, but as relics of a bygone era. Bourke is emblematic of an increased effort to objectify the cultural practices of *mexicanos*, interpreting them as superstitious and backward people of the premodern world. The poetics of dislocation that I have argued for are about such a process, and it is here that a corollary between the efforts of Bourke, Tranchese, and the San Antonio Conservation Society can be detected.

Tranchese's misreading of the meaning of *devoción* for Don Leandro and his project of rearranging and publishing with translation a text of *Los Pastores* are in accordance with Bourke's cultural practices. On one level, Tranchese appreciates and seeks to maintain popular religious practices, especially as a means of warding off the perils of secularization; but on another level, his efforts at translation, redaction, and cathexis for a proper chronological order reveal his inability to comprehend the social insights that inform Don Leandro's resolve to "aser [*sic*] pastores" (to be and perform *Los Pastores*). There is no doubt that this European-trained Jesuit was a modern man. His work against poverty and the perils of the poor through the channels of government-funded social programs attest to this. But an even more significant indicator of Tranchese's modernism is his inability to realize how the performers of *Los Pastores* could experience the sacred through performance. Devotion, for Tranchese, is not the experience of wholeness and sociability, but the incantation of religious doctrine; it is not the experience of communitas, but the declaration of ritual creeds and sacred prayers; it is not the social conviviality of *barrio* life, but orthodox adherence to prescribed rules.

Tranchese's concern with chronological order and biblical realism and his insistence on proper orthography are emblematic of a wider concern for order and similitude. Ritual, for him, is an act of proper representation that is attentive to authenticity in text, order, and expression. Ritual is about the correct presentation of a sacred text, whereas for Don Leandro and his performers *Los Pastores* is an act of social engagement through devotion. Although there are certain to be various social and cultural texts that inform devotions, they are not a priori texts to be replicated, but events that stand alone as the product of emergent forms, contexts, talents, and poetics.

Devoción, for Don Leandro, is an act of making social members, of crafting solidarity and sociability that are at the heart of forging a social identity. After one has experienced geographic, economic, and social displacement, the ability to actively relocate one's identity and social place through devotion is an act of empowerment. As studies in the sociology and anthropology of religion have demonstrated, religion functions as a means of collective community and myth making (Berger 1967; Durkheim [1915] 1965; Geertz 1973; Turner 1969). Whether perceived as a practice that constitutes models "of" or "for" social reality (Geertz 1973), or as a ritual process that produces social cohesion (Turner 1969), religious practice is germane to the social and cultural making of meaning. *Los Pastores,* and the desire for devotional performance, is the medium that allows Don Leandro to forge a sense of sociability, solidarity, and communal identity. His understanding of *devoción* stems from a premodern cultural complex that understands performance in public to be a social affair. If "man made himself in public," as Richard Sennett (1974:18) writes about the eighteenth century, public performances of devotion such as *Los Pastores* were part of the public repertoire that led to a shared identity for these early performers.

The efforts of the San Antonio Conservation Society represent a similar stance toward *Los Pastores* as that found in the actions of Tranchese and Bourke. The Conservation Society's efforts, however, signal the arrival of the modern practice of cultural displacement for touristic amusement, whereby people discover themselves through the cultural productions of others (MacCannell 1976). What merits preservation, from the Conservation Society's point of view, is the event of *Los Pastores,* one that represents an authentic Mexican tradition, not the social relations and devotional intentions that produce it. In their desire to protect *Los Pastores,* the Conservation Society's members displace this event from its social and devotional links and promote it as a cultural product for touristic attraction.

By 1950, the shift from devotion to diversion in the touristic arena was complete. Isolating and preserving the performed text contributed to cultural fetishism, whereby the event was preserved but the social relations and experience from which it is made were mystified. Today, the purpose of the Conservation Society, taken from its handbook, is to "preserve and to encourage the preservation of historic buildings, objects and places related to the history of Texas . . . to educate the public, especially the youth of today and tomorrow with knowledge of our inherited regional values" (1988/1989). Their intent is noble, but their affect is to interpret the cultural experiences and expressive forms of *mexicanos* as artifacts, without the very values of sociability essential to their making. This organization is representative of modern institutions, and my critique, in part, is not directed at them specifically but at the general mechanisms of modernity they enact that reproduce the cultural practices of others in ways that displace them from the social processes and meanings held for those who produce them. "Modernized people," Dean MacCannell (1976:30) writes, "released from primary family and ethnic group responsibilities, organize themselves in groups around worldviews provided by cultural productions." Such efforts give rise, MacCannell (1976:32) continues, to "a modern form of alienation of individuals interested only in the model or life-style, not in the life it represents." Such is the case of the mission performance: tourists and Conservation Society members alike express an interest in the event while failing to recognize the social conditions of both the performers and the experience from which the event emerges. Here, spectators also face a form of alienation by failing to engage the life of the event. Instead of experiencing the social conviviality, that found in the gifting of performance, they engage the makers of *Los Pastores* only tangentially, if at all, as agents of amusement. Although it is not surprising to see the mission event displace other meanings, the church domain merits further comment.

Modern Catholicism, like other major religious entities, is a bureaucratic institution. Its size and orthodox ideological apparatus (to turn a phrase of Althusser's) require that it be so. But with bureaucracy and regulation comes the loss of personalization and an increase in alienation, especially in the United States, where religious pluralism prevails and official religious affiliation is a private affair. As Peter Berger (1967:134), speaking of the demise of religious cohesion, states: "The world-building potency of religion is thus restricted to the construction of sub-worlds, of fragmented universes of meaning, the plausibility structure of which may in some cases be no larger than the nuclear family."

The church is limited in providing a place where ritual and devotional processes can foster a socially and culturally cohesive vision of the modern world, since such a vision has been fragmented and privatized. The church, unwilling to relinquish its authority in these matters, attempts to provide a forum where practices like *Los Pastores* are exhibited, but with little success. The institutional structure is not willing, nor is it designed, to provide a space for the tenuous and unpredictable outcomes of communitas. Solidarity and sociability are forms of power and self-identification, processes that threaten institutional religion, especially its orthodoxy. In place of this, the church provides a venue where the nativity story is dramatically represented, but displaces the solidarity founded on the gifting of performance. Like the mission, the church domain is a place where *Los Pastores* can be viewed as a cultural production, while at the same time erasing the socially cohesive relations of gift-giving.

Even with these displacements, there emerges a type of social bonding I have called the gifting of performance. Through relationships of gifting and reciprocal action, the gifting of performance forges a sense of community based on sociability. It is not that the relations produced through gifting are inherently more meaningful than others, but that the presentation and giving of self extends social bonds that potentiate social networks. In times of crisis, at moments of political significance, these relationships transfer into forms of social practice that extend sociability to acts of mutual aid, social concern, and, when available, economic resources. Gifting and reciprocity imply a give and take, a mutual interaction and engagement of self that draws people into networks of solidarity.

The significance of *Los Pastores* in the modern world is varied. The *barrio*-home performance is recentered as one of devotion and ritual discourse, which leads to social obligation. Although devotion is invoked in the church domain, its practice reveals a different process. As in the mission, audience members experience the event from afar, both socially and spatially. Both the mission and church domains dislocate the meanings produced in the *barrio*-home, recentering them as forms of religious entertainment and touristic amusement.

The meanings of *Los Pastores,* those that fall between devotion and diversion, function as forms of signification. Ranges of signification, values, and the emergent relations of sociability are critical for understanding *Los Pastores* and its ability to construct meaning. In some domains, solidarity relations emerge as the dominant ones, shaping the cultural schema of performative interaction, whereas at other events, recenterings through an inchoate, extended religious affiliation, as in the church, or romanticized visions of tradition and "the past," as in the mission, lead to events that amuse more than cleave. The making of *Los Pastores* embodies a local site where the ability to construct one's identity, as well as that of the Other, either as members of a social group through the idiom of devotion, or as actors that perform their roles for the amusement of outsiders, is a socially symbolic act. And, as in all kinds of performances, the ability to direct what occurs on stage is a powerful, potentially political, and often contested affair.

Notes

INTRODUCTION

1. John Igo (1967) identifies this text and its performance as the "Granados-Tranchese" version, to indicate the editing and reorganization undertaken by Tranchese. The local troupe, however, recognizes Don Leandro as its founder and so I have chosen to refer to this text as the Granado version of *Los Pastores*.

2. The study of medieval popular culture has flourished in recent years, especially in the work of Bakhtin (1984), Burke (1978), and Davis (1975). Although these scholars differ in their intellectual approaches and concerns, each has attempted to reevaluate the role of popular culture, especially its relationship to the established cultural forms of elite classes.

3. By analyzing *Los Pastores* as the conjuncture of the "dramatized" and the "dramatic" I attempt to understand this performance, following Bakhtin (1981:255), as a "totality" in which these two components "are indissolubly united in a single but complex event."

4. Edward Bruner (1986:6) expresses this same sentiment when he states that "the relationship between experience and its expressions is always problematic." I would emphasize that history is an essential, however absent, component in the organizing logic of culture and cannot be underestimated in this endeavor. The efforts of Jameson (1971, 1981) have been quite influential in foregrounding the place of history in the study of literary forms.

1. THE SOCIAL AND DRAMATIC STAGE

1. The essays in Poyo and Hinojosa (1991) contribute significantly to the historical understanding of San Antonio during this early period.

2. The shift from a cattle and pastoral economy to industrial agriculture is one that must be seen within the larger social climate in which the Battle of the Alamo and México's loss of the Southwest in the U.S.-Mexican war occur. Various scholars have

written about this era from a number of perspectives, including the following: Barrera (1979), De León (1982, 1983), García (1981), Montejano (1987), and Weber (1973).

3. All performers up to the mid-1970s were men, except for those playing the role of Gila, the shepherdess, and that of the Angel, which was played by a young boy outfitted in a white dresslike garment.

4. A nationally recognized Mexican-American arts organization, dedicated to the restoration of Mexican-American art forms, is located one block from the church. Its staff consists of professional artists, musicians, and writers who sponsor workshops and performances covering several genres of Mexican-American artistic forms. In the two years I performed with the troupe, there was no interaction between the performers and the officials from this organization. Like many arts agencies, their understanding of Mexican-American art involves the construction and reproduction of "invented traditions" (Hobsbawm and Ranger 1983). Although I am not critical of these endeavors, the absence of any formal relationship suggests the development and training of Mexican-American artists with little or no interest in the noncommodified, folkloric, forms of expressive culture that are indigenous to this area.

5. Of the three domains of performance, a home is the most common. Nearly all the homes we performed in were located in the West Side *barrio*. The significance of this domain, one that emerges when contrasted with that of the church or the mission, stems from both its home and *barrio* social coordinates. As a result, I refer to this domain as that of the *barrio*-home; for expediency, however, I will also refer to it as the "home" or *barrio* performance.

6. In 1993, the performers acquired wireless microphones for use at church locations. However, only five of the characters were equipped with these, while others were still barely audible.

2. FROM SPAIN TO SOUTH TEXAS

1. On the occasion of Corpus Christi, the auto was performed on *carros,* or floats, and paraded through town.

2. Except for the *Auto de los Reyes Magos,* there are no examples of this dramatic form available for the period between the twelfth and early fifteenth century.

3. Two other writers who follow the tradition of Vicente are Diego Sánchez de Badajos, who wrote the *Farsa de la salutación,* and Bartolomé de Torres Naharro, who wrote the *Farsa del sordo* and the *Diálogo del Nacimiento* (Rael 1965:17).

4. The works of Natalie Zemon Davis (1975) and Peter Burke (1978) on the force of popular humor and culture in the Middle Ages offer views similar to those provided by Bakhtin (1984).

5. Many of these first missionaries have been credited with documenting the linguistic and cultural practices of the indigenous people of México. What remains unfortu-

nate is that we have only the records and observations of these Spanish agents and not those of the preconquest cultures and societies of this period.

6. Pedro de Gante's influence was so widespread that by the end of the century, schools modeled after his own were in existence at Tlatelolco, Tiripitio, and elsewhere.

7. While one of Rael's hypothesis is that the *pastorela* was brought into the Southwest by Franciscan missionaries, Marie discusses two other options: one, that the *pastorela* was brought by the first Spanish settlers who migrated north into this area; or two, that later colonists who migrated after the settlement of this area brought the *pastorela* with them.

8. Igo (1985) includes the Granado version in his count. The Heinrich Collection has two versions of the Granado text in its possession: the first is the original publication by the Treviño brothers, and the second is a typed version dated 1920.

9. The *San Antonio Express* reported several other performances in subsequent years: December 25, 1890, and January 10, 1893. I wish to express my appreciation to Tim Matovina for referring me to these references.

10. The Heinrich Collection contains several manuscripts that date to the early twentieth century: the Torres manuscript from Eagle Pass, Texas, has a possible date of 1905; a manuscript from Juan D. Rodriquez of Laredo dated 1918; another manuscript from Laredo, dated 1939 and connected with St. Augustine Church, entitled *El Nacimiento de Mesías;* and three manuscripts from Mission, Texas, by Juan Luna dated November 28, 1922; by José Ruiz with no date; and another by Gilberto Rentería dated 1936.

3. STORY AND STRUCTURE

1. Igo (1985), among others, has referred to the *infierno* as the "hellmouth," a name that descends from the Middle Ages when such dramatizations featured the mouths of huge dragons or serpentlike demons painted on walls. Shoemaker writes of Christmas celebrations in 1581, which feature "una boca de infierno," or hellmouth (Shoemaker 1935:49), and in some instances a curtain, as the Guadalupe players use, marks the entrance to the mouth (Shoemaker 1935:51).

2. The personification of the metaphysical world is discussed by Bakhtin (1981:150): "Folkloric man demands space and time for his full realization; he exists entirely and fully in these dimensions and feels comfortable in them."

3. The Granado text includes a choral part, written for the shepherds, that could be considered an aspect of the liminal world. In the performance, however, there are no markers to indicate when the shepherds are performing as "shepherds" or as members of a "chorus." More important, the performers themselves do not treat the chorus as a distinct role but see the two parts as one and the same. As a result, I treat all the actions of the shepherds as structurally contained within the referential world.

4. The rosary signifies another anachronism since it represents a tradition that started several hundred years after the birth of Christ.

5. In this sequence of events, the hermit plays the religious hero who crosses a boundary to lead his people out of danger. Examples of this in the Judeo-Christian tradition are Moses, Jesus (who descends into hell), and the Good Shepherd. This pattern is an example of what Northrop Frye (1957) refers to as the "quest-romance."

6. Consentino's (1982) study of Mende storytellers provides a similar example of the manipulation of time.

4. POETIC PERFORMANCES

1. Limón (1992), in an analysis that combines Bloom's theory of poetic influence with the critical Marxism of Raymond Williams and Fredric Jameson, shows how the heroic *corrido* tradition of South Texas influenced later poetry of the Chicano movement.

2. Paredes (1958a), McDowell (1975), and Limón (1992) all comment that the sung octosyllabic line changes meter, producing a different phonological line than its recited form.

3. The second edition of the Tranchese-Granado text, published in 1978, contains an appendix with all the musical transcriptions for the first verse of each sung part of *Los Pastores*. The appendix was added by Sister Carmelo Montalvo, O.S.B.

4. Turner and Seriff (1987) provide an interpretation of altar making among German-American women in Texas. Although this group is ethnically different, the principle of a gender-based expressive culture related to the construction of home altars is instructive for this case as well.

5. HISTORICAL POETICS AND CULTURAL PRACTICE

1. A more geographically and socially relevant work on the way cultural poetics have influenced the study and social life of *mexicanos* in South Texas is that of José Limón (1994).

2. Acuña (1981), De Leon (1982), Montejano (1987), and Weber (1973) provide synthetic studies of this particular period. For a somewhat later period see García (1989).

3. For an economic analysis of the Texas-México border area see Hansen (1981).

4. José Limón (1994) refers to this period, and the activities of John Bourke in particular, as that of "war" and "anthropology."

5. Others, it seems, made their feelings about Bourke known as well. In 1895, the publishers of *El Bien Público* wrote an article, "War against Peace or a New Attila," which reviewed the legal accusations against Bourke (Porter 1986:295).

6. This is not to say that *mexicanos* did not resist. They did, and in ways that were

significant. But the encroachments by the dominant order were too extensive and powerful, creating a sense of democratic apartheid in parts of South Texas that was to last for several generations. See Paredes (1978) for his particular view on cultural conflict on the border.

7. See De León (1983) and De León and Stewart (1985) for more information about the social climate in Texas at this time. For a more descriptive study see Foley et al. (1977).

8. In translating Don Leandro's polysemous term *aser* (from *a ser* and *hacer*) as "to be and perform" I am giving equal voice to the essential and active senses of this word. This translation is important for understanding Don Leandro's conception of performance as an active process.

9. To this point, Richard García (1991:27) states: "San Antonio between 1900 and 1930 needed labor for urbanization and industrialization, and the Mexicans—the existing native population and emigrating one—were the source that would build San Antonio and the Southwest."

10. For a more detailed look at Tranchese's activities and their impact on the City of San Antonio, see Richard García (1991).

11. Tranchese's actions are consonant with the kind of Catholic radicalism that was emerging at the time, especially as promoted by Dorothy Day and the Catholic Worker's Movement. On one level, Tranchese, like Day, was a strong advocate of social reform, while at the same time preserving the status quo within the institutional church. For more of Tranchese's views on *Los Pastores* see Tranchese (1941).

12. This text is taken from a photograph housed at the collection of the Institute of Texan Cultures, #70-289.

SAN ANTONIO TEXAS ENERO DE 1949
UN POQUITO DE HISTORIA

Don Leandro Granado,
Nativo de la ciuidad urapuato guanajuato México
Vino a esta ciuidad de San Antonio Texas
el 27 de febrero de 1894
En México comense aser Pastor en 1884
y en esta ciuidad comense aser pastor el 1913
y desde entonses comense a ascrevir este Libro
llebando la representacion amuchos ogares
y Siguierndo aciendolos todos los años
y este año 1949 con el fabor de Dios y Su Santa-
gracia el 27 de febrero cumplire 75 años
y conciderando que ya no boy apoder aser
pastores Siertamente muy apesar mio . . .
y viendo que el padre Carmel tiene muy
vuena boluntad para Seguir llebando ala
practica esta Representacion de los pastores
Contoda mi bolundad y Contodo cariño
le Regalo mi libro de pastorela para que

el no deje que sepierde esta tradicional
deVocion y cuando el Muera ho se cambie
le deje una copia a su Susesor para que
Siga llebandose asu Representacion en la
Iglecia de N.S. de Guadalup de San Antonio
Texas y Rueguen a Dios por el que escrivio
estas Mal Escritas Linias

Leandro Granado
415 Elvira St
San Antonio Texas

nota
Esta es una comprobacion de que yo Leandro Granado le cedi el derecho de este libro
al Rv. padre Carmel Tranchese

13. Northrop Frye (1957:137), writing on the displacement of myth to realism, describes a process that applies to Tranchese: "But to make it [myth] plausible, symmetrical, and morally acceptable story a good deal of displacement is necessary, and it is only after a comparative study of the story type has been made that the metaphorical structure within it begins to emerge."

14. I want to thank Tim Matovina for drawing my attention to this early reference as I was preparing an earlier draft of this discussion (Flores 1993).

15. Bauman and Briggs (1990:76) write that the ability to relocate a performance from one context to another is an issue of social power.

6. MEMORY, PLACE, AND CONTEXTUALIZATION

1. Limón (1989) provides a salient reading of *chingaderas*, linking their performance to a discourse of social critique.

2. Paul Connerton (1989:37) states: "Our memories are located within the mental and material spaces of the group." My concern here is to show how material spaces contain features (architectural, semiotic, spatial alignment) that are the loci of historical and popular memory.

3. The linguistic repertoire of Chicanos, Mexican Americans, or *mexicanos* in South Texas is one composed of various forms of Spanish, English, and combinations of the two sometimes referred to as "bilingualism with diglossia" (Limón 1982:30). A number of historical and political factors are responsible for the unique development of these lexical, syntactical, and morphological forms. See Limón (1982) and Elías-Olivares (1979) for further information on this process.

4. The hermit's interjections transform Luzbel's monologue into dialogic speechplay, breaking Luzbel's authoritative discourse through this ludic device. Bakhtin (1981) provides an insightful discussion of the salience of authorial voices and challenges to their monolithic authority like the one improvised by the hermit in this speechplay.

5. On the topic of men's sexual joking, and for an alternate reading from that provided by many of the early Mexican intellectuals who wrote on this subject, see Limón (1989).

6. For an overview of other "markers" of performance, see Bauman (1977), Bauman and Sherzer (1974), and Duranti and Goodwin (1992), and Hymes (1981).

7. Soja (1989) provides a cogent, insightful, and critical perspective on the relationship between social space and other facets of social life.

8. The use of tradition as a means of legitimizing one's practice has been explored by a number of social theorists. See Handler and Linnekin (1984), Hobsbawm and Ranger (1983), and Shils (1981). Bauman (1992) provides a discussion of the active process of "traditionalizing" as it emerges in the act of performance itself.

9. The role of women is quite significant since such participation follows patterns discussed by Sacks (1989:543) as the way "in which women's unwaged work creates community-based and class-based social ties of interdependence that are key to neighborhood and household survival."

10. The information on which this paragraph is based is taken from the 1988–89 *Yearbook* of the San Antonio Conservation Society. A copy of this document is housed in the reference room of the library of the University of Texas at San Antonio.

11. This serves as an example of what Davydd Greenwood (1989:172) refers to as "local color," or the commoditization of culture that accompanies tourism.

7. GIFTING AND PERFORMANCE

1. By connecting performance to practice, Bauman (1986a:132) is drawing on a tradition that stems from Marx's (1978:145) eighth thesis on Feuerbach that says: "Social life is essentially practical."

2. This is not to ignore or deny the walls of isolation caused by alienation and exploitation. Such isolations are real, devastating, and controlling. But again, as Williams (1973, 1977) has shown, hegemony works less through coercion than by invitation. For a discussion of hegemony that is more sociolinguistically oriented, see Woolard (1985).

3. Eagleton (1978:65) presents a discussion of this point as it applies to literary texts.

4. At a critical stage in the development of this chapter, I reread Limón's insightful article, "Western Marxism and Folklore" (1983b). He concludes with some probing thoughts on the relationship between folklore as process and gifting as a metaphor for that process. It took a while, but Limón's ideas finally germinated into my comments here and elsewhere (Flores 1994). I want to thank Professor Limón for allowing me the opportunity to explore his initial insights in a manner that I hope does not misrepresent them.

5. Hyde is not unique in this matter—Mauss ([1925] 1990), in his classic formulation on this subject, arrived at a similar conclusion much earlier.

6. It is important to underscore that this engagement does not preclude or negate

the fact that relations within this event may be unequal; that is, differences of gender, class, and status still prevail. As Strathern (1988:161) shows, enchainment is still very much a part of any relationship based on gifting, and I would add, sociability.

7. Turner and Seriff's analysis (1987:457) also explores how gifting relates to the interpersonal relations that go into the building of a home altar by women: "Gifting on the woman-centered occasion of St. Joseph's is not a competitive or obligatory act, nor is it a public form of manipulation, propitiation, or pacification of one's neighbors or one's gods. We suggest that it must be understood, instead, as a testament to intimacy—a kind of intimacy that is predicated in the values of reproduction." Whereas Turner and Seriff focus on intimacy in relations to women's gifting, my focus, while comparable, is on sociability as the result of communal gifting through performance. See Kay Turner (1982) for another discussion of Mexican-American home altars.

8. Vélez-Ibáñez (1980, 1983) demonstrates how social networks facilitate a number of economic and political support services.

9. In similar fashion, Abrahams (1972b) shows how Christmas on St. Vincent leads to shared experiences and related forms of reciprocity.

10. In discussing the pottery of Helen Cordero, Barbara Babcock (1986:325) states that the market destination of these figurines does not influence the values and beliefs with which they are made. The members of Los Pastores, in similar fashion, perform with the same rigor and beliefs as they would in the other two domains, although they do sense that the interactive dimensions of performance that emerge in the mission venue are different.

11. In a recent article on the semiotics of tourist art, Jules-Rosette (1990:11) states that "the process of creation and production remain the unexplored dimensions of tourist art." I would suggest that this performance analysis, and its relationship to tourism, is one effort, however small, at addressing this void.

8. BETWEEN DEVOTION AND DIVERSION

1. By focusing on the dialectics of desire and its obstacles, Frye (1957), in very certain terms, anticipates Jameson's (1981) later theorizing about the ideology of form and its dialectics.

2. For a discussion of Chicano narrative forms as vernacular modernism see Limón (1992).

References Cited

Abrahams, Roger D. 1972a. Personal Power and Social Restraint in the Definition of Folklore. In *Toward New Perspectives in Folklore,* eds. Richard Bauman and Américo Paredes, pp. 16–30. Austin: University of Texas Press.

———. 1972b. Christmas and Carnival on St. Vincent. *Western Folklore* 31:275–89.

———. 1981. Shouting Match at the Border: The Folklore of Display Events. In *"And Other Neighborly Names": Social Process and Cultural Image in Texas Folklore,* ed. Richard Bauman and Roger D. Abrahams, pp. 303–21. Austin: University of Texas Press.

Abu-Lughod, Lila. 1986. *Veiled Sentiments: Honor and Poetry in a Bedouin Society.* Berkeley: University of California Press.

Acuña, Rodolfo. 1981. *Occupied America: A History Of Chicanos.* New York: Harper and Row.

Althusser, Louis. 1965. *For Marx.* London: Allen Lane.

———. 1971. *Lenin and Philosophy and Other Essays.* New York: Monthly Review Press.

Appadurai, Arjun, ed. 1986. *The Social Life of Things: Commodities in Cultural Perspective.* Cambridge: Cambridge University Press.

Babcock, Barbara. 1986. Modeled Selves: Helen Cordero's "Little People." In *The Anthropology of Experience.* ed. Victor Turner and Edward Bruner, pp. 316–43. Urbana: University of Illinois Press.

———, ed. 1978. *The Reversible World: Forms of Symbolic Inversion.* Ithaca, N.Y.: Cornell University Press.

Bakhtin, Mikhail. M. 1981. *The Dialogic Imagination.* Austin: University of Texas Press.

———. 1984. *Rabelais and His World.* Bloomington: Indiana University Press.

Barrera, Mario. 1979. *Race and Class in the Southwest: A Theory of Racial Inequality.* Notre Dame: University of Notre Dame Press.

Barthes, Roland. 1972. *Mythologies.* New York: Cape, Hill and Wang.

———. 1987. *Criticism and Truth.* Minneapolis: University of Minnesota Press.

Bauman, Richard. 1977. *Verbal Art as Performance.* Prospect Hills, Ill.: Waveland Press.

———. 1986a. Performance and Honor in 13th-century Iceland. *Journal of American Folklore* 99:131–50.

———. 1986b. *Story, Performance, and Event.* Cambridge: Cambridge University Press.

————, ed. 1992. *Folklore, Cultural Performances, and Popular Entertainment: A Communications-Centered Handbook*. Oxford: Oxford University Press.

Bauman, Richard, and Roger. D. Abrahams, eds. 1981. *"And Other Neighborly Names":Social Process and Cultural Image in Texas Folklore*. Austin: University of Texas of Austin.

Bauman, Richard, and Charles Briggs. 1990. Poetics and Performance as Critical Perspectives on Language and Social Life. *Annual Review of Anthropology* 19:59–88.

Bauman, Richard, and Joel Sherzer, eds. 1974. *Explorations in the Ethnography of Speaking*. Cambridge: Cambridge University Press.

Berger, Peter. 1967. *The Sacred Canopy: Elements of a Sociological Theory of Religion*. New York: Doubleday Books.

Bernstein, Richard. 1983. *Beyond Objectivism and Relativism: Science, Hermeneutics, and Praxis*. Philadelphia: University of Pennsylvania Press.

Bourdieu, Pierre. 1977. *Outline of a Theory of Practice*. Cambridge: Cambridge University Press.

Bourke, John. G. 1893. The Miracle Play of the Rio Grande. *Journal of American Folklore* 6(21):89–95.

————. 1894a. The American Congo. *Scribner's* 15(May):590–610.

————. 1894b. Popular Medicine, Customs, and Superstitions of the Rio Grande. *Journal of American Folk-lore* 7(April–June):119–46.

————. 1895. The Folk-Foods of the Rio Grande Valley and of Northern Mexico. *Journal of American Folk-lore* 8(January–April):41–71.

Briggs, Charles. 1992. "Since I am a Woman, I Will Chastise My Relatives": Gender, Reported Speech, and the (Re)production of Social Relations in Warao Ritual Wailing. *American Ethnologist* 19:337–61.

Bruner, Edward M. 1986. Experience and Its Expressions. In *The Anthropology of Experience*, ed. Victor Turner and Edward Bruner, pp. 3–32. Urbana: University of Illinois Press.

Bruni, Mary Ann S. 1985. *Rosita's Christmas Wish*. San Antonio: Texart Services.

Burke, Peter. 1978. *Popular Culture in Early Modern Europe*. New York: Harper and Row.

Campa, Arturo. 1934a. *Spanish Religious Folk Theatre in the Spanish Southwest*. (First Cycle). Albuquerque: University of New Mexico Bulletin (5)1.

————. 1934b. *Spanish Religious Folk Theatre in the Spanish Southwest*. (Second Cycle). Albuquerque: University of New Mexico Bulletin (5)2.

Cardenas, Gilberto, Jorge Chapa, and Susan Burek. 1993. The Changing Economic Position of Mexican Americans in San Antonio. In *Latinos in a Changing U.S. Economy*, ed. Frank Bonilla and Rebecca Morales, pp. 160–83. Newbury Park, Calif.: Sage Publications.

Castañeda, Carlos. 1932. The First American Play. *The Catholic World* 124(January):429–37.

Cole, M. R. 1907. *Los Pastores: A Mexican Play of the Nativity.* Boston: Houghton, Mifflin.

Connerton, Paul. 1989. *How Societies Remember.* Cambridge: Cambridge University Press.

Consentino, Donald. 1982. *Defiant Maids and Stubborn Farmers: Tradition and Invention in Mende Story Performance.* Cambridge: Cambridge University Press.

Crawford, J. P. Wickersham. 1911. The Pastor and Bobo in the Spanish Religious Drama of the Sixteenth Century. *Romantic Review* 2(4):376–401.

Culler, Jonathan. 1975. *Structuralist Poetics.* Ithaca, N.Y.: Cornell University Press.

Curtis, Albert. 1955. *Fabulous San Antonio.* San Antonio: Naylor.

Davis, Natalie Zemon. 1975. *Society and Culture in Early Modern France.* Stanford, Calif.: Stanford University Press.

de la Teja, Jesús F., and John Wheat. 1991. Béxar: Profile of a Tejano Community, 1820–1832. In *Tejano Origins in Eighteenth-Century San Antonio,* ed. Gerald E. Poyo and Gilberto M. Hinojosa, pp. 1–26. Austin: University of Texas Press.

De León, Arnoldo. 1982. *The Tejano Community, 1836–1900.* Albuquerque: University of New Mexico Press.

———. 1983. *They Called Them Greasers: Anglo Attitudes toward Mexicans in Texas, 1821–1900.* Austin: University of Texas Press.

De León, Arnoldo, and Kenneth L. Stewart. 1985. A Tale of Three Cities: A Comparative Analysis of the Socio-Economic Conditions of Mexican-Americans in Los Angeles, Tucson, and San Antonio. *Journal of the West* 24(2):64–74.

Diekemper, Bernard. 1985. The Catholic Church in the Shadows. *Journal of the West* 24(2):46–53.

Donovan, Richard B. 1985. *The Liturgical Drama in Medieval Spain.* Toronto: Pontifical Institute of Medieval Studies.

Douglas, Mary 1966. *Purity and Danger.* London: Routledge and Kegan Paul.

———. 1990. Foreword to *The Gift: The Form and Reason for Exchange in Archaic Societies,* by Marcel Mauss, trans. W. D. Halls, pp. vii–xviii. New York: W. W. Norton.

Driggs, Howard R., and Sarah S. King. 1936. *Rise of the Lone Star: A Story of Texas Told by Its Pioneers.* New York: Frederick A. Stokes.

Duranti, Alessandro, and Charles Goodwin. 1992. *Rethinking Context.* Cambridge: Cambridge University Press.

Durkheim, Emile. [1915] 1965. *The Elementary Forms of the Religious Life.* New York: The Free Press.

Eagleton, Terry 1978. *Criticism and Ideology: Marxist Literary Theory.* London: Verso.

Elías-Olivares, Lucía. 1979. Language Use in a Chicano Community: A Sociolinguistic Approach. In *Sociolinguistic Aspects of Language Learning and Teaching,* ed. J. B. Pride, pp. 120–35. Oxford: Oxford University Press.

Estrada, Francisco López. 1974. *Los Libros de Pastores en La Literatura Española.* Madrid: Editorial Gredos.

Everett, Donald E. 1975. *San Antonio: The Flavor of Its Past, 1845–1898*. San Antonio: Trinity University Press.

Fernandez, James. 1986. *Persuasions and Performances: The Play of Tropes in Culture*. Bloomington: Indiana University Press.

Flores, Richard R. 1992. The *Corrido* and the Emergence of Texas- Mexican Social Identity. *Journal of American Folklore* 105:166–82.

———. 1993. History, "Los Pastores," and the Shifting Poetics of Dislocation. *Journal of Historical Sociology* 6:164–85.

———. 1994. "Los Pastores" and the Gifting of Performance. *American Ethnologist* 21(2):270–85.

Foley, Douglas E., with Clarice Mota, Donald Post, and Ignacio Lozano. 1977. *From Peones to Politicos: Class and Ethnicity in a South Texas Town 1900–1987*. Austin: University of Texas Press.

Frye, Northrop. 1957. *Anatomy of Criticism*. Princeton, N.J.: Princeton University Press.

García, Mario T. 1981. *Desert Immigrants: The Mexicans of El Paso, 1880–1920*. New Haven, Conn.: Yale University Press.

———. 1989. *Mexican Americans: Leadership, Ideology, and Identity, 1930–1960*. New Haven, Conn.: Yale University Press.

García, Richard 1991. *Rise of the Mexican American Middle Class*. College Station: Texas A&M University Press.

Garciadueñas, José R. 1939. *Autos y Coloquios del Siglo XVI*. Mexico: Universidad Nacional Autonoma.

Geertz, Clifford. 1973. *The Interpretation of Culture*. New York: Basic Books.

Godelier, Maurice. 1977. *Perspectives in Marxist Anthropology*, trans. Robert Brain. Cambridge: Cambridge University Press.

Goodwin, Marjorie H. 1980. He-Said-She-Said: Formal Cultural Procedures for the Construction of a Gossip Dispute Activity. *American Ethnologist* 7:674–95.

Granado, Leandro. 1949. *Letter to Carmel Tranchese*. San Antonio: Institute of Texan Cultures, San Antonio, Texas.

Green, Thomas A. 1981. Introduction: Special Issue on Folk Drama. *Journal of American Folklore* 94:421–32.

Greenblatt, Stephen. 1980. *Renaissance Self-Fashioning*. Chicago: University of Chicago Press.

Greenwood, Davydd J. 1989. Culture by the Pound: An Anthropological Perspective on Tourism as Cultural Commoditization. In *Hosts and Guests: The Anthropology of Tourism*, 2d ed., ed. Valene L. Smith, pp. 171–86. Philadelphia: University of Pennsylvania Press.

Hagner, Lillie Mae. 1940. *Alluring San Antonio*. San Antonio: Naylor.

Hagy, Loleta. 1933. *Christmas in Our Little Mexico*. San Antonio: Home and Club Official Monthly Publication, City Federation of Women's Club 4:5–6.

Hall, Stuart. 1981. Notes on Deconstructing the Popular. In *People's History and Socialist Thought,* ed. Raphael Samuel, pp. 227–40. London: Routledge and Kegan Paul.

Handler, Richard, and Joyce Linnekin. 1984. Tradition, Genuine or Spurious. *Journal of American Folklore* 97:273–90.

Hanks, William F. 1987. Discourse Genres in a Theory of Practice. *American Ethnologist* 14:668–92.

———. 1989. Text and Textuality. *Annual Review of Anthropology* 18:95–127.

Hansen, Niles 1981. *The Border Economy.* Austin: University of Texas Press.

Hirschfield, Dorothy. 1928. Los Pastores. *Theatre Arts Monthly* 22(December):903–11.

Hobsbawm, Eric, and Terence Ranger, eds. 1983. *The Invention of Tradition.* Cambridge: Cambridge University Press.

Hyde, Lewis 1983. *The Gift.* New York: Vintage Books.

Hymes, Dell. 1974. *Foundations in Sociolinguistics: An Ethnographic Approach.* Philadelphia: University of Pennsylvania Press.

———. 1981. *"In Vain I Tried to Tell You": Essays in Native American Ethnopoetics.* Philadelphia: University of Pennsylvania Press.

Igo, John N. 1967. *Los Pastores: An Annotated Bibliography with an Introduction.* San Antonio, Tex.: San Antonio College.

———. 1985. Los Pastores: A Triple Tradition. *Journal of Popular Culture* 19:131–38.

Inkley, Bebe C., ed. 1976. *Los Pastores.* The Newsletter, San Antonio, Tex.: San Antonio Conservation Society. 14(12).

Jakobson, Roman. 1960. Linguistics and Poetics. In *Style in Language,* ed. Thomas Sebeok, pp. 350–77. Cambridge, Mass.: MIT Press.

Jameson, Fredric. 1971. *Marxism and Form.* Princeton, N.J.: Princeton University Press.

———. 1981. *The Political Unconscious.* Ithaca, N.Y.: Cornell University Press.

Jones, Michael Owen. 1975. *The Hand-Made Object and Its Maker.* Berkeley: University of California Press.

Jules-Rosette, Bennetta. 1990. Semiotics and Cultural Diversity: Entering the 1990s. *American Journal of Semiotics* 7:5–26.

Kammen, Michael. 1991. *Mystic Chords of Memory: The Transformation of Tradition in American Culture.* New York: Vintage Books/Random House.

Kapferer, Bruce. 1986. Performance and the Structuring of Meaning. In *The Anthropology of Experience,* eds. Victor Turner and Edward Bruner, pp. 188–206. Urbana: University of Illinois Press.

Keeler, Ward. 1987. *Javanese Shadow Plays, Javanese Selves.* Princeton, N.J.: Princeton University Press.

Lafaye, Jacques. 1976. *Quetzalcóatl and Guadalupe: The Formation of Mexican National Consciousness 1531–1813.* Chicago: University of Chicago Press.

Lévi-Strauss, Claude. 1963. *Structural Anthropology.* New York: Basic Books.

Leyva, Joseph. 1951. *A Genetic Study of Los Pastores.* Master's thesis, Trinity University, San Antonio, Texas.

Limón, José E. 1974. El Primer Congreso Mexicanista de 1911: A Precursor to Contemporary Chicanismo. *Aztlán* 5:85–117.

———. 1982. El Meeting: History, Folk Spanish, and Ethnic Nationalism in a Chicano Student Community. In *The Spanish Language in the United States: Sociolinguistic Aspects*, ed. Jon Amastae and Lucía Elías-Olivares, pp. 301–32. Cambridge: Cambridge University Press.

———. 1983a. Folklore, Social Conflict and the United States-Mexico Border. In *Handbook of American Folklore*, ed. Richard Dorson, pp. 216–26. Bloomington: Indiana University Press.

———. 1983b. Western Marxism and Folklore: A Critical Introduction. *Journal of American Folklore* 96:34–52.

———. 1986. *The Return of the Mexican Ballad: Américo Paredes and His Anthropological Text as Persuasive Political Performance*. Working Paper Series 16. Stanford Center For Chicano Research.

———. 1989. *Carne, Carnales,* and the Carnivalesque: Bakhtinian *Batos,* Disorder, and Narrative Discourse. *American Ethnologist* 16:471–86.

———. 1992. *Mexican Ballads, Chicano Poems: History and Influence in Mexican-American Social Poetry*. Berkeley: University of California Press.

———. 1994. *Dancing with the Devil: Society and Cultural Poetics in Mexican-American South Texas*. Madison: University of Wisconsin Press.

Long, Jeff. 1990. *Duel of Eagles: The Mexican-U.S. Fight for the Alamo*. New York: William Morrow.

Lowery, Janette S. 1938. *Annunciata and the Shepherds*. New York: Gentry Press.

MacCannell, Dean. 1976. *The Tourist*. New York: Schocken Books.

McDowell, John H. 1975. The Mexican Corrido: Formula and Theme in a Ballad Tradition. *Journal of American Folklore* 85:205–20.

Marie, Sister Joseph I. 1948. *The Role of the Church and the Folk in the Development of the Early Drama in New Mexico*. Ph.D. diss., English Department, University of Pennsylvania.

Martin, Randy. 1985. Dance as a Social Movement. *Social Text* 12(Fall):54–70.

Marx, Karl. 1964. *The Economic and Philosophic Manuscripts of 1844*, ed. Dirk J. Struik, trans. Martin Milligan. New York: International Publishers.

———. 1967. *Capital: A Critical Analysis of Capitalist Production*, vol. 1, ed. Frederick Engels, trans. Samuel Moore and Edward Aveling from the Third German Edition. New York: International Publishers.

———. 1978. Thesis on Feuerbach. In *The Marx-Engels Reader*, ed. Robert C. Tucker, pp. 143–45. New York: W. W. Norton.

Mauss, Marcel. [1925] 1990. *The Gift: The Form and Reason for Exchange in Archaic Societies*, trans. W. D. Halls. New York: W. W. Norton.

Montejano, David. 1987. *Anglos and Mexicans in the Making of Texas, 1836–1986*. Austin: University of Texas Press.

Nelson-Cisneros, Victor B. 1975. La Clase trabajadora en Tejas, 1920–1940. *Aztlán* 6:239–65.

———. 1978. UCAPAWA Organizing in Texas, 1935–50. *Aztlán* 9:71–84.

Obeyesekere, Gananath. 1990. *The Work of Culture.* Chicago: University of Chicago Press.

Ortner, Sherry. 1990. Patterns of History. In *Culture through Time,* ed. Emiko Ohnuki-Tierney. Stanford, Calif.: Stanford University Press.

Paredes, Américo. 1958a. *With His Pistol in His Hand: A Border Ballad and Its Hero.* Austin: University of Texas Press.

———. 1958b. The Mexican Corrido: Its Rise and Fall. In *Madstones and Twisters,* eds. M. Boatright, W. Hudson, and A. Maxwell, pp. 91–105. Dallas: Southern Methodist University Press.

———. 1964. Pastorela. In *Buying the Wind,* ed. Richard M. Dorson, pp. 466–79. Chicago: University of Chicago Press.

———. 1966. The Décima on the Texas-Mexican Border: Folk Song as an Adjunct to Legend. *Journal of the Folklore Institute* 3:154–67.

———. 1978. The Problem of Identity in a Changing Culture: Popular Expressions of Culture Conflict along the Rio Grande Border. In *Views Across the Border: The United States and Mexico,* ed. Stanley R. Robe, pp. 68–94. Albuquerque: University of New Mexico Press.

Parisot, Rev. Pierre F. 1899. *The Reminiscences of a Texas Missionary.* San Antonio: Johnson Brothers.

Pearce, T. M. 1956. The New Mexican "Shepherds' Play." *Western Folklore* 15:77–88.

Peña, Manuel. 1985. *The Texas-Mexican Conjunto.* Austin: University of Texas Press.

Perry, George S. 1948. Rumpled Angel of the Slums. *Saturday Evening Post* 221:32–47.

Peyton, Green. 1946. *San Antonio: City in the Sun.* New York and London: Whittlesey House, McGraw-Hill.

Porter, Joseph C. 1986. *Paper Medicine Man: John Gregory Bourke and His American West.* Norman: University of Oklahoma Press.

Poyo, Gerald E., and Gilberto M. Hinojosa, eds. 1991. *Tejano Origins in Eighteenth-Century San Antonio.* Austin: University of Texas Press.

Pratt, Mary Louise. 1986. Fieldwork in Common Places. In *Writing Culture: The Poetics and Politics of Ethnography,* ed. James Clifford and George Marcus, pp. 27–50. Berkeley: University of California Press.

Quilas, Antonio. 1986. *Métrica española.* Barcelona: Editorial Ariel.

Rael, Juan. 1965. *The Sources and Diffusion of the Mexican Shepherds' Plays.* Guadalajara: Libreria la Joyita.

Raley, Helen. 1924. Christmas according to Lope De Vega. *San Antonio Express.*

Ravicz, Marilyn E. 1970. *Early Colonial Religious Drama in Mexico: From Tzompantli to Golgatha.* Washington: Catholic University Press.

Rebel, Herman. 1989a. Cultural Hegemony and Class Experience (Part One). *American Ethnologist* 16:117–36.

———. 1989b. Cultural Hegemony and Class Experience (Part Two). *American Ethnologist* 16:350–65.

Richmond, Douglas W. 1980. *La Guerra de Texas se renova:* Mexican Insurrection and Carrancista Ambitions, 1900–1920. *Aztlán* 11:1–32.

Ricoeur, Paul. 1979. The Model of the Text: Meaningful Action Considered as a Text. In *Interpretive Social Science: A Reader,* ed. Paul Rabinow and William M. Sullivan, pp. 73–101. Berkeley: University of California Press.

Robe, Stanley. 1954. *Coloquios de pastores from Jalisco, Mexico.* Berkeley: University of California Press.

———. 1957. The Relationship of Los Pastores to Other Spanish-American Folk Drama. *Western Folklore* 16:281–89.

Russell, Jeffrey B. 1984. *Lucifer: The Devil in the Middle Ages.* Ithaca, N.Y.: Cornell University Press.

Sacks, Karen B. 1989. Toward a Unified Theory of Class, Race, and Gender. *American Ethnologist* 16:534–50.

Sahlins, Marshall. 1972. *Stone Age Economics.* Chicago: Aldine.

Saldívar, Ramón. 1990. *Chicano Narrative: The Dialectics of Difference.* Madison: University of Wisconsin Press.

San Antonio Conservation Society. 1988–89. *Yearbook.* On file at the University of Texas at San Antonio Library.

San Miguel, Guadalupe, Jr. 1987. *"Let All of Them Take Heed": Mexican Americans and the Campaign for Educational Equality in Texas, 1910–1981.* Austin: University of Texas Press.

Sennett, Richard. 1974. *The Fall of Public Man.* New York: Knopf.

Shils, Edward. 1981. *Tradition.* London: Faber and Faber.

Shoemaker, William H. 1935. *The Multiple Stage in Spain during the Fifteenth and Sixteenth Centuries.* Princeton, N.J.: Princeton University Press.

Soja, Edward. 1989. *Postmodern Geography: The Reassertion of Space in Critical Social Theory.* London: Verso Press.

Stallybrass, Peter, and Allon White. 1986. *The Politics and Poetics of Transgression.* Ithaca, N.Y.: Cornell University Press.

Strathern, Marilyn. 1988. *The Gender of the Gift.* Berkeley: University of California Press.

Sugranes, Rev. Eugene. 1921. San Antonio's Time Honored Christmas Play Brought here by Fr. Margil in the Seventeenth Century. *San Antonio Evening News.* San Antonio, Texas.

Taussig, Michael. 1980. *The Devil and Commodity Fetishism in South America.* Chapel Hill: University of North Carolina Press.

———. 1993. *Mimesis and Alterity: A Particular History of the Senses.* New York: Routledge.

Tranchese, Carmelo, SJ. 1941. Los Pastores: Miracle Play. *Extension* (December):11.
————. 1949. Foreword. *Los Pastores: A Christmas Drama of Old Mexico,* ed. Carmelo Tranchese and Leandro Granado. San Antonio: Treviño Brothers.

Turner, Kay. 1982. Mexican-American Home Altars: Towards their Interpretation. *Aztlán* 13(1&2):309–26.

Turner, Kay, and Suzie Seriff. 1987. "Giving an Altar": The Ideology of Reproduction in a St. Joseph's Day Feast. *Journal of American Folklore* 100:446–60.

Turner, Victor. 1969. *The Ritual Process.* Chicago: Aldine.
————. 1974. *Dramas, Fields, and Metaphors.* Ithaca, N.Y.: Cornell University Press.
————. 1982. *From Ritual to Theatre.* New York: Performing Arts Journal Publications.
————. 1986. Dewey, Dilthey, and Drama: An Essay in the Anthropology of Experience. In *The Anthropology of Experience,* ed. Victor Turner and Edward Bruner, pp. 33–44. Urbana: University of Illinois Press.

Van Gennep, Arnold. 1960. *The Rites of Passage.* Chicago: University of Chicago Press.

Vélez-Ibáñez, Carlos. 1980. Mexicano/Hispano Support System and Confianza: Theoretical Issues of Cultural Adaptation. In *Hispanic Natural Support Systems,* ed. B. Valle and W. Vega, pp. 45–54. Sacramento: California Department of Mental Health.
————. 1983. *Bonds of Mutual Trust: The Cultural Systems of Rotating Credit Associations among Urban Mexicans and Chicanos.* New Brunswick, N.J.: Rutgers University Press.

Waugh, Julia N. 1955. *The Silver Cradle.* Austin: University of Texas Press.

Weber, David J., ed. 1973. *Foreigners in their Native Land.* Albuquerque: University of New Mexico Press.

Weber, Max. 1946. *From Max Weber: Essays in Sociology.* New York: Oxford University Press.

Weiner, Annette B. 1976. *Women of Value, Men of Renown: New Perspectives in Trobriand Exchange.* Austin: University of Texas Press.

Williams, Raymond. 1973. *The Country and the City.* New York: Oxford University Press.
————. 1977. *Marxism and Literature.* Oxford: Oxford University Press.
————. 1981. *The Sociology of Culture.* New York: Schocken Books.

Wolff, Kurt H. ed. 1950. *The Sociology of Georg Simmel.* New York and London: The Free Press.

Woolard, Katheryn A. 1985. Language Variation and Cultural Hegemony: Toward an Integration of Sociolinguistic and Social Theory. *American Ethnologist* 12:738–48.

Young, Karl. 1933. *The Drama of the Medieval Church.* Oxford: Clarendon Press.

Index